TONY MACAULAY grew up in the 1970s at the top of the Shankill Road – an experience that has shaped his life and inspired his writing. Following successful spells as a paperboy and a breadboy, he has gone on to spend more than thirty years working for peace and reconciliation both in Northern Ireland and abroad. Tony is also a writer and broadcaster, contributing regularly to Radio Ulster for more than ten years. His first two books, *Paperboy* and *Breadboy*, were critically acclaimed bestsellers. *All Growed Up* is his third book.

ALL GROWED UP

WHAT BREADBOY DID AT UNIVERSITY

TONY MACAULAY

·THE·
BLACK
·STAFF·
PRESS

First published in 2014 by Blackstaff Press
4D Weavers Court
Linfield Road
Belfast BT12 5GH

With the assistance of
The Arts Council of Northern Ireland

Typeset by KT Designs, St Helens, England

Printed in Berwick-upon-Tweed by Martins the Printers

A CIP catalogue for this book is available from the British Library

ISBN 978 0 85640 934 9

www.blackstaffpress.com

Follow Tony on Twitter @tonymacaulay

Some names and identifying details have been changed
to protect the privacy of individuals.

For Big Isobel
and Lovely Lesley

CONTENTS

INTRODUCTION

I was a student. It's there on my CV. In 1982, I departed West Belfast to go where few people from the Upper Shankill had boldly gone before: to university.

Belfast in the eighties was like an episode of *Dallas*; lovely to look at and plenty of drama but basically the same sad, sorry story repeated week after week. I escaped to the New University of Ulster in Coleraine to become an intellectual, a socialist and a New Romantic. I was full of aspirations – like a futuristic car rolling off the production line in the DeLorean Motor factory. I yearned for peace in a time of Troubles. I dreamt of a bright future in a country convulsed by the past.

I was more naive than you could possibly imagine.

VALENTINE'S DAY

I was a sex symbol, so I was. As a result of my recent triumph on the stage as Riff, the leader of the Jets, in *West Side Story* the entire first form girls' hockey team at Belfast Royal Academy adored me. Who could blame them? I was seventeen years old now and shaving twice a week. My new-found height and deeply broken voice, combined with the aroma of Hai Karate aftershave, demonstrated to the world that I was a real man now. The same wee girls that once laughed at me for being a mere bread van delivery boy from up the Shankill now giggled with desire through their braces as I strode manfully toward them across the playground. I could disrupt a game of hopscotch in front of the junior girls' toilets like Charlton Heston parting the Red Sea in the Bible. Thomas O'Hara said a wee ginger girl with pigtails and a patch over one lens of her pink National Health glasses had even fixed a photograph of me to the inside of her locker door with pink bubble gum after seeking me out among the glorious rugger boys in the school magazine. It was a picture of me clicking my fingers on stage in a T-shirt, and in the heat of desire, this adoring fan had ripped out my image the way I sometimes did

1

with the nicest ladies in the bra section of the *Great Universal Club Book*. My adhesion to a girl's locker door put me up there in the same league of desirability as Adam Ant with the make-up and Shakin' Stevens with the denims. I had Bo Derek coming out of the sea in a wet swimsuit on the inside of my locker door. It was evident that I was a sort of Bo Derek to the first form girls of Belfast Royal Academy. The only difference between me and these other sex symbols was that I hadn't actually had sex yet. I was a wee good livin' fella and sex before marriage was a sin, even if you could get someone to do it with you.

Our school production of *West Side Story* had received excellent reviews, except for one by a swanky lower-sixth girl with a lisp who wrote a review for her English Language class critiquing my performance as 'somewhat derivative' and 'frankly nothing more meaningful or artistically substantial than a poor impersonation of The Fonz'. I pulled her hair in the school dinner queue and mimicked her lisp, shouting, 'Did that feel derivative, thnobby knickerth?' She started to cry and I felt guilty while eating my pink custard and coconut sponge cake because I had hurt a girl and I was supposed to be the only teenage pacifist from West Belfast.

It was Friday 12 February 1982, the last day of school before Valentine's Day and the third most important day in my life after passing the eleven-plus and getting saved at the caravan site in Millisle. Everyone in Northern Ireland was still arguing about the Troubles and how it was the other side's entire fault. Everybody in Belfast was raging about the lay-offs at the DeLorean Motor factory in Dunmurry where they built fancy space-age cars that no one could ever afford to buy. But I had more important matters on my mind. A few weeks ago I had received an official letter informing me that 12 February was the day of my interview for a place at university. I was just a wee lad from up the Shankill, although I had been a very good paperboy and an excellent breadboy, but today I was preparing for the next big step up the ladder of my career. There were very few jobs in Belfast and there was talk of redundancies in the foundry where my father had worked all his life. In those days, a good job in Belfast was as rare as a hug on the peace line, and I knew what I must accomplish to progress in this limited job market. I could listen to my mother and try to get a good job in the bank so that I could come up in the world and move to Bangor. I could obey my granny and become a Presbyterian minister and get a house for free for preaching the Gospel. But I had grander ambitions, because I wanted to be the next Terry Wogan on BBC1, and if I hoped to become a great broadcaster with an Irish accent, simply helping my father as the assistant DJ at the Westy Disco every Saturday night would not suffice. To transform myself into a professional I needed to go to university and become a student and an intellectual. Titch McCracken said all students did was smoke marijuana and support the IRA, but I was undeterred. I was determined to grasp the opportunity to go where very few of my peers from the Upper Shankill had boldly gone before. I wanted to be like Captain James T. Kirk, seeking out new worlds and civilizations, except with books instead of phaser guns. After all, this is what my father had been working for in the foundry all these years. This was the reason why my mother had sewed thousands of dresses for posh ladies up the Lisburn Road to wear to dinner dances at the Chimney Corner Hotel.

No one in my family had ever earned a degree, though there had been great expectations a few years ago when my big brother got into Queen's University. I had never seen my father so proud. My big brother loved the social life but he hated studying economics and eventually gave it up for a good job in Shorts. Now it was my turn, and I was determined to see it through until my graduation day, when I would get to wear robes and a funny hat with a tassel. I had applied to the New University of Ulster to take a BA honours degree in Media Studies. I understood that this was the best route for me to pursue if I wanted to become a great journalist like the ones in America that got Richard Nixon into trouble, or at least to have my own chat show on BBC1 interviewing Ronnie Corbett and Joanna Lumley. The university was, as the name suggested, 'new'. It was in Coleraine, which was somewhere beyond Glengormley and near Portrush, where you went on Easter Monday for fish and chips, a paddle in the sea and a ride on the ghost train in Barry's Amusements. John Hume said it was an injustice that the new university had not been built in Derry, which was Catholic for Londonderry.

However, on this momentous day I had pressing business to conduct at school before catching the train to Coleraine. Every year the School Charity Committee, of which I was a long-serving member, organised a school postal service for Valentine's Day. It was a very successful charitable enterprise; the pupils paid 10p for a school stamp, the Valentine's Day cards were delivered during second period and lots of children in Africa were saved. This year Valentine's Day was on a Sunday so the cards were delivered on Friday while we were still at school – it was probably a sin to send love cards on the Sabbath anyway.

I was certain that the film-star status I had attained in the wake of *West Side Story* meant I would receive more cards than any other boy in my class. Second period was Maths and, as Miss Brown with the nice smile and sensible shoes patiently explained the meaning of an indecipherable equation, I was busy daydreaming about receiving more Valentine's Day cards than Timothy Longsley. This was very important to me because Timothy was a rugby-playing genius who lived up the Antrim Road in a mansion with an avocado bidet and a flowering cherry tree. All the girls fancied Timothy and he knew it. He snogged them and chucked them away like chewed-up sticks of Wrigley's gum in the playground. Today was a rare opportunity for me to beat him at something.

My love life had become very complicated in recent years. It was like an episode of *Dallas* but with fewer shoulder pads, because John Frazer's in Gresham Street didn't stock them yet. When I split up with Judy Carlton, it was almost as shocking as when Agnetha and Björn got divorced. Knowing me, knowing her, there was nothing we could do. After Judy, I went out with Lindsay Johnson with the breasts and the New Wave hair. Lindsay loved peace and God and was even more good livin' than me. She was a very good kisser but Jesus told her to chuck me to revise for her A levels. This breakup seemed to be less of a shock to the middle sixth form than my estrangement with Judy. It was more akin to when Frida and Benny completed the ABBA marriage breakdown. Now I was a man and shaving twice a week I was learning from painful personal experience the truth of the lyrics of 'The Winner Takes It All'.

As Miss Brown continued with a reasonable explanation of a most unreasonable A level question, I waited impatiently for the school post to arrive, fiddling with a stapler the teacher had absentmindedly left on my desk. I could see from the clock above the blackboard that it was nearly ten o'clock. This was the exact time I knew I had to leave school to go home and put on my good suit before taking a black taxi into the city centre to the train station.

'My cards had better hurry up!' I whispered to Aaron Ward, who was sitting in front of me. Aaron was brilliant at rugby and cricket and anything involving running or balls, but I liked him anyway.

'What are you like, wee lad?' he replied.

'I've an interview at the NUU today,' I said proudly.

'You're not going to Toytown next year, are you?' he asked.

'Toytown' was what people who wanted to go Queen's University condescendingly called the New University of Ulster.

Just then, the door of the classroom burst open and in my excitement I stapled my thumb.

'Tony!' cried Miss Brown with a genuine shriek of concern.

Denise Clyde and Joanne Gault stared in horror at my bloody thumb, and from the back of the classroom I heard a hearty snort from Timothy Longsley.

'What are you like, wee lad?' repeated Aaron Ward.

I pretended that the injection of a staple through my flesh had not hurt in the least as I extracted it from my throbbing thumb. I then had to suck my thumb to stop the bleeding and I hit a reddener because I realised I must look just like Linda Milligan, who still sucked her thumb when doing the hardest maths questions and cried when she didn't get an A.

Oblivious to the bloodbath at my desk, two spotty third formers from the charity committee began to deliver the Valentine's Day cards to the desks of the most beloved in the class. Thomas O'Hara got one small card with lipstick kisses all over it and Denise Clyde got one huge card in a pink envelope with 'SWALK' written all over it. This was not, as I first suspected, the acronym for yet another new paramilitary organisation, because apparently these letters stood for 'Sealed With A Loving Kiss'. Everyone said Denise's card was from Frankie Jones and, judging by the flush of his cheeks, I agreed. Frankie was the class expert on sex, both theory and practice – albeit mostly solo – and was not usually embarrassed by anything. His uncharacteristic blushes just proved to the whole Maths class that he had sent the card to Denise. It seemed that Frankie wanted a relationship with a real live female rather than the women in the pages of the well-thumbed *Playboy* magazines hidden in his schoolbag, which I never once peeked at during break times when no one was looking.

Finally it was my turn to receive the post. It soon became clear that the two clever third formers were deliberately keeping me to the end for dramatic effect. In fact, I felt a drum roll would have been appropriate. As the post girls approached my desk and opened the mailbag my senses were struck with the overpowering scent of Charley perfume, which had been lovingly sprayed on each card. Firstly the girls produced three small brown envelopes, like the ones my father sometimes borrowed from the office in the foundry. Two of these envelopes contained rather amateur handmade cards from girls who had obviously been watching too much *Blue Peter*, but it was the thought that counted. The other brown envelope contained a note in strangely familiar handwriting, which read, 'Who would wanna send YOU a Valentine card, ya big fruit?' I wondered how my big brother had managed to infiltrate the school postal system. Next, I was presented with a pile of bright white envelopes, containing a selection of Charlie Brown, Paddington Bear and 'Love is …' cards. It seemed that every girl in the school wanted a cartoon character to endorse her expression of love for me. After this I was handed five medium-sized cards in pink envelopes, which must have cost a bomb in the smoke-damage sale in Eason's. Finally, after a short but dramatic pause similar to the one just before Michael Aspel announced who'd won Miss World, the post girls revealed two enormous pink envelopes. One of these giant envelopes was covered in glitter and was sticky with strong, sweet-smelling glue. My pile of cards now covered half the surface of my desk. This reminded me of when they emptied out the votes from Rev. Ian Paisley's ballot boxes onto big tables to count at the King's Hall in the elections. The class spontaneously gave me a round of applause, which was a bit of a relief as this turn of events could have easily left me open to jealous hostility from the less idolised in the class. Miss Brown looked on in genuine amazement as I opened my cards, staining each of them with blood from my stapled thumb which rather fittingly matched the red lipstick kisses on the envelopes. The opening of every new envelope revealed a fresh expression of undying love. I had never read so many versions of 'Roses are red, violets are blue' in my life. I sensed that the whole class was impressed by the grand total of fourteen, yes *fourteen*, cards on my desk. This was more than I had ever received on my birthday, including the year I was in bed with the chickenpox and a bottle of Lucozade. I was certain the other boys were jealous but the girls seemed thrilled to have the privilege of sharing a classroom with a sex symbol. I knew I should remain humble despite being blessed with the good looks and charisma to attract such worship, but I couldn't resist the temptation to turn to Timothy Longsley and mouth 'Sickener!' with a victorious smile. It was only when I turned back towards Miss Brown and her valiant efforts to redirect our attention to algebra that I noticed the clock now said 10.20 a.m.

My heart skipped a beat. I was late! I had to go! I had a bus to catch and a good suit to put on and a black taxi to take down the Shankill Road to catch a train to Coleraine to become a graduate and a famous broadcaster.

'Excuse me, Miss, I have to go to my university interview now, so I do,' I explained quickly to Miss Brown, handing her a note from my mammy, putting on my duffle coat and gathering together my school books and fourteen, yes *fourteen*, Valentine cards. As I pushed towards the door I dropped a Paddington Bear card and Linda Mulligan picked it up, flicked her attempted Purdey bob, fluttered her eyelashes and said suggestively, 'I wonder who sent you this one?'

'What are you like, wee lad?' I heard Aaron Ward say as I left, slamming the classroom door behind me.

As I ran across the playground and out the front gates of BRA, the imposing granite structure of the ancient Crombie building looked down upon me and seemed to 'tut' heavily. How could a pupil from this prestigious grammar school be late for the most important academic appointment of his life? This was worse than being late for Oul Mac's paper round, or Leslie McGregor's bread round, or the morning service in Ballygomartin Presbyterian Church. I darted past a British Army saracen and a foot patrol of soldiers with big boots and guns and camouflaged faces. Panic set in because I knew it looked as if I was running away from a situation, and I prayed that my grammar school scarf, duffle coat and selection of Charlie Brown Valentine's Day cards would be a good enough alibi for any allegations that I was fleeing the scene of a terrorist-related crime. Thankfully, the foot patrol ignored me, apart from one young soldier who aimed his gun at me for practice.

I carried on running and arrived in a sweat at the bus stop. I hoped the bus hadn't been hijacked that day and prayed that one would come soon. I waited impatiently for ten minutes until I decided it would be quicker to run the three miles home across the peace lines than rely on a bus to take me into the city centre and then risk trying to find another bus up the Shankill. Reliable public transport was as rare as forgiveness in 1980's Belfast. As I raced up the Cliftonville Road I was conscious that the large pink envelopes sticking out of my schoolbag and smelling of Charley perfume would not be beneficial if I encountered any wee hoods intent on beating me up for being a snob or a Protestant or both. But I soon arrived safely on the Crumlin Road and dashed up one side of the road on the Protestant pavement between the peace walls and past the big Catholic chapel beside Ardoyne where the IRA lived. Suddenly two teenage girls, who were obviously mitching millies, emerged from beside the Ardoyne shops and began to follow me. I considered the possible humiliation of being the victim of a female sectarian attack and hurried on. However as the girls drew closer, smoking and twirling their chewing gum on their fingers, one of them said, 'You're lovely, wee lad. You look like Paul Young, so you do!' I was very flattered because Paul Young was a brilliant singer whose hair I copied with gel from Boots. Had I not been in such a hurry I would have stopped and discussed with these girls from the other side how we could build peace across the barricades together because I was the only Protestant pacifist on the peace line, but there wasn't even time for peace-making today! I carried on running but was certain I heard the other girl saying, 'Wise up, wee girl. Yer man's a boot!'

I leapt across the peace line like a determined rioter hurdling a petrol bomb and scurried up Twaddell Avenue, past the prim Protestant hedges of customers I delivered bread to every Saturday morning from the Ormo Mini Shop. It was a cold February day but I was sweating like a pig, though the merciful Belfast drizzle on my face helped to cool me down. I swept past The Eagle newsagent shop on the Ballygomartin Road where Oul Mac was busy loading hundreds of *Belfast Telegraph*s into his new red Ford Transit van to distribute to his latest crew of paperboys, including my wee brother who was dutifully following in my professional bootsteps.

'Bout ye, Mac?' I shouted to my former employer as I flitted by.

Oul Mac turned around and stared at the strange figure in a duffle coat sprinting past with pink envelopes falling out of his school bag. A look of vague recognition crossed his wrinkled face as he took a drag of a cigarette and pulled up his trousers, which were now held up by string that had once bound together batches of newspapers. As I turned the corner towards the Glencairn estate I could hear Oul Mac in the distance shouting, 'What in the name of Jaysus was that?'

Finally I had to zip up the Ballygomartin Road, past the Westy Disco hut, the site of my greatest snogs, past our church and then up the tortuously steep hill to our estate. When I arrived at our rickety front gate I checked the time. According to my new digital watch it was 10.59, which is digital for 'nearly 11 o'clock'. I retrieved the front door key from underneath the doormat, dropped my Valentine-laden school bag in the hall and climbed the stairs three shag-piled steps at a time. I changed as swiftly as Superman in a telephone box, and within seconds I was out of my school uniform and in my leather brogues and good blue suit, which was 20 weeks at 99p from the *Great Universal Club Book*. To complete this breakneck transformation I splashed on some of my father's Old Spice to make me smell older and less sweaty and put on a skinny red leather tie like the one Michael Jackson wore, although Michael's tie probably wasn't reduced to half price in the bomb-damage sale in John Frazer's.

I was going to make it! My sprint home had saved time. It was 11.15 a.m. when I left the house in my good suit, clutching my interview letter and a piece and jam I had hurriedly made in the kitchen. I could catch a black taxi down the road in five minutes and make it to the train station before noon. I was elated knowing that, in spite of the awful risk I had taken earlier that day, I *could* have it all after all! I could receive the most Valentine cards for any boy in the long history of BRA and be en route to my place at university within an hour. As I waited at the bus stop, I thanked God for looking after me and keeping me from being late or shot.

As the minutes beeped away on my digital watch, though, I began to fret. What was keeping the black taxi? I hadn't seen any vehicles on the main road for a while. Was the road being blocked to save Ulster? Had the Provos blown up more shops in the town to free Ireland? Friday was always the most popular day of the week for bombs in Belfast.

'Listen, love, there's trouble down the road and all the buses and taxis is off!' shouted Billy Cooper's granny from across the street. She was one of my best bread customers in the estate, especially on a Saturday morning.

'And don't forget my pan and my plain and my two soda and two pataita the marra mornin'!' she added.

This was typical of Belfast! Just when I was about to do something important the Troubles got in the way. I had to start running again. This time I jogged down the Ballygomartin Road, taking a shortcut through Woodvale Park and past a tree with a faded carving of 'Tony Loves Sharon' in the bark. Then I scooted down the road, past the Shankill graveyard where lots of children had died much too young many years ago, passing 'His and Hers' hairdressers where they permed my mother and all the local pensioners. I flew past the falling-down Stadium Cinema opposite 'Spin a Disc' where I bought all my 45s, and the Shankill Library where I had borrowed all the Narnia books and *The Hobbit*. I ran on and on, past all the churches and pubs and King Billy murals, passing all the great wee shops and the smell of salt and vinegar from Beattie's Fish and Chip Shop. By the time I reached the city centre I was out of breath and had an awful stitch in my side, so the queue at the security gate where you got searched for bombs provided a welcome opportunity for a rest. Once I had been thoroughly frisked by a fat man with hairs up his nose I checked my digital watch again. It was 11.49, which was digital for 'nearly too late for the twelve o'clock train to Coleraine'! I zoomed towards the train station as fast as I could but my shins were very sore now from sprinting in my good brogues from the bargain bucket in MacManus's Shoes. I tried to convince myself that I might just make it. By the time I got to the train station it was 11.55. In the queue, a granny with a shopping trolley dropped her purse, and I helped her retrieve it with a level of urgency that seemed to disturb her. After she had completed the longest purchase of a return ticket to Lisburn in the history of Northern Ireland Railways, I bought my ticket and tore towards the platform as my watch beeped noon. Arriving on the platform, I could not believe my eyes – the last carriage of the Coleraine train was just disappearing out of the station! My heart sank like a poor swimmer in the Ormeau Baths. I imagined I was in one of those black and white movies on BBC2 on a Saturday afternoon that made my mother cry. My sweetheart had been waiting for me on the train so we could run off together and live happily ever after in Paris, but I was late and she had departed alone, heartbroken in the mistaken belief that I no longer wanted to be her lover. A friendly railway man with one buck tooth interrupted my Hollywood reverie.

'If you run quick, son, you might still catch the bus to Coleraine!' he advised, pointing me towards the bus station across the bridge. Off I loped again. What if I missed the bus too? How could I get a degree if I couldn't even use public transport? I was annoyed at myself and there was no one else to blame, not even my big brother or the Provos. All of my father's overtime at the foundry would come to nothing because I had been so proud and big-headed over getting more Valentine cards than anyone else in my class. I recalled the words of Rev. Lowe in church, 'Pride cometh before a fall.' My fall was cometh-ing, so it was.

I reached the bus station, exhausted and perspiring heavily through my good suit. The bus to Coleraine was driving off dispassionately. It was within spitting distance, but I was too late and too tired and upset to spit. This was worse than turning up at City Hall to watch the Twelfth parades after all the bands had already marched to the Field. My career prospects were devastated. As I stood alone in the bus station I had to try hard not to cry in public. This would only have completed my humiliation – boys weren't allowed to cry because it meant you were a homosexual. It was pathetic – I was seventeen years old now and shaving twice a week but all I wanted to do was cry and tell my mammy.

I found one of the least vandalised telephone boxes, which as usual smelt of pee, and I looked up the telephone number for Mackie's in the dirty *Yellow Pages*. My mother was working in the wages office of the foundry now, because the pay was better than sewing dresses and she no longer had to stay at home all the time to look after us.

'Can I speak to Mrs Macaulay in wages, please?' I asked. 'I'm her son.'

'Yes, love, just hang on a wee minute,' said the operator.

'What's wrong?' shrieked Mammy. A phone call at work usually meant someone was ill or dead, so I reassured her that I was neither. I confessed that I had missed the train and said I didn't know what to do and whined that I was never going to get into university and would end up signing on the dole in Snugville Street for the rest of my life.

'Oh my God, wee fella. That head of yours is full of sweetie mice!' was her initial response, but then she came up with a solution.

'Come on you up to the foundry and get the car keys from your daddy and drive up to Coleraine yourself in the new car. I'll phone the university and tell them you're going to be late.'

This was the perfect solution. Wee Betty was a brilliant problem solver. Of course, her family did give her lots of opportunities to practise.

'I don't know what we're goin' to do with you, son,' were the final words on the phone before the pips went and my 10p ran out. Within seconds I was off and running again. This was worse than being chased by wee hoods when I was collecting the money on a Friday night paper round. It was more physically demanding than a month of Saturday morning bread delivery with the Ormo Mini Shop. The strain on my legs was greater than when I was forced to do a three-mile cross-country run up the Cavehill by a spiteful PE teacher as punishment for being crap at rugby.

The most direct route to the foundry was up the Grosvenor

Road on the Catholic side of the peace wall, past lampposts flying Irish tricolours instead of Union Jacks, so I knew the journey would be treacherous. As I galloped past murals of Bobby Sands, my granny's words were ringing in my ears, 'Them Hunger Strike muriels are a blinkin' disgrace!' At any moment I could be stopped by an IRA man and exposed as a wee Prod and a legitimate target. This possibility accelerated my pace considerably up the Grosvenor Road and alongside the Royal Victoria Hospital. I feared I would be inside the hospital soon on an operating table having bullets removed without anaesthetic like a good cowboy shot by a gang of outlaws in the Wild West. This terror spurred me on as I crossed the Falls Road at hijack corner, keeping my head down and at the same time trying to look nonchalant at speed in good brogues, a suit and tie. What would happen if the people of the Falls Road mistook me for a tick man or a Mormon being chased from door-to-door duties?

Mercifully, I arrived unscathed at the front door of the Mackie's offices where my mother was waiting in her good beige anorak from the British Home Stores January sale. She was biting her nails and she looked relieved to see me.

'I don't know what we're going to do with you, wee lad. Your head's in cloud bloody cuckoo land!'

'It's not my fault, Mammy, the buses were off and I'm sweltered and my legs are killin' me and I've got a desperate stitch in my side!'

'You'll have to run down to the Albert Foundry and get the car keys from your Daddy!' she said urgently. 'Now away you go and don't be worrying, it'll be all right, love, so it will.'

I scooted down the side street off the main Springfield Road where millions of men in overalls went to work every morning and headed towards the huge metal gate at the entrance to the foundry.

'I'm Eric Macaulay's son, he's the foreman from Engineering 2 and I need to see him for an emergency!' I explained to the security man on the gate.

He looked me up and down and decided that I was not a terrorist disguised in a cheap suit and Michael Jackson tie attempting to blow up the factory for Ireland.

'Go on ahead, son, yer da's a right fella, so he is!' he said gruffly.

I had never set foot in the foundry before, and when I reached the factory floor I stopped, struggling to take it all in. There was nothing light or comforting or soft here. It was huge and hot and sweaty and noisy and I was surrounded by serious-looking men wearing protective goggles. There was molten metal, sparks flying in every direction and a cacophony of metallic clanks and bangs that made me jump. I had galloped straight into hell! It was like a scene from a post-apocalyptic science fiction movie, but this was real life on the Springfield Road. Mackie's was like *Mad Max*! It dawned on me that my father was a hero like Mel Gibson, struggling to survive every day in a hostile environment for the sake of his family. I had heard many stories about the foundry – the hard work, the good men, the poor pay and the bad bosses – but I had never experienced the reality of it before. This was where my father had worked for thirty years so that I would never have to.

'No son of mine is gonna spend his life breakin' his back for buttons!' he would say.

I was suddenly very conscious of my formal attire. The men working around me wore overalls stained with oil and I stood out like an Orangeman at a Novena. The grease and sweat on the men's faces made me feel clean and privileged and lazy. I noticed all the men had chunky dirty hands that made mine look white and soft, like a lady's hands in a Fairy Liquid commercial. I stuck my hands in my pockets, certain these hard working men were thinking to themselves 'What the hell's a wee soft snob like that doin' in a place like this?'

I had started moving back towards the door when an older man with kind eyes and blue overalls tapped me on the shoulder.

'You're not supposed to be in here, son,' he said, sensing my discomfort.

'I'm Eric Macaulay's son and I need to see him for an emergency!' I shouted over the clamour of industry, trying not to sound too grammar school.

'Aye, yer da's a right fella, so he is. He's very proud of you theee wee boys!' he said kindly as if he'd known me all my life.

He patted me on the back just for being my father's son, and pointed to a sort of office with dirty plastic windows in the corner of the foundry.

'Yer da's over there!' he said.

I was never so glad to see the back of my father's baldy head. As I approached the office, ducking flying sparks en route, I could see that Dad was standing in the office surrounded by a group of tough-looking men in overalls who hung on his every word. They

were looking at a huge piece of machinery on a big metal table. When I reached the door Dad was explaining how to fix this monstrous clump of cogs in the same way he once tried to explain to me how to fix my remote control Dalek when my big brother kicked off its sucker just for badness. Suddenly he noticed his very clean son in a suit at the door of his foundry office. He stopped immediately and strode towards me in a manner that suggested both concern and anger.

'Here's the car keys, ya stupid wee glipe!' he said, throwing them at me. 'Are you gonna throw away your chances of not endin' up in a place like this because your head's in the bloody clouds?'

'It's not my fault! The buses were off and I'm sweltered and I've got a desperate stitch,' I replied, catching the car keys by the key ring with one hand, and cupping the pain in my side dramatically with the other.

But as soon as I had uttered those words I felt guilty. The men in this place knew what it was like to be sweltered and have a stitch in their side every day. Until that moment I had been truly ignorant of the daily life of a working man. My bread round was a Sunday School picnic compared to this.

'Are you gonna stand there like a wee prig, or are you gonna get your arse outta here?' my father demanded.

I turned to make my way towards the car park and he added, 'Now away you go and don't be worrying, it'll be all right son, so it will.'

Within two minutes I was in the foundry car park and there it was before me — our brand new car. The humiliating days of the Ford Escort respray were behind us now. This was the first time we had ever been able to afford a brand new car on hire purchase, and now that I had finally passed my driving test I could drive it with pride. It was a brand new green Simca. A Skoda was deemed less reliable and a Lada was slightly outside of our price range. I called it 'The Green Dream Machine' but Timothy Longsley called it a 'Simp Car'. I jumped into the gleaming green vehicle, settled into the faux suede driver's seat, turned the ignition key and began my epic journey to university.

As I left West Belfast I turned on our very first car radio and The Jam were singing 'A Town Called Malice'. As I rocketed up the motorway, leaving behind all that was familiar, that odd-lookin' wee man from Soft Cell was coincidently singing 'Say Hello, Wave Goodbye'. When I reached the edge of the city I felt like an Apollo astronaut about to break free from the earth's gravitational pull for the first time. I was all alone driving north of Glengormley for the first time in my life. For a moment I forgot that I was late for my university interview. When the Radio 1 DJ, Peter Powell with the perm, introduced Orchestral Manoeuvres in the Dark's new single it seemed like the perfect theme tune for my hopeful new beginnings. I turned up the radio to full volume and, with the grand synthesized sounds of 'Maid of Orleans' filling the interior of the Simca, imagined I had just stolen my grandaddy's red Cadillac convertible from Southfork Ranch in *Dallas* and was speeding along Route 66 in sunglasses and a Stetson hat on my way to become the richest and most famous man in America. I was dead excited, so I was!

2

SEA, SAND AND STUDENTS

I was lost, so I was. I had driven up the motorway alone for the first time ever. This was against the law for a newly-qualified R driver, so I was very aware that at any moment an undercover RUC patrol might apprehend me and I would end up being interrogated in a cell in Castlereagh rather than the university in Coleraine. After several secret failures I had finally passed my driving test. The driving examiner had congratulated me with the encouraging words, 'And for God's sake will you stop driving like a bloody granny!' So far, my driving had caused an unexpected mix of conflict and confusion in my life. On one occasion, my mother nearly had a canary because I breathed in tight whilst squeezing the car through the tiny gap between a bin lorry and a Chrysler Sunbeam on the Shankill Road.

'The car doesn't get any smaller by you breathin' in, ya eejit!' she shrieked, hitting me across the back of the head with the Green Shield stamps book from the glove compartment while my big brother sniggered in the back seat. There is no truth whatsoever in his allegation that I then lost my temper, called my dear mother 'a fuckin' oul goat', stormed out of the car and had to walk home in the rain. On another memorable evening I was stopped at a police checkpoint on the way home from a rock gospel concert in Glengormley Presbyterian. Hundreds of us had enjoyed Andy McCarroll & Moral Support playing Christian punk and a dozen girls had queued up at the end to seek Andy's counsel on getting saved.

'Your eyes are poppin' outta your head, son', observed an RUC man with a moustache before inviting me to blow into his Breathalyser.

'But I've just got contact lenses for my birthday and they're dead sore, so they are,' was my honest explanation.

Of course, my sober breath proved my innocence, but I was affronted that I had been accused of such evil on my way home from an evangelical event where only minutes before I had been praising Jesus with electric guitars. My only intoxication that night had been spiritual.

'Why are youse picking on me instead of being out catching terrorists?' I wondered.

On the day of my interview though, the problems really began once I left the security of the motorway. I was certain I had followed all the signs to Coleraine. I had passed Ballymena, where they loved money and Paisley, and ended up in Ballymoney, where Titch McCracken said the Lost Tribe of Israel lived. This theory now seemed plausible to me, because I myself got lost very quickly in Ballymoney. I knew for a fact that there was a brilliant bike rider from Ballymoney called Joey Dunlop, so I imagined I was Joey in a big race driving around the one-way system in laps, and eventually I found my way back onto the main road to Coleraine. I was excited to be nearing my future. I knew very little about Coleraine apart from the fact it was near the Giant's Causeway and the people up there made cheese in the same way that people in Cookstown made Geordie Best sausages. Once I arrived in Coleraine town centre, however, I was lost once more. I tried to find the route on my father's AA map of Ireland but for some reason it didn't include the streets of Coleraine, and when I couldn't fold the map up again properly I ended up cursing and throwing the whole crumpled mess on to the back seat. The wee orange light came on in the Simca dashboard indicating that I was running out of petrol and I realised I had only the change from my train fare in my pocket. I started to panic and sweat yet again. I was aware I was driving too fast. I couldn't find the road to the university anywhere. I was driving around in circles past pubs and churches for ages. Then at last, to my enormous relief, I recognised the tall building from the front cover of the university prospectus in the distance. The New University of Ulster was basically a cement skyscraper in a big field beside a lovely river. It was the only skyscraper in Coleraine, although it wasn't anywhere near as tall as the Empire State Building or Divis Flats. As I finally approached this place of learning, Bucks Fizz were singing 'The Land of Make Believe' on the radio (Bucks Fizz were a sort of English ABBA who had their skirts dramatically shortened when they were making their minds up). I surveyed the imposing institution before me and concluded that the university was accurately named because it looked very 'new' indeed, even though the campus looked more like the DeLorean Motor factory than Queen's University. The main building was connected to other smaller buildings by what appeared to be an exceptionally long bus shelter spanning the middle of a big field. Hordes of cold-looking students in jeans were walking up and down the bus shelter with books under their arms and, contrary to Titch McCracken's assertions, not one of them was smoking marijuana. I instantly wanted to be one of them. I imagined myself in a new pair of jeans from John Frazer's in Gresham Street, carrying books by poets and philosophers that were too complicated to read and going to lectures given by bearded men with English accents on every possible '-ology'.

Mrs Grant in our street had a son at university in England, although he seemed to have been there for years and never came home. She was very proud of her genius son and managed to mention his university status in almost every conversation. My mother had recently dared to compete while queuing in the post office for her family allowance, informing Mrs Grant that her Tony had an interview at the New University of Ulster, so he did. Mrs Grant reportedly replied that her son was at a proper university with red bricks. I thought this was an odd boast to make because all the poorest houses in Belfast were built with red bricks. It had never occurred to me that red bricks were a symbol of academic prowess. In West Belfast, red bricks were for throwing at the Brits. When I parked the green Simca and bounded up the million steps to the front door I couldn't spot a single red brick lurking in the architecture of the New University of Ulster.

In the glass entrance doors to the main building my reflection showed a flustered-looking wee lad in a blue suit with a slightly askew Michael Jackson tie and a sweat-soaked fringe. I looked more like a very young member of Kraftwerk after an Olympic race against Sebastian Coe than a proper student, but I was already two hours late for the interview so there was no time to fix myself. I dashed past a scale model of the university campus up to the reception desk, and a grumpy security man directed me towards another building at the far end of the longest bus shelter in the world. Running along this passageway I appreciated how the plastic wall on one side protected me from the icy wind, but I felt very self-conscious being so well-dressed compared to the proper students with their punky hair and snarly mouths.

Unbelievably, when I arrived on the far side of the campus I got lost once again. I had never been later or more lost in my life. This latest building was a maze of narrow corridors with confusing numbers on all the doors. I was more panicked than ever. It was nearly five o'clock and if I didn't arrive soon I was certain the professors would have to forget about me and go home or their dinners would be burnt. At my lowest point I opened one promising-looking door and a mop and bucket smelling of boke fell out. I was close to tears. I didn't deserve this! Today was supposed to be my big opportunity to come up in the world but everything was conspiring against me! Just as I was on the brink of giving up and returning to beg the surly security man for help, I turned the corner into a long corridor and found a row of chairs and a door marked 'Interviews: Do Not Disturb'. A small, spotty teenager was on the seat nearest the door. He was wearing faded jeans and a red T-shirt with a picture of a longhaired man in a beret. I assumed he was a fellow potential student who was also here to begin his intellectual transformation. He looked sweaty and nervous and he was staring down at his Dr Marten's, which reminded me of the boots I once hid money in to avoid hoods and robbers on my paper round when I was a wee kid.

'Are you here for the Media Studies interview?' I asked breathlessly.

'Aye,' he replied, looking up briefly.

This teenager had even more spots than me and I could tell from personal experience that he picked them. I breathed a deep sigh of relief and sat down beside him. Once I had caught my breath, I decided to make friends with my future fellow academic.

'What's your name?'

'Marty. What's your name?'

'Tony. Where you from?'

'Derry.'

Catholic, I thought.

'Where you from?'

'Belfast.'

'You wanna do media?'

'Aye.'

Just as we were really starting to get along, I asked, 'Do you think there are many people trying to get a place on this course?'

'Aye,' replied Marty seriously. 'Let's hope there aren't too many fuckin' snobs from the likes of Belfast Royal Academy!'

I blushed and then replied very quickly, 'Aye, right 'nuff!'

'What football team do ye support?' he asked.

'Leeds United,' I replied.

I didn't support any football team but I always answered Leeds in such circumstances in case the person posing the question thought I was a homosexual.

'That's soccer,' he corrected me sternly. 'What *football* team do ye support? I'm a Derry man.'

I realised he was talking about the Catholic football they played in Irish in Crossmaglen so I desperately tried to think of the name of a team, but I didn't know any. My father always changed channels when they were showing a GAA match on TV because he feared the BBC was using the sport to try to seduce us into a United Ireland. Mercifully the door opened then, and a bearded professor wearing brown corduroys appeared, just like on the Open University on BBC2. He ushered out a very attractive blonde girl wearing denim shorts like Daisy in *The Dukes of Hazzard*.

'Thank you, Marina,' he said in a deep voice.

As our eyes followed Marina's denim shorts down the long corridor, I noticed that Marty and I actually did have something in common, though I was surprised to see that the professor held his gaze on Marina's Daisy Dukes for a much longer period than either Marty or myself did. For a minute he seemed deeply distracted, as if he was thinking about something most absorbing. I assumed this was what happened when you became an intellectual. Eventually, his thoughts returned to his next two interviewees and I put up my hand to ask a question.

'You don't have to put your hand up here,' he said kindly. 'This is not school. We are not instruments of control and conformity here.'

I had no idea what he was talking about but I lowered my hand obediently.

'Sorry,' I said hoping he wouldn't take marks off me for this mistake. 'I'm Tony Macaulay and I was supposed to be here at three o'clock but there were lots of bombs scares and riots in Belfast, so there were, and I ...'

'It's okay, your mother phoned to say you'd missed the train and you were in a bit of state. You're the one from Belfast Royal Academy aren't you?'

I felt Marty wince beside me. My being at BRA seemed to offend him.

'Yes,' I confessed, blushing. Marty stood up.

'I'm Marty Mullen from Derry and I was here on time and I have a right te be seen first!' he said defiantly.

I wished I could be this confident with a professor.

'Come on ahead, Marty,' said the professor and ushered my competition into his office. 'Just two more after you,' he added, looking somewhat weary.

I was confused. When I went to primary school I was a snob because, unlike my classmates in the Council estate, I lived in a semi-detached house, and when I went to grammar school I was a pleb because I came from up the Shankill. I had assumed that my social inferiority would be even more acute at university, but it seemed from my limited interaction with Marty Mullen that here I might be a snob again. Was I going to have to hide who I was and where I was from for the rest of my life? Before this thought could gain any traction, a tall young man appeared at the end of the corridor. He was wearing a Columbo raincoat, army combat trousers, suede ankle boots and a tablecloth scarf around his neck like Simon Le Bon from Duran Duran. I had never seen any of these New Romantic-type clothes available over 20 weeks at any price in the *Great Universal Club Book*. This guy looked as if he'd just stepped off the stage of *Top of the Pops*. I noticed how relaxed he was, even though I guessed he was also attending an interview to decide on the rest of his life. He didn't seem to notice me at all at first, such was the intensity of his concentration on the music from his Sony Walkman.

'Hi,' he said in an English accent.

'Bout ye?' I replied.

He looked slightly confused by my greeting. He offered me his hand.

'I'm Byron Drake from Romford, Essex,' he said confidently.

'I'm Tony Macaulay from Belfast, so I am.'

There was that confused look again.

He was friendly and confident and looked like a proper student even though he hadn't even got on the course yet. I liked him straight away. It was a new experience for me to feel less confident than my peers. Following my triumph on the stage in *West Side Story* I was more confident than most boys at my school, but I had only met two possible peers here and they both seemed much more confident than me. I shook Byron's hand and he looked me up and down with a sympathetic smile, the same way I looked at my wee brother when he forgot to brush his hair before going to church.

'What are you listening to?' I asked.

'Joy Division,' he said, as if these two words were truly sacred.

'Ah yeah, "Love Will Tear Us Apart". That's class, so it is.' I said.

This was true because it was a brilliant song and you could sing along to the chorus, like 'Super Trouper'.

'Too commercial,' he stated with great authority. 'The album tracks are far better. Which album do you like best, Tone?' he enquired.

I was amazed at how quickly I had become 'Tone'. I didn't know the name of any Joy Division albums.

'Er … the early ones,' I ventured. 'Before they became too commercial.'

I knew this was the right answer because Ian Forrester at school always said this about Adam and the Ants and he knew about such matters because he read the *New Musical Express*. When Adam and the Ants went to number one in the charts for the first time, the band's name was Tippexed off half the school bags in middle sixth the next day.

'Me too,' replied Byron. 'Their early stuff is really, really dark.'

'Yeah', I agreed.

'Really, really deep', said Byron.

'Yeah,' I nodded sagely.

'Yeah, Tone. Really, really dark and really, really deep.'

We nodded together knowledgeably for a few seconds. I was relieved that I had managed to disguise my ignorance of the more obscure compositions of Joy Division.

'What's your favourite band, Tone?' he asked.

ABBA, I thought.

'Pink Floyd' I said quickly.

Now I was thinking on my feet. This conversation was proving to be good practice for coming up with the correct answers for my impending interview. My grown-up cousin Derek had hundreds of albums by all of the most critically acclaimed rock bands that you couldn't sing-along with and I remembered him talking enthusiastically about 'The Floyd'.

'Ah, old school, Tone,' he said. 'And what's your favourite Floyd album?'

Pause.

'Oh, all of them,' I replied as if it was too difficult to choose from my entire Pink Floyd collection. Little did Byron know that the solitary Pink Floyd record I owned was the single of 'Another Brick in the Wall' even though I was still annoyed that it had kept ABBA's 'I Have a Dream' off the Christmas number one spot in 1979.

'Some Floyd is almost Nietzschean, you know,' pronounced Byron.

I had no idea what he was talking about but it sounded clever, and with his English accent Byron was immediately my superior. It dawned on me that I had a very long way to go if I were to become an authentic intellectual at university. I clearly had a great deal to learn, and Byron Drake was streets ahead of me. He was the same age as me but he looked like a student and sounded like an intellectual. Beside him I felt unworldly, ill-informed and immature. He listened to proper music that you couldn't sing-along to, and I was just some wee good livin' fella from up the Shankill. Beside Byron Drake I felt like I was Titch McCracken!

'Are you a Protestant or a Catholic?' he asked, more directly than was the norm among the natives. 'And what the hell are you guys over here fighting over religion for anyway?'

I was about to attempt an explanation on how it wasn't as simple as that and I was going to explain that I was, in fact, a Protestant pacifist from the peace line, when the professor's office door opened. Marty Mullen brushed rudely past me , the spots on his flushed face glowing from the pressure.

'Good luck, Tone!' said Byron.

I quickly escaped into the interview room, where thankfully the questioning was much less demanding

One hour later I was back in the green Simca driving out of the university, and after all the panic of the day, I could finally start to relax. I was certain that the professor had been impressed when I told him I wanted to be a great journalist like Woodward or Bernstein or Wogan. The theme from 'Hill Street Blues' was playing on the car radio and I imagined I was a tough, no-nonsense American cop on patrol in my police car on the look-out for drug dealers and pimps. I had just been for an interview with Captain Frank Furillo for promotion in the precinct, and now I was on an undercover mission to clean up the mean streets. However my daydream was interrupted when a sign with a picture of a bucket and spade and saying 'Welcome to Portsewart' appeared before me. I was so busy wondering whether the answers to all the questions had been intellectual enough that I had taken a wrong turn, and instead of taking the road back towards Belfast I was heading towards the sea.

As I motored on down the hill, a vast expanse of dark blue

ocean opened up in front of me. The sight of the sea took my breath away. As I approached the water, the crests of the choppy waves reminded me of the drawing on the cover of *The Cruel Sea*, which had cost me £1.50 in fines to the Shankill Library after I lost it down the back of the sofa. I turned the corner to avoid driving into the sea and saw the sea foam blowing across the road and a sign which said 'Atlantic Circle.' This was the Atlantic Ocean! I had driven to the very edge of Northern Ireland and the next stop was America! If I put a message in a bottle here it would float across the Atlantic Ocean and wash up at the feet of the Statue of Liberty.

A few minutes later I turned a sharp corner to find a beautiful little harbour with old wooden boats and sea spray splashing over the walls. Then I was driving along a street with shops on one side and the sea on the other. It was as if all the shops on one side of the Shankill Road had been demolished and replaced with a beach. The wee orange light on the dashboard was still warning that I needed to buy petrol so I decided to stop the car and ask in one of the shops if they had a petrol station in Portstewart. I parked the car within a few feet of the waves and walked along the windy promenade. I found a small but irresistible amusement arcade and wasted 50p on several games of *Pac-Man*, but the ghosts kept getting me no matter how fast I tried to eat the wee dots. Next I discovered an old-fashioned ice cream café called Morelli's. Inside it was like a 1950's American diner, like the one in *Happy Days*, with lots of mirrors and big long glasses with straws. The café had huge old black-and-white pictures of the Giants' Causeway and Dunluce Castle on the walls. It was cold and wet outside so there were very few customers purchasing pokes and 99s. I surveyed the menu of delights above the counter and ordered an indulgent knickerbocker glory with my train fare change. I had never seen an ice cream constructed on such a scale before. The knickerbocker glory in Morelli's was like a poke for the Queen. I ate it alone but the ice cream made me shiver, so I had to return to the counter to order a hot drink to warm me up again. I was impressed at the variety of the food and beverages available outside of Belfast. I opted for another new taste from the menu called a Russian Tea, which I assumed was something communists drank in between vodkas. This exotic beverage was basically hot tea with a slice of lemon, served in a long glass instead of a wee cup and saucer and without milk or a Marie biscuit. The nice lady behind the counter gave me directions to the petrol station and I wrote them down on a napkin. By this stage I thought all the excitement was over but there was more drama to come, even though the day had already contained all the drama of an episode of *Dallas*, but without the oil or sex. On my way to the petrol station I noticed a sign for the beach. It seemed a shame to visit the seaside and not to go to the beach even if it was too cold and dark to build a sandcastle or go for a wee paddle on the shore. As I followed the signs I discovered, to my utter amazement, that you were actually allowed to drive your car on to the beach. This was irresistible, and so I steered the green Simca onto the sand and sped along Portstewart Strand, swerving past the larger clumps of seaweed. I imagined I was Lawrence of Arabia from my mother's favourite film, riding a camel with sand dunes on my left and waves on my right. At the end of the beach I found an old concrete army sentry post from World War Two which I used as a public convenience, as the Russian Tea and icy winds had stimulated my kidneys considerably. When I returned to the car to drive back to the petrol station, though, yet another disaster had struck. The back wheels were stuck in the sand! The more I revved my engine, the deeper the wheels embedded in the soft wet sand. The poor green Simca reminded me of the the evil man in the pith helmet who had fallen into sinking sand after trying to shoot Tarzan on BBC2. I tried to dig the wheels out with my bare hands in my good blue suit but my efforts failed and my good brogues filled up with sand too. I tried to remember what I had learned in Scouts about survival but there were no ropes anywhere to tie knots in. Instead I grabbed a piece of driftwood and used it as an improvised spade. Lord Baden Powell would have been proud of me. In spite of this ingenious improvisation, my frantic efforts achieved nothing. I was stranded on the strand, cold, wet, exhausted and all alone. Then, as I stood up straight to rub my aching back, I realised to my horror that the tide was coming in! It was only a matter of time before the waves were lapping at the hubcaps of the green Simca. This was the first new car my father had ever been able to afford to buy on hire purchase and soon it was going to be submerged in the Atlantic Ocean like the *Titanic* and my da would kill me! Not even a DeLorean could survive this.

I sprinted back down the beach to seek help but the beach seemed longer on foot and once again I was sweating and panting and developing a painful stitch in my side. I ran as fast as I could but the soft sand seemed to deliberately slow me down, like in one of those nightmares where you're running away from exterminating Daleks but you're paralysed and can't run at all. Just as I was about to come up in the world I was on the verge of disaster again. What would I say to my father? Sorry, Daddy, the Portstewart Provos hijacked the Simca and drove it into the sea?

I was beginning to regret the knickerbocker glory, but just as the exotic dish seemed like it might make a violent return I spotted the lights of a huge hotel close to the beach. I ran up the steps to the Strand Hotel, past a sign advertising a disco in the basement, and arrived at the reception desk, upset and dishevelled. A middle-aged woman with a big hairdo, glasses and make-up like Sybil in *Fawlty Towers* looked me up and down. I half expected Basil to arrive on the scene.

'My daddy's Simca is sinking in the sand and the tide's comin' in and he'll kill me!' I spluttered pathetically.

Shaking her head and without speaking to me, Sybil lifted the telephone and dialed a number. After a few seconds the person picked up.

'Young William, love, there's another one stuck on the beach here. Can you sort this wee crater out, hey?'

Within half an hour a helpful farmer arrived on a tractor with a towrope. Young William looked about sixty years old. I wondered what age Old William might be. My rescuer reminded me of the workingmen in the foundry earlier today, except he had a country accent that sounded almost Scottish and he smelt of farm rather than oil. Of course, by this point I had sweated so profusely that I smelt worse than any farm.

If only I had brought my Hai Karate aftershave with me, I

thought, at least I could mask my BO a bit.

'Youse boys from Belfast think youse know everything but youse boys from Belfast know nothin',' said Young William kindly as we made our way towards what I feared would be the first Simca submarine.

Thankfully the waves had only just begun to lick around the front wheels of the precious family car. Young William appeared unconcerned, and within minutes the endangered vehicle had been hitched up and towed to safety. I thanked him at least a dozen times and felt wick that I had no money to give him.

'Just you be more careful next time, young sonny ma lad,' he said as he departed in his big green tractor. It seemed to me that this Massey Ferguson was Thunderbird 2 sent by International Rescue and Young William was actually Scott Tracy himself, now on his way back to Tracy Island, rather than to feed the pigs near Aghadowey.

With what little physical and mental energy I had left I managed to find a little petrol station called Larkhill where an old man put the petrol in for you. I offered him 90p – which, minus the cost of a knickerbocker glory, a Russian Tea and a game of *Pac-Man*, was all I had left from my train fare change – to buy a drop of petrol which I prayed would be enough to bring me back home to Belfast.

Thankfully the journey home was uneventful, and when I finally arrived back under the comforting shadow of the Black Mountain I turned up the car radio to blast out Tight Fit's 'The Lion Sleeps Tonight'. As I sang along to the 'awhimaways' my mind drifted from my interview to my beach trauma, to Byron and Marty, knickerbocker glories, student life and Bo Derek. Arriving home I was subjected to a further interview by my parents on what the professor had asked me and what I thought of the university and if I had made any wee friends and why were my good brogues full of wet sand and when was I going to get my head out of Cloud Nine and wise up a bit. When I finally got to bed that night I dreamt that I was a student with books under my arm, walking through the longest bus shelter in the world and listening to Joy Division on a Sony Walkman, and the tide was coming in and Young William and Bo Derek were coming in a floating DeLorean to save me. In spite of all the drama of the day, the whole experience simply made me want to become a student more than ever. I was determined to study hard and pass my A levels and go to the New University of Ulster. I was going to get off Cloud Nine and become confident and an intellectual and dead mature and all, so I was.

3

BREADBOY NO MORE

For the next four months I continued to dream of becoming an undergraduate with blue jeans and big books. Following my brief encounter with Byron Drake, I decided that I needed to extend my musical and literary repertoire in more credible directions. I borrowed the biggest, longest and heaviest book I could find in the whole of the Shankill Library. It was called *War and Peace* and it was by a famous author called Leo Tolstoy, who was a sort of C.S. Lewis of Russia. Then I bought a cassette by a serious New Romantic band called Spandau Ballet. Most of their lyrics made no sense, proving that they were really, really deep. I bought an extended play Spandau Ballet record called 'Instinction'. This was my first twelve-inch single purchase since ABBA's 'Lay All Your Love on Me'. The difference between my two twelve-inches was that no one understood 'Instinction', proving that it was music for the more cerebral music fan. The only ABBA song I had difficulty deciphering was 'Bang-A-Boomerang' on their *Greatest Hits* album and I was pretty sure Benny and Björn were not attempting to affirm their intellectualism on that particular track.

I studied diligently for my English A level but I struggled to revise with any sense of purpose for my Maths and Physics exams. The careers advice from Belfast Royal Academy was 'Do Science!' and although I was much more interested in studying History and Politics to help me understand the world better, I ended up studying Maths and Physics at A level because I got an A in these subjects in my O levels. My parents did not dare contradict the headmaster's advice that my future lay in science alone, but I put up sufficient resistance to be allowed to continue with English because it was my favourite subject and I had won school prizes in English for being so good at it, so I had. Due to my unusual combination of subjects I ended up in a very small English A level class with just five other classmates. The educational advantages of a smaller classroom were enhanced considerably by the fact that the other five pupils were attractive girls. Our teacher was Mr Dyson, a brand new young teacher who was so enthusiastic about William Shakespeare and Jane Austen that I actually looked forward to going to his classes. Mr Dyson talked to us and listened to us like we were adults and he gave the impression that school might be about enjoying learning and not just about passing exams. Mr Dyson wrote proper poetry and laughed at me when I tried to impress him by using too many gargantuan words in my effervescent essays on 'the metaphor of the moor' in the work of Thomas Hardy.

During these months I focused almost entirely on the future. It was the best approach to take when you lived in a city that was always looking to the past. Soldiers and paramilitaries and children and shoppers continued to die on the streets every week, and a few days after every awful killing came the sad sight of suffering families walking behind the coffins. I didn't care which flag they put on the coffin; all I saw were the heartbroken mothers and weeping wives and small children with tears and snatters clutching wilting flowers and walking behind dark hearses in the rain. Every funeral I saw made me more of a pacifist but I noticed it made many people hate the other side even more. I was weary listening to the same old arguments on the television news. *Scene Around Six* felt like it was being repeated more often than *Columbo*. The only fact Catholics and Protestants seemed to agree on was that 'themuns started it'. I closed my ears to the men who justified or condemned one slaughter but not another. I refused to listen to 'ah, but what about when yousens did that to us' again and again and again. This ugly clamour faded into the background when I surveyed the faces of shattered families shuffling behind those coffins in the rain. Sometimes I wanted to climb up on to the dome of the City Hall and scream down at the whole city, 'What about your bloody children?' But I realised that such language would be inappropriate for a Sunday School teacher and I was afraid I might slip and fall off the dome and end up in the Royal for stitches.

While the rest of the world was more interested in Margaret Thatcher going to war against Argentina in the Falkland Islands, the Troubles went on and on, and unemployment in Belfast went up and up. The DeLorean Motor factory in Dunmurry closed down and everyone was completely scundered. When they shut down the big Enkalon factory in Antrim it seemed as if the whole of Northern Ireland would soon be shut down. Every night on

Good Evening Ulster Gloria Hunniford told us who else had lost their jobs. Even the shipyard in East Belfast, where they built the most famous ship that ever sank, was laying off hundreds of workers. My parents were worried that Mackie's would be next and feared they would end up on the dole and we would lose the green Simca and our house and everything. The spectre of unemployment made my successful education more important than ever.

At long last, the day of my A level results arrived. To gain a place on the Media Studies degree course I needed a minimum of two Cs. On hearing this news in the sixth form common room, Timothy Longsley felt compelled to comment that this proved I was destined for a 'Mickey Mouse course at a Mickey Mouse university'. I replied that Media Studies was not a 'Mickey Mouse course' and there was nothing wrong with Mickey Mouse anyway because Walt Disney was a genius, so he was.

Having received loads of As in my O levels, expectations were high that I would exceed the requirements, but as I had failed to make a significant breakthrough in my understanding of mechanics in the months leading up to my Maths and Physics exams I wasn't so certain. The news of my eleven-plus and O levels had arrived by post, but on this occasion I could phone the school office and be informed of my results by a human being. I had butterflies in my stomach when the clock struck nine o'clock and I reached for the telephone. My parents were at work in the foundry and my big brother was watching cricket on the television while my wee brother played in the backyard on the new skateboard that had replaced his punctured spacehopper.

'Hello, it's Tony Macaulay. I'm calling for my A levels, so I am.'

'Yes, dear,' said the friendly school secretary. 'Just let me look it up …'

I held on to the phone as if I was Captain James T. Kirk on my communicator, waiting to hear from Lieutenant Uhura whether it was possible to beam me up from an alien planet on the brink of destruction.

'You got a B in English …'

Disappointing – I was supposed to get an A in English.

'An E in Maths …'

That's a fail!

'And an E in Physics.'

That's another fail!

'Thank you,' I said meekly, and hung up the phone.

'Well what did you get, ya big swot?' shouted my big brother.

I took a deep breath.

'One B and two Es,' I answered humbly.

The guffaws in the living room drowned out the sound of the cricket commentary from Lord's Cricket Ground for several overs.

'William friggin' Shakespeare only got a B in English!' he roared.

I was badly shaken, but I realised that I needed to calm down and work out if a B and two Es were equivalent to two Cs. If not, I was doomed to work as a breadboy in the Ormo Mini Shop for the rest of my life.

'Buzzzzzzzz!' mocked my big brother, now lying on his back

on the living room floor. 'B-E-E, buzzzzzzy bee!'

'Shut yer bake, you,' I cried. 'At least I'm not a drop-out like *some* people. I'm trying to count if it adds up to two Cs.'

'Sure it's official now. An E in Maths – you don't know how to count!'

He ran outside to the backyard to share the good news with my wee brother.

'The big fruit failed! Buzzzzzzz!'

As my siblings began a celebratory game of 'keepy uppy' in the backyard I did the maths once, then twice, and finally breathed a sigh of relief when I worked out I had just made it. I had scraped just enough points to be accepted onto my chosen course at the New University of Ulster.

It's a good thing I didn't want to go to Queen's, I thought.

I decided to phone some school friends for reassurance. Nearly everyone had got As and Bs and was going to university in England, though Linda Mulligan cryptically told everyone she got 'a C and two other very high grades' and Aaron Ward was similarly nonspecific but sounded even more disappointed than me. Once I was satisfied that I had secured my place at university, however, my heart stopped pounding and I phoned my mother at the wages office in the foundry.

'I got in!' I said triumphantly.

'Oh my God, wait 'til I tell your father! What did you get?'

'One B and two Es,' I replied somewhat less triumphantly.

'Buzzzzzzzzzz!' went my wee brother, who was now imitating the sound and motion of a bumblebee as he flew up and down the hallway on his skateboard.

'I told you I didn't want to do science but yousens made me do it,' I complained.

'Well, maybe if you'd done a bit less coortin' round Glengormley,' she replied.

Maybe my mother was right. Maybe Lindsay Johnson had been right all along to obey Jesus and chuck me to revise more for her A levels. When my father arrived home that night he didn't even mention my grades. He shook my hand formally and said, 'This son of mine is going to university'.

Once the disappointment of my grades had passed the realisation that I really was on my way to university began to sink in. Within a few days the official offer letter from the university arrived and I was elated. All my aunts and uncles sent me congratulation cards with money inside and everyone on our street was impressed. Auntie Mabel gave me a big hug and a Kit Kat and my Auntie Hetty said I was 'a quare smasher'. Mrs Piper warned me to be careful because most students were IRA sympathisers and Mr Black said, 'Aye, so you think you're better than the rest of us now, don't you?'

Over the next few weeks I would have to find somewhere to live in Coleraine and prepare to move out of my childhood home. In all the excitement, I almost forgot that academic study and soda farl delivery were incompatible, and I realised that I had some important business matters to deal with. Although I had once thought that this day might never come, it was no longer possible to continue with my career as a breadboy.

On my final Saturday morning as executive assistant to Leslie McGregor in the last Ormo Mini Shop in the world, I was wakened at six o'clock as usual by the depressing news on Downtown Radio. This was followed by the farming round-up on the price of pigs in Portadown and an uplifting new single called 'Come on Eileen'. It seemed as if Dexy's Midnight Runners were urging me to pluck up the courage to inform Leslie of my resignation, even though my name wasn't Eileen. I had planned to inform Leslie immediately, before the delivery of a single bap, but when I arrived into the van I noticed that the master breadman was on particularly cheery form. There was a special offer on the Veda loaves and apparently he had just been given another high-level security briefing by the chief inspector of the RUC.

'C'mere til I tell ye, son,' he said, smiling with every tooth he could still muster. 'Them Vedas'll go like hot cakes the day and the police has stepped up security in the estate because of intelligence.'

I was loath to spoil his good humour by announcing my imminent departure so soon. I was certain he would be devastated and struggle to find a sufficiently trustworthy successor, so I decided to hold off with my resignation until our mid-morning break. Leslie had parked the van behind the boarded-up shops across from the UDA community centre and, as we sat down for our customary can of Lilt and a Florence cake that was past its sell-by date, I finally plucked up the courage to share the bad news. Leslie and I had been colleagues for years now. Together, we had dutifully delivered bread to the customers of the Upper Shankill through riots, bomb scares and snowstorms. His customers referred to me as 'The Wee Lad' – not just any old wee lad, *The* Wee Lad. In the quiet moments between customers on

Saturday mornings, Leslie and I had stood between the shelves of plain loaves and potato farls discussing religion and politics and the perfect wheaten bannock.

'You know the way I got into university with my A levels and all?' I said.

'Yes, you did well, young lad. Your father's as proud as punch, so he is.'

'Well, er, when I move up to university I won't be home every weekend … and there's nothin' wrong with bein' a bread boy or nothin', so there's not, er … but I'm going to have to give it up. But I'll stay on until you find someone else …'

'Aye, young Mark's startin' next week,' Leslie interrupted.

This was not the response I had expected.

'Sure he did a grand job with the extra pan loaf orders for sandwiches for the Field when you were away with the youth club for the Twelfth fortnight.'

I was relieved that the news of my departure was not as devastating as expected but my obvious dispensability came as something of a shock. Leslie had obviously been planning for this eventuality for some time, which proved that my mother's assessment of his business acumen was correct. 'His nibs is no dozer, so he's not,' she often said.

Leslie was about to launch into a fulsome tribute to my career when Billy Cooper's granny climbed up the steps of the Mini Shop.

'A pan, a plain, two soda and two pataita,' she said.

With this interruption we were on our way again. Leslie generously informed all subsequent customers that 'The Wee

Lad' was leaving and this produced a few extra tips from my best customers such as Miss Adams, who was not related to Gerry.

'Only always do your best, young man,' said Miss Adams. 'Your best is only always what you can do.'

Mrs McAlister, who lived beside the peace line and had cages on her front windows, gave me a kiss on the cheek, and her daughter Naomi gave me a big hug from her wheelchair.

Only Big Duff, as was fitting of a paramilitary commander, held back on fulsome praise.

'Oh, aye,' he said. 'Another one leavin' his community.'

It was the first time I had heard Big Duff refer to it as my community. Usually he called it *his* community. Why was it only my community when I was leaving?

When my final bread round was complete, Leslie left me home to my front door. I shook his hand like a man and thanked him for everything. I said I would still see him at church sometimes and would still help out on the Sunday School excursion, especially if he needed someone to make sure the McLarnon twins didn't shoplift sticks of rock from the amusement arcade in Newcastle. As I was leaving, he patted me on the back and handed me a whole box of Tunnock's Tea Cakes, which were normally kept for Christmas celebrations and funerals. As he drove off he pressed the big red button on his dashboard and gave me a parting 'diddle-dee-ding, diddle-dee-ding, diddle-dee-ding'. The familiar sound of the Ormo Mini Shop echoed around the red brick walls in our street. I couldn't have asked for a better send off. I was on my way now, so I was.

MOVING ON

'Hello?' said Mammy, picking up the telephone. 'Och yes, dear,' she continued in her best Gloria Hunniford voice, 'I'll just fetch him for you now. Toneeee!'

My mother was being so polite it seemed that either Mrs Thatcher or the Queen had called. As I approached the hall she put her hand over the mouthpiece of the phone and whispered, 'It's Aaron Ward from school. His daddy's a dentist, you know.'

'Yes, I know,' I said, rolling my eyes. Every time I mentioned Aaron Ward's name my mother said, 'His father's a dentist, you know.' I bet if Aaron mentioned my name in his house, no one in his family ever said, 'His father's a foreman in the foundry, you know'.

'Bout ye, Aaron?'

'Bout ye.'

'Well, did you get in?'

'Aye.'

'Class!'

'Are you sharin'?'

'Digs?'

'Aye.'

'Aye!'

This was good news. Aaron had got a place on a new course about computers in the New University of Ulster and we had just agreed that we were going to share something called 'student digs' at Coleraine, which basically meant neither of us would have to live alone. I was relieved that at least one of my mates from school wasn't going to Queen's or England because now I would have one existing friend to start my first year of university with. I always got on well with Aaron even though he was brilliant at sport and he thought my head was cut.

'Here, if we get a flat in Portstewart we can play *Pac-Man* in the Musies every day and eat Knickerbocker Glories in Morellis.' I said excitedly.

'What are you like, wee lad?' replied Aaron.

When I informed my mother that I was going to be sharing a flat with Aaron Ward she was on the phone to my Auntie Doris almost immediately.

'Our Tony's going to share a house with Aaron Ward. His father's a dentist, you know.'

'So what?' Dad shouted from the living room, where he was watching a film about Jacques Cousteau finding fascinating fish on BBC2. 'All yer man does is look down people's gobs all day.'

Our search for accommodation proved to be more difficult than Aaron and I had expected. I couldn't afford the Halls of Residence and Aaron had secured his place on the course too late to get a room there. So one day, Aaron borrowed his father's Rover and we travelled up the motorway to Coleraine to explore our options. My disappointment at not being able to afford Halls was considerably reduced when we arrived at the university; the Halls of Residence reminded me of the Weetabix Flats on the Shankill Road, and they were being demolished because they were deemed unfit for human habitation. We visited the Students' Union to get housing advice and met Conor O'Neill who was wearing a Tyrone Gaelic football tracksuit. Conor explained that he lived in a flat near the train station in Portrush because the bedrooms in Halls were smaller than the minimum size of a prison cell under the Geneva Convention, and this was typical of Thatcher's Britain.

'Oooh, Thatchurr! That wummin,' he said as his rosy cheeks went an even deeper shade of red. 'Oooh, Thatchurr!'

We thanked him for his advice and took away a list of rental properties to explore in Coleraine, Portstewart and the nearby seaside resort of Portrush. This North Coast region was known locally as the Triangle because the three towns were located on the points of a geographical triangle. This use of geometric shapes to describe a neighbourhood appealed to me, and I wondered if the Falls and the Shankill with the peace wall dividing the two parallel roads could become known as the Parallelogram. Aaron and I stopped at a rusty red telephone box and made a few viewing appointments for lettings that were within my price range. I knew that Aaron could probably afford to pay more than me, because his father was a dentist, you know, but he seemed happy enough to try to find something habitable and affordable enough for both of us. Our first stop was an eight bedroom terraced house in Portrush which was a few miles along the coast from Portstewart. Portrush was where you went on Easter Monday on the train and hoped there were no fights between drunks in your carriage on the way home. It had never occurred to me that people lived in Portrush all year round, and not just in caravan sites in July. Before entering the first property the landlord explained through bad breath that we would be sharing with six other lads and that if any one of us broke anything all eight of our deposits would be withheld. He then told us that he hoped we were not on drugs and showed us several damp bedrooms with stained mattresses on old-fashioned beds and wardrobes with woodworm. Finally he told us it would cost us £30 per week (more than twice what I could afford on my student grant) and that we would be evicted if we paid late and he hoped we would come to know the Lord Jesus Christ as our own and personal Saviour. I didn't bother to explain to him that I was already saved because he probably would have demanded proof of my spiritual credentials, and having seen his piggin' property I just wanted him to leave us alone.

'Thanks very much, we'll think about it,' Aaron said politely, presumably referring to both the accommodation and the Lord.

'I feel sick,' I said to Aaron once the landlord left us with three pages of house rules. 'I'm not sleepin' on no pissy mattress in a dirty hole like that. I'd rather sleep in a tent. I'm serious!'

'I think a tent might just blow away up here, Hiawatha!' replied Aaron.

After several more visits to similarly stinking properties with equally obnoxious landlords I began to lose heart. Nobody had warned me about this. I thought the main strain in going to university would be of an intellectual nature. No one told me you had to live in a dump. In Belfast, if you didn't go to university and got a good job in the bank and still lived at home with your parents you were expected to put some money into the house for your keep, but your mammy still did the shopping and the washing and cooked your dinner. I was realising that student life was going to be much harder than I had expected. After an exhausting day of disappointment I suggested that Aaron take his father's car onto the beach for a laugh, but he declined as he had heard that stupid eejits got their cars stuck in the sand there all the time.

'They do not!' I exclaimed with as much incredulity as I could muster. 'Some people are as thick as champ, aren't they?'

As Aaron and I travelled home we discussed whether we would ever find somewhere decent to live in the Triangle.

'If we had a TARDIS,' I posited, 'we would have plenty of room because it's bigger on the inside than the outside, and we could travel in time and space and arrive in Coleraine before we left Belfast and we could go back in time to hear all our lectures all over again if we missed one or didn't understand everything the first time.'

'What are you like, wee lad?' said Aaron.

A few days later Aaron's father came to the rescue, as if our accommodation problem was a rotten tooth requiring a root canal. Mr Ward must have put out the word on the dentist grapevine that his son needed accommodation in the Triangle and that a reduced price would help accommodate his son's wee friend who didn't have an awful lot. The reward for such a deal would be the use of the Ward's holiday apartment in the Algarve. It was unfortunate that my father had previously sold our caravan in Millisle, as I was certain access to our holiday home in County

Down would have made the offer even more enticing. This time I borrowed the green Simca and Aaron didn't laugh at it too much when I collected him from his big house up the Antrim Road. Naturally, he had a flowering cherry tree in his front garden. I had never been to the toilet in Aaron's house but I was convinced his bathroom had an avocado bidet. This time when Aaron and I arrived in Portstewart, several friendly homeowners gave us a cuppa tea and a digestive biscuit before showing us around nice summer holiday homes with radiators in the bedrooms. During one such tour, the landlord had a moment of enlightenment.

'I know the place for two boys like you,' he said. 'Mrs Flood takes a couple of good livin' students every year and her house is lovely. She'll even make your dinner for you.'

I liked the sound of this immediately, although Aaron seemed a little perturbed to be placed in the same good livin' category as me. The man called Mrs Flood to arrange an appointment, and within the hour Aaron and I were ringing the doorbell of the Strand Beach Guest House and admiring the view of the Atlantic Ocean from the front step. A well-dressed older lady with big glasses, kind eyes and a friendly smile answered the door and looked us up and down quickly before inviting us inside for a cuppa tea and a slice of Battenberg cake. Mrs Flood's living room was bigger than the whole downstairs of my house, with huge windows overlooking the sea and a giant potted plant in the corner. The walls of every room were covered with expensive-looking wallpaper and the entire house was bereft of woodchip. Aaron and I had a lovely chat with Mrs Flood and learned that she was a widow with two dogs and one grown-up daughter who still lived at home, but all three were presently out for a walk on the beach. I wondered exactly how grown-up her daughter might be and knew Aaron was thinking the same thing. Mrs Flood explained to us that she enjoyed the company of students as long as they were no bother. We assured her that we would be no bother at all. Aaron explained that he played rugby and cricket and was from the Antrim Road where his father was a dentist. I added that my father worked in industry and I was a Sunday School teacher from quite close to the Antrim Road and I enjoyed the theatre. We had 'no bother' written all over us. Mrs Flood told us that being away from home for the first time wasn't easy and we would probably need a bit of looking-after. I couldn't believe it – we had found a mammy in Portstewart! Then Mrs Flood showed us into what would be our shared bedroom. It had a double bed for Aaron, a single bed for me, a desk for Aaron to study at and a wee table for me. Our room had an ensuite bathroom that was bigger than our bathroom at home, even after Daddy had knocked down the wall between the toilet and the bath with the sledgehammer he had borrowed from the foundry. The bathroom suite and wallpaper were all a bit too pink for our taste, and the toilet had a doily ballerina toilet roll holder on top of the cistern, but I was certain we could cope with this minor discomfort when Mrs Flood explained that the cost was only £10 per week including our breakfast and dinner. We were landed!

A few short weeks later I had to pack my bags and move out of home. I was permitted the use of the Simca for a Saturday to transport all of my worldly goods from my Belfast bedroom to my new room in Portstewart. I packed two suitcases of clothes and a box of books and filled several Stewarts supermarket bags with various other essentials such as my new Sony Walkman, my music cassette collection, digital clock radio and a half-full bottle of Hai Karate aftershave. While I was packing the car, I heard the familiar 'diddle-dee-ding' of the Ormo Mini Shop and gave Leslie a wave when he stopped outside Mr Black's house.

'Two soda and a packet of flies' graveyards and hurry up, in the name of blazes!' shouted Mr Black from his front step.

That was one part of customer service that I didn't miss.

'C'mere 'til I tell ye, there's a situation down the Road,' called Leslie from the van. 'Take it easy nigh, we're not doin' too bad, so we're not. I'll send The Wee Lad over in a minute.'

Young Mark leapt down the steps of the van with great enthusiasm. I was shocked at how quickly my mantel of The Wee Lad had been appropriated.

Once the boot and back seat of the Simca were full I returned to my bedroom for a final check in case I had forgotten anything essential, like my passport or my Clearasil spot lotion or my well-thumbed Good News Bible. The room was not completely bare because I knew I would be coming home every other weekend to have my clothes washed and to stock up on tins of Yellow Pack baked beans; however, as I stood at the door and looked inside, it seemed as if my personality had already departed. The sellotape which had held up my Agnetha poster for years had torn off some of the woodchip wallpaper. I sighed as I remembered all the nights I had gone to bed feeling warm and safe in this wee room, even those nights when I could hear shooting outside and the sound of bombs exploding down the Road. As I reflected on my happy childhood I realised my mother was standing behind me, observing me observing my room. She was crying, so I gave her a big hug. After all those years of her comforting me when I skinned my knees or my big brother decked me it felt as if I was comforting her for the first time

'Sure I'll be back at the weekends with my washing,' I reassured her.

'But it'll never be the same,' she said drying her eyes as she always did when she realised there was nothing she could do about something sad – like when they axed Meg Richardson from *Crossroads*.

'You be careful up there now, won't you?'

'Sure I'm always careful, Mammy.'

'Aye, but your head's in cloud cuckoo land half the time, love.'

'Well, as Granny would say, I'm all growed up now, so I am.'

I felt like Bobby Ewing reassuring Miss Ellie after Jock had died in a mysterious plane crash in South America. I gave wee Betty another big hug and kiss on the cheek.

'Don't you worry about me, Mammy', I said, knowing fine rightly she would worry about me anyway.

When I left the house that day, my whole family came out to the front step to wave goodbye. My father put his arm around my mother as they waved, my wee brother looked on solemnly from his skateboard, and my big brother spat out his chewing gum, rolled it into a missile and fired it at the green Simca as I drove off. This only emphasised the magnitude of the change that was taking place in my life. I was leaving home, so I was.

5

FIRST IMPRESSIONS

'Why are you goin' up there, wee lad?' asked Irene Maxwell after a particularly vigorous boogie to 'Fame' by her fellow Irene (Cara) at the Westy Disco.

I often watched costume dramas on BBC1 on a Sunday night, and I had noticed that, when posh English people went to university in Oxford or Cambridge, they called it 'going up'. I was certain this use of academic language would impress everybody. However, when I told Irene Maxwell I was 'going up' to Coleraine she did not fully understand the significance of my words.

'So what? My aunties always go up to Coleraine on the train for shoes in the January sales,' she replied.

It seemed that Irene's passionate desire for me was passing when she added, 'Sure what do I care, wee lad? You can go up to wherever the hell you like. "I'm gonna live forever, I'm gonna learn how to fly",' she sang right into my face with a devil-may-care look in her eyes and a strong smell of shandy on her breath.

The Human League started playing and Irene flipped her large, floppy New Romantic fringe and returned to the dance floor to do the Robot. She continued to glance over at me and wink suggestively every time it came to the chorus of 'Don't You Want Me Baby'. It was getting late and all I really wanted was a fish supper from the chippy on the West Circular Road.

When my 'going up' day finally arrived it was very cold and windy on the North Coast, and this turned out to be excellent preparation for the next three years. In fact, when I got off the train to walk up the field from the university halt to the skyscraper, I was sure I was going to die of exposure like Captain Scott of the Antarctic. I was wearing my brand-new, tight-fitting Wrangler jeans from John Frazer's (which, as fashion demanded, were uncomfortably snug round the jimmy joe region), my favourite blue bomber jacket and a pair of new gutties from the *Great Universal Club Book*. But this casual student attire could not protect me from the icy winds, and I wondered if I would have to borrow an old-fashioned vest and long johns from my granda to survive in this hostile climate. By the time I reached the one million steps up to the front door of the main university building my hands were numb and my feet were freezing. I hadn't shivered so much since I was a paperboy, and for the first time I truly appreciated how cold Luke Skywalker must have felt on the Planet Hoth in *The Empire Strikes Back*. I ran up the concrete steps two at a time, partly to warm myself up and partly as a symbolic leap into academia. I felt like I was about to begin advanced Jedi training with Master Yoda.

When I stepped inside the New University of Ulster there were students in blue jeans everywhere, but not one person I recognised anywhere. Aaron Ward had arranged to meet me beside the model of the university in the reception area but there was no sign of him.

'Good morning,' I said cheerfully to a ginger student with a beard standing on his own at the model.

'Is it?' he replied, spitting his chewing gum on the floor.

'Hiya, I'm a fresher in Media Studies,' I said to a spiky-haired undergraduate in a leather jacket.

'Bully for you!' he said sarcastically in an English accent, and walked off, sneering.

This unfriendliness was a quare gunk, and my excitement dissipated faster than a shopper in a bomb scare at the Co-op Superstore. Everyone around me seemed happy and confident, and they were all chatting and laughing with their friends about what they had been doing all summer. I felt like Norman No-Mates. This was terrible! At last I was a proper student at university – a real live fresher, boldly going where no one from my family had gone before – but I felt lost and alone and out of place. What was a wee lad from up the Shankill doing in a place like this anyway? A slap around the back of my head brought me back to my senses.

'Where were you, wee lad?' said Aaron.

I never thought I would be so happy to be slapped around the head by a rugger boy.

'The Fresher's Fair is this way,' he said pointing to a fluorescent poster, and we began the first of many thousands of treks across the longest bus shelter in the world towards the Students' Union.

The Fresher's Fair sounded brilliant. It was where you found out about how university worked and all the different clubs and societies you could join. As we approached the SU, I noticed a vaguely familiar spotty face. It was yer man from Derry from the day of my interview. He was wearing Wrangler jeans and a

Wrangler jacket and was accompanied by two other fellas wearing the exact same outfit. They looked more like a gang of wee hard men from down the Shankill than a cohort of undergraduates.

'Bout ye?' I said. 'Marty Mullen, right? You got in then?'

'Oh aye, the interview. You're from Belfast aren't ye?' Marty said.

Thankfully he seemed to have forgotten the 'Royal Academy' part.

'Yes and you're from Londond– … You're from Derry,' I replied, catching myself on just in time to avoid a sectarian incident.

'Aye, and so are these two wans here,' said Marty Mullen introducing his clones.

'Right, dead on. Bout ye?' I said to Marty's mates in a masculine but friendly tone.

'What about ye?' they answered in unison.

'He's from Belfast too,' I said, in an attempt to draw Aaron into the conversation.

'What about ye?' said Marty.

'Bout ye,' said Aaron.

'What about ye?' said Marty's clones.

'Bout ye,' said Aaron

'We're going over to the Fresher's Fair,' I said excitedly, interrupting the flow of the conversation.

'It's pure shite!' said Marty.

'Oh, right. See ya.' I replied cheerfully, wondering if I was ever going to make any new friends in this place.

The Fresher's Fair reinforced just how little I had in common with Marty Mullen; it was anything *but* shite. There were stands for banks and insurance and travel cards and other boring stuff, but there were also lots of stands where people the same age as me invited me to join their clubs. When Aaron announced at the rugby club stand that he had played for the Glorious First XV rugby team at BRA he was practically mobbed, so I continued to explore the hall on my own. I avoided most of the sports clubs but picked up a leaflet for the canoe club because I had enjoyed canoeing with the Greenhill YMCA in the Mourne Mountains and had only capsized once. The political clubs fascinated me. I picked up a membership form for Greenpeace because they saved whales and accepted a CND pen to help get rid of nuclear weapons. Amnesty International offered me a goody bag full of leaflets explaining how they helped people who were put in prison for no good reason. My father said Amnesty International supported the IRA, so I decided not to join up until I had read their literature and decided for myself whether they were pacifists or Provos.

The Students' Union had leaflets about getting involved in Rag Week, when you put on fancy dress, put dirty jokes in a magazine and threw flour over everyone for charity. The Students' Union also had a bar to spend your grant in and an office where you could get advice on money and housing if you spent all your money in the bar too quickly. As I walked passed the Student's Union stand I recognised Conor O'Neill, who had given us such helpful housing advice, explaining to several wide-eyed freshers that in Thatcher's Britain student grants would be cut so that working-class people couldn't go to university. This came as no surprise to me as Maggie had already cut free school milk, but poor Conor was getting very red in the face over it.

'Oooh Thatchurr!' I heard him say as I made my way towards the sanctuary of the religious societies. Maybe if I joined one of the religious clubs I would meet other good livin' people like me who might want to make friends but might not want to have sex or drink. As I made my way in the direction of the sanctified corner a crowd of freshers in front of me made a sharp about-turn when one of them gave the warning cry, 'Watch out! God Squad ahead!'

Even though the Christians were all located in one corner, I got the distinct impression that they didn't sit comfortably together. I detected more of a sense of competition and resentment than spiritual unity between the chaplaincies, the Student Christian Movement and the Christian Union. The Student Christian Movement stand caught my eye first because it had posters about peace and justice and helping poor people in the Third World. This sounded good to me, and I wondered if I might finally meet another Christian who was a pacifist. There were only a couple of people sitting at this stand, though, and they didn't look very happy. The Christian Union stand was much bigger and had lots of attractive girls giggling and handing out brightly coloured leaflets with sunsets, crosses and kittens. When I made the mistake of asking the Student Christian Movement guy what the difference between his club and the Christian Union was he got very cross indeed and started ranting about 'right-wing conservative evangelical fundamentalists', pronouncing each syllable as spitefully as possible. He seemed to really hate the Christian Union, which didn't sound very Christian to me. A portulent vicar with a red face and a double chin hanging over his dog collar was walking around all the chaplaincy stands as if he was in charge of all things God-related, and I was surprised to see that he was also scowling at the friendly girls at the Christian Union stand. I worried that a peace wall might have to be erected there and then to prevent hostilities from breaking out. Meanwhile, the lovely girls from the Christian Union were asking me what my name was and what course I was doing and where I was living and which church I went to and if I was saved or going to hell. One of the loveliest girls explained, with a sparkling smile, that the chaplaincies and Student Christian Movement weren't proper born-again Christians and that's why they were so cross. Having weighed up the differences in theological emphasis I decided to join the Christian Union, with all the lovely girls. The first meeting was on Thursday night, and I made a note of this with my new CND pen in my new Amnesty International diary.

Once I had my religion and politics sorted out I searched for something else to join just for fun. The Film Club looked good but I was studying this on my course anyway, so it was the Drama Club that captured my attention with posters showing scenes from various famous Shakespeare plays. I had enjoyed studying *Hamlet* at school and, according to Mr Dyson, it was one of Shakespeare's greatest hits. I began to dream of being cast in an iconic role in one of the greatest plays of all time; however, just as I was getting dead excited and trying to remember the lines of a few soliloquies, Aaron slapped me on the back of the head.

'Musies!' he said.

Sure enough, at the back of the Students' Union hall, behind the Socialist Workers' stand, stood two arcade machines. Aaron and I raced towards them, upsetting a pile of Socialist Worker magazines on the way. The two men on the Socialist Workers' stand looked genuinely disappointed, having obviously thought that two freshers were running toward the ranks of socialism with greater enthusiasm than they had seen for years. Aaron begsied *Asteroids* first and of course he was brilliant at blowing up all the meteorites in space, like Han Solo. However, I decked him at the *Frogger* machine because I was highly skilled in jumping onto logs without falling into the swamp or getting eaten by crocodiles. After spending £5 each, we went into the uni bar for a Coke and disapproved of all our fellow freshers who were wasting their student grants on drink when they had rent to pay and food to buy. We then spent another £5 on the arcade machines before catching the bus back to Portstewart for a delicious mince and mash dinner prepared by Mrs Flood.

During our first week of living together it became clear that, although Aaron and I were very different, we might be able to cope with sharing a room. I had only ever shared a room with my big brother and he was good at rugby too, so I expected that Aaron might also want to beat me up for fun a few times a week. Aaron obviously got enough practice in scrums on the rugby pitch, though, as he didn't feel the need to assault me at all. In fact, he didn't get too excited about anything, really. Yes, he did laugh at my ABBA cassette collection and my Cliff Richard gospel album, and he did threaten to throw me out if I ever started dressing like 'one of them fruits' on the cover of my Spandau Ballet cassette, but apart from these musical conflicts we got on okay most of the time. Aaron preferred to listen to edgier music, such as Chris De Burgh, Christopher Cross and Chris Rea. It seemed there was no singer-songwriter called Chris that he did not adore. Once we had agreed that headphones were the best compromise, everyone was happy, including Mrs Flood, who did not appreciate the echoes of either 'Gimme Gimme Gimme' or 'Patricia the Stripper' at full volume while she was baking scones for the Gospel Hall. Mrs Flood's daughter Gwen proved to be a helpful ally in such circumstances, even though it was clear from the day we moved in that she did not fancy either of us. If me and Aaron were bickering brothers, Gwen was our peace-making big sister.

When Thursday evening arrived, Aaron and I headed down to Lecture Theatre 17 for our first Christian Union meeting. I wasn't sure what to expect, but I hoped it wasn't going to be like church. We arrived slightly late because we had been arguing in the library about whose course was the best. Aaron said Computer Studies was the future and Media Studies was a Mickey Mouse course taken by weirdoes with pink hair. I put up a strong defence, because in my first lecture I had learned that all the roads were going to be dug up soon to put in cable television so everyone would be connected and have twenty TV channels, and computers could never do anything like that.

When we stepped inside LT17, I was amazed to find that the room was full. In my experience, religion was a minority sport – church was always half empty and no matter how old I got I always seemed to be the youngest person attending any religious meeting, apart from christenings. There must have been at least a hundred students there and they were all chatting and laughing and very few of them looked like squares. None of the people I had met on my course were there because it was happy hour in the uni bar. As soon as we entered the room, Aaron and I were enveloped by a group of lovely girls, as if we were Wham! arriving in the *Top of the Pops* studio. Most of the girls were from Portadown and called Heather, but we made lots of other new friends as well. One of the Heathers introduced us to a big, friendly country girl called Lesley.

'My old boss was called Leslie, too! It's a boy's name,' I joked, referring to my former employer in the Ormo Mini Shop.

'Sure, Tony's a girl's name,' she replied.

Aaron laughed.

Lesley smiled with very attractive teeth and continued, 'I'll have to boss youse Belfast boys about a wee bit now youse are up here, so I will!'

Lesley had a remarkably strong country accent, lilting somewhere between Ballymena and the Scottish Highlands.

'Love your accent, so I do,' I said.

'You've no idea! You're the one with the accent,' she retorted. 'Do you always go up at the end of your sentences in Belfast?' she said in a mock Belfast accent, still smiling.

It had never occurred to me that country people might make fun of the Belfast accent the same way we made fun of theirs. Aaron laughed. We decided we liked this girl.

'You'd never get bored with her around,' I whispered.

'She wouldn't give you a chance,' replied Aaron.

At this point Aaron could not resist the urge to tell one of the Heathers that he had played rugby in the Glorious First XV rugby team at Belfast Royal Academy, and he was once again mobbed by adoring sports fans. It still felt like we were Wham!, but now Aaron was George Michael and I was the other one. This did, however, give me the opportunity to make some friends of my own. I met a gang of other good livin' fellas from Ballymena, who were very interested in cars and the Heathers from Portadown. They referred to each other as 'boys' but most of them were called Bill, Billy, Willy or William, apart from the boys who had surnames as first names. After a friendly chat about the wonders of the new Ford XR3 with Billy Barton and Hamilton Johnston, the boys were distracted by the arrival of an old mate from the Young Farmers' Club in Ballymoney.

'Hey, boy, what's the craic, hey?' they chorused, and I moved along to the next group.

Nobody ignored me or was rude to my face in here. Next, I got chatting to a small group of English students and was introduced to Clive Ross, who said God had told to him to come to Coleraine for a religious revival. On hearing this, one of the lovely English girls said, 'Praise Jesus! That's really just kinda beautiful.' She was wearing a T-shirt that said 'Jesus Rocks' which was not a phrase Rev. Lowe had ever uttered in the pulpit of Ballygomartin Presbyterian Church.

'I'm Tara,' she said with a charismatic smile.

As I shook hands and introduced myself to the group, I started to feel at home at university for the first time. I had a sense that I belonged here, even though these young people were all so different from me. In fact, I had never been part of such a diverse group of people in my life. There were Presbyterians and Baptists and Brethren and Church of Ireland and Pentecostals all in the same room. There were students from Birmingham and Sussex and China and Bushmills. I was aware that I myself contributed to this rich diversity, because there was no one else here from up the Shankill. We were such a multi-denominational, multicultural gathering that I even met two black people and a Catholic.

I was wondering if this was what heaven would be like when Aaron slapped me around the head and reminded me that we had to hitch a lift home soon or Mrs Flood would give our chicken pie and mash to the dogs.

That night, as I lay in the dark on my pink bed sheets, I contemplated my first impressions of university life. For years I had taken for granted the friends I had known since I was a wee boy, who thought I was dead-on just because I was Tony. Here, though, almost every friendship was brand new, and I had to try hard to impress people if they were even going to. be bothered with me. I had made some new friends, of course, but some students simply didn't want to know me. Across the room Aaron was snoring with the all the ferocity of the tiger in Bellevue Zoo. I lay awake and listened to the waves roaring in the distance. I wondered if I would enjoy my new life up here. I feared I might hate it. I was insecure, so I was.

6

BECOMING AN INTELLECTUAL

I had three years to make it as an intellectual, so I had no time to waste – but before navigating ideology, philosophy and sociology, I had to find my way around the university campus. There were two libraries at either end of the longest bus shelter in the world and the main library was the size of ten Shankill Libraries and had more shelves than a thousand Ormo Mini Shops. I spent many hours in this library trying to keep warm, chatting up lovely girls from the Christian Union and looking up fascinating books and articles about 'the ideology of mass communications' and 'the gender politics of Hollywood' on the same microfiche machines they used in science laboratories on spaceships. The university had a huge concert hall with thousands of windows called The Diamond. It was like the university's good room because it had expensive curtains and a piano and was only used on special occasions. In Belfast they had ceased the construction of buildings with lots of windows long ago because of all the car bombs, so it was a rare wonder for me to stand in a building with so much light allowed in. To reach The Diamond from the main library you had to walk across an indoor bridge with a shop, a bank and big pot plants. Marty Mullen winked and nudged me when he told me they weren't the only pot plants on campus, as if this was some big secret. I was surprised because Marty didn't strike me as an enthusiast of domestic horticulture.

There was so much to learn and so little time to learn it before your next assignment was due. University was not like school; if you didn't turn up or do your work, no one gave you detention or phoned your parents – you just failed and that was that. I was determined not to fail so I tried hard to understand everything and pass all my assignments, but becoming an intellectual proved to be even harder than I had expected. At school, you just learned things off by heart and tried to remember it all for the exam, but here they didn't always give you the answer and sometimes the lecturers said there was *no* right answer. In seminars you were expected to have an opinion and someone always argued that whatever you said was wrong. My head was spinning with the new language of semesters and modules and 2:1s and 2:2s and trying to have an opinion on everything.

Every semester I was allowed to choose some of my own modules, so as well as studying mass communications and media production, I was able to study social psychology and the conflict in Northern Ireland. I even had another go at the War Poets. Every new subject demanded more time spent in the library, struggling to understand everything and being terrified someone might ask me a question which would expose how little I had grasped. Byron Drake was always asking me demanding questions. I bumped into him in the second week of term in the Students' Union café after a particularly challenging game of *Frogger*.

'Hey, Tone,' he said.

'I remember you from the interview day. You're Byron,' I replied.

'Thanks for the reminder, Tone.'

He was dressed even more like a New Romantic now, with a long tweed coat and a frilly shirt and suede ankle boots like Steve Strange, who probably lived up the street from Byron's house in England. Byron had also grown a fringe that permanently hid one of his eyes even though he flicked it away constantly, and he wore a scarf like Yasser Arafat during the bongs on the *News at Ten*. As he sat down beside me, I noticed he was carrying a copy of the *Guardian* newspaper and a paperback book, the title of which I couldn't quite make out.

'What's your book?' I asked.

Byron removed his Walkman headphones as if this question required a considered response and showed me the slim volume he was carrying. The book was titled *The Catcher in the Rye*.

'Classic,' he pronounced. ' J. D. Salinger. Have you read it?'

'No,' I answered, deciding that a modicum of honesty might be necessary if we were to become friends. 'What's it about?'

'Oh, it's very, very deep,' he said somberly, 'and very, very, dark. Almost Nietzschean. Changed my life. What are you reading?'

The 1982 *Doctor Who Annual* and my *Everyday with Jesus* bible reading notes, I thought.

'Oh a wee bit of Tolkien and quare bit of C.S. Lewis,' I replied.

At least this was true. By this stage in my life I had borrowed everything hobbit-related and all of the Narnia books from the shelves of the Shankill Library, but Byron seemed unimpressed. I wondered how I might claw back some credibility, then I remembered that I had been renewing my loan of *War and Peace* for months now in preparation for this moment.

'I've started reading *War and Peace* too. Classic, so it is.'

'Listen, Tone,' Byron said. 'The world is full of people who have *started* reading *War and Peace*.'

I noticed that Byron had a habit of exaggerating his fringe-flick every time he said something particularly clever.

'Some of Tolstoy is really, really dark …' I attempted before Byron interrupted me.

'I've always preferred *Anna Karenina*.'

'Is she better than Tolstoy? I've never read any of her stuff,' I said innocently, assuming Anna Karenina was like a Russian Enid Blyton.

'Dostoyevsky said it was flawless as a work of art,' said Byron, ignoring my question and flicking his fringe yet again.

Who? I thought, concluding that I had another Russian to look up on the microfiche machine in the library before my next encounter with Byron Drake.

I nodded knowledgeably every time a professor or student mentioned a book or a writer or an '-ism' or an '-ology', but inside I was fretting over how little I knew about anything. Was this what all the other students had been learning at A level while I was failing Physics and coortin' round Glengormley? I had so much catching up to do, and it wasn't just a matter of knowing the most important people and ideas in world history; at university they insisted on you having your own opinion and being able to prove that you were right. I wasn't used to having my own opinion on anything apart from who was the best pop band ever and who was the best Doctor Who. Up until this point in my life I was secure in my understanding of how the world worked – knowing the goodies from the baddies, who was right and who was wrong – but in my first semester at university this certainty was turned on its head.

It had always been satisfying to know that I was one of the goodies in the world, but in lectures, discussions and tutorials, I quickly learned that I had been a baddie all along! First I discovered that, in spite of all I had heard from heaven and earth, Protestants in Northern Ireland were actually the bad guys, like white South Africans and Israelis. Apparently Protestants were the 'dominant elite of British imperialism in Ireland'. It had never occurred to me before that I was an elite anything, although it was true that I had once been a pretty elite paperboy, and Geordie Best was an elite footballer and he was a Protestant from the Cregagh Road. In all my years of laughing at posh English twits in *It Ain't Half Hot, Mum* on BBC1 I had been blind to the fact that I was part of this ruling class. One of my lecturers even compared Protestants to the Raj of the British Empire in India. Obviously the university lecturers knew a lot more about life than me, but I was certain none of them had never been up the Shankill as most of the people there could barely afford a car on hire purchase, never mind an elephant and a wee man to fan them.

Just as I was coming to terms with my new-found privileged status I made another major discovery. I learned that the IRA were *not* terrorists after all, but freedom fighters against the British invaders, which now included me! I found it very hard to stop calling the IRA terrorists because I had been terrified of them all my life. If the Provos decided you were a legitimate target and wanted to kill you then you had no chance, and freedom fighters were allowed to kill people if a country refused to give them equal rights, even after they had asked nicely. I was even more shocked to learn that the UDA and UVF were actually secret agents of the British state, because I could not imagine anyone less like James Bond than Big Duff in the estate, and Mrs Big Duff wasn't remotely like Pussy Galore. I was prepared to reconsider many of my opinions but I was still a pacifist, and I still took the position that it was wrong for anybody to blow you up at the shops or shoot you at your front door, no matter what you called them.

As if this re-education wasn't traumatic enough, I then had my eyes opened to the fact that Russians were not the worst baddies in the world after all. You see, being left wing or right wing was even more important than being Catholic or Protestant, although I noticed at university that Catholics were generally more left and right and Protestants tended to be more right and wrong. I learned that left wing was clever and good and right wing was middle class and bad. Left was right because of Karl Marx and Vanessa Redgrave. Right was wrong because of Adolf Hitler and Margaret Thatcher. Communism was left and because left was right and Russians were communists, it turned out Russians were right after all. I decided that I was probably more left than right because helping poor people in the Third World and being a blessed peacemaker sounded quite left wing to me, and I got very angry when the *Sun*, a right-wing newspaper, gloated over killing

Argentinians in the Falklands War.

But I was in for another intellectual earthquake: Christians were baddies too! No one at Ballygomartin Presbyterian Church had ever told me that religion was a drug to stop people asking questions of bourgeoisie capitalists. Christianity was apparently a tool of oppression responsible for the deaths of millions of innocent people throughout history, though this had never been mentioned in Sunday School while I was colouring-in pictures of Jesus feeding the five thousand. My father was an atheist, but he just thought my faith was harmless nonsense. At university it seemed that Christians were murderous monsters – unless they were freedom fighters, of course.

'Religion is for weak people who cannot think for themselves,' announced the professor at the beginning of a lecture on how to edit a video. He was looking straight at me, and I was sure an informer had spotted me at the Christian Union and I was about to be thrown off the course before I could oppress someone. Outside lectures, I met lots of clever students who made jokes about the Christian Union being full of boring squares who didn't know how to enjoy themselves. I thought this was most unfair because the Christian Union had a welcome supper for freshers in the church hall with tray bakes and lemonade. Billy Barton from Bushmills had a motorbike so he couldn't possibly have been considered a boring square.

'Hey, boy, what's the craic, hey?' Billy would say every time he met you. He was always on the lookout for some craic, so it was most unfair to label him as boring. I once tried to engage Billy in a discussion on the Palestinian situation but his eyes glazed over.

For Billy there was clearly very little craic in the Middle East, but that didn't mean he was boring.

Once I had recovered from the initial shock of my world being turned upside down, I accepted that if I wanted to fit in with my peers I would have to keep my head down. If I was exposed as a wee good livin' Protestant from up the Shankill I would fail university for a cert! But I could only pretend to be someone else to a certain extent, so I had to find a way of becoming an intellectual while also staying true to myself. After reading lots of books in the library and thinking so hard my brain hurt, I found the perfect solution; I would become a Christian socialist. My mother's grandfather had been a member of the Communist Party, and my father used to vote for the Northern Ireland Labour Party before the Troubles swept it away, so there was socialism in my blood and I knew my family would be happy. But I wasn't prepared to give up my faith just to satisfy everyone else, so Christian socialism was the answer. Malcolm Muggeridge was a very clever intellectual on TV and he seemed to be a Christian socialist so it was obviously possible and intellectually acceptable. This proved to be a difficult tightrope to tread, however, because most socialists I knew hated Christians as much as they hated Maggie Thatcher, and most Christians were suspicious that socialists would try to ban them and put them in prison like in Russia and China. I risked upsetting both my lecturers *and* the lovely girls in the Christian Union. I was still trying to make new friends and not alienate everybody and I didn't want to end up sitting on my own in the canteen at lunchtime like all the weirdo students.

Whenever I needed to work it all out, I abandoned the

library and took long walks along the beach. I loved the solitude of Portstewart Strand when it was cold and dark and windy. There I was alone to come to my own conclusions – or at least the conclusions that would keep most people happy most of the time. As I trudged along the sand, the churning waves reflected my inner turmoil. It was really, really dark and really, really deep – almost Nietzschean – but sometimes I just wanted to just go for a poke in Morelli's.

Once I had built an ideological foundation it was easier to cope with the daily dismantling of my worldview. I was able to put up a few arguments in my defence in my essays, if not in public in front of a hostile audience of peers and professors. As my re-education progressed, I noticed that minorities were always goodies and majorities were always baddies. I felt like a minority every day at university, but I longed to be part of a socially acceptable minority where I could be the victim and not just the wicked oppressor all the time. Then one day, while studying for a test in Social Psychology, I stumbled upon an article in a psychology journal about how left-handed people were a minority that had been discriminated against throughout history. I had never been so glad to be left-handed in my entire life. At last, I was part of a minority and a victim of discrimination! I had suffered like many thousands of left-handed people before me. I remembered my granny's stories about back in her day, when left-handed people were forced to write with their right hand in school and got caned if they disobeyed. It seemed that when it came to handwriting, left was wrong and right was right. I had never been able to afford a proper left-handed guitar like Paul McCartney and had to settle for restringing a right handed guitar and playing it upside down with the plectrum guard in the wrong place. I realised now that this was what John Hume called 'injustice'. The article also said that left-handedness was a result of minor brain damage at birth. Although I was slightly offended by this theory, it meant that I was also a sort of disabled person, and this put me in another official minority category that no one would dare to question. I could argue that the government never did anything to help me with my disability like giving free left-handed scissors to schools and therefore left-handed people were discriminated against and this was typical of Thatcher's Britain. I decided to write an essay on the human rights abuses of left-handed people, but I ran into trouble when I read some articles that said discrimination against left-handed people came from the Bible and was propagated by the church. This was so unfair! Just when I had found an oppressed minority where I belonged I discovered that I was probably oppressing myself. There was even a technical term for this – I was suffering from 'internalized oppression'. I looked up a Bible reference book and found one example in the Old Testament where God chose left-handed people over right-handed people, but that was because they were good at throwing stones. I decided not to use this reference in my essay as I assumed that I would lose marks for quoting the Bible, and I didn't want to suggest that God approved of stone-throwing as there was enough it going on where I came from.

After many months of struggling I eventually found an '-ism' I could agree with. As part of my Women in Film Noir module, I had to read all about feminism for the first time. In between watching movies with sexy black and white femme fatales played by actresses like Rita Hayworth, I learned that women had always been discriminated against and were never allowed to hold power – except for Margaret Thatcher, but she was worse than a man. Some of my professors brought up feminism in almost every lecture. They explained that power structures were patriarchal and excluded women, and gave lots of examples from the media and big companies and politics and churches (who were the cause of it all in the first place). Inequality for women seemed very unfair to me and I had always enjoyed *Cagney & Lacey*, so it was great to see all my lecturers – who were all men, every single one of them – standing up for women. I assumed that becoming a feminist would impress the more politically astute girls on my course who fancied Billy Bragg and Che Guevara, but this didn't appear to work for our most outspoken feminist lecturer. He appreciated women so much made that he made lots of suggestive jokes and leered at them, like Benny Hill when he chased women around in their underwear on UTV. One of the cleverest girls described this feminist role model as 'more lecherer than lecturer' and accused him of being a bigger hypocrite than a Christian, to which I smiled and said nothing.

The following weekend when I was home in Belfast, I decided to inform my mother that I had become a feminist. I was certain she would appreciate that, now I was an intellectual, I was going to argue for greater equality for her and my granny. This would prove to her the benefits of the education that she had worked so hard to secure for me. I waited until *Match of the Day* was on in the living room and she was alone in the kitchen doing the dishes.

'I've become a feminist,' I said proudly, handing her a plastic bag containing two weeks' worth of dirty clothes.

'You're a *what*?' she asked, looking startled by the revelation.

I assumed she would appreciate my newfound solidarity with her in the fight for women's rights, so her reaction confused me.

'I'm a feminist,' I repeated.

'Oh dear God, don't be tellin' me that and don't be tellin' your father,' she said. 'Don't you be gettin' any funny ideas up there at that university. You can forget about that right now and get yourself a nice girlfriend like your big brother.'

I was confused, so I was.

7

WHEREVER I LAY MY HAT, THAT'S MY HOME

In my first year at uni I managed to make it home to Belfast every other weekend, or more often if I had no money or extra laundry. I travelled up and down to Belfast on the train so often I got to know which carriages had working heaters and clean seats. One weekend I would be taking long walks along the beach in Portstewart, working out my ideological position on the important political, social and economic issues of the world, and the next I would be at home in Belfast doing some shopping down the Road and watching *Doctor Who* on the sofa (rather than behind the sofa as the monsters didn't scare me anymore). I had two homes, two beds and two lives; I even had two libraries. In Coleraine I had to remember to borrow all the best books for my assignments before other keen students borrowed them first, and in Belfast I had to remember to go back to the Shankill Library to renew my loan of *War and Peace* over and over again. After many months of living between my two homes, it occurred to me that I wasn't just the spitting image of Paul Young – especially when I used sticky gel from Boots on my hair – his music also reflected my life when he sang 'Wherever I Lay My Hat, That's My Home.'

In Coleraine there was hardly any sign of The Troubles and I was free to be a student, a socialist and an intellectual; back in Belfast there were still bomb scares and shootings and army checkpoints every weekend. It seemed as though nothing ever changed at home, but as the months went by, I began to notice that I wasn't the only one who was changing.

My big brother had such a good job in Short's that he was going to get married and move to Bangor, in spite of the fact that this most desirable of suburbs was miles away from the cricket club and the bookies on the Woodvale Road. He didn't beat me up for fun anymore and spent most of his time at home in the sitting room with his girlfriend. Meanwhile, my wee brother had continued the family tradition by bucking the trend on the Shankill, passing the eleven-plus and getting into grammar school. On his first day at Belfast Royal Academy the PE teacher asked him if he was like his eldest brother or 'the other one that did drama'. When my wee brother replied that he was a talented rugby player like his eldest sibling, the PE teacher simply said, 'Good.' Although I had no desire to be a great sportsman, when my wee brother reported this conversation to me I abandoned my pacifist principles and imagined I was a cat burglar in a black suit like the Milk Tray man, and in my mind I broke into the school gym and burst every one of the PE teacher's balls.

I was noticing changes among the older generation, too. My father was worried about being made redundant because of the stupidity of all his bosses, of which he maintained there were far too many anyway. Worryingly, he was making as many visits to the Wine Lodge for cans of Carlsberg Special as my mother made to the Mace for cans of baked beans, and I began to hate the sight of those gold-coloured beer cans, because the more he drank the more he slabbered. He continued to keep up to date with the latest technology, investing in the newest must-have gadgets – including a Betamax video recorder which he used to record Bonnie Tyler on *Top of the Pops* – but he seemed to have given up on some of his other hobbies. He was neglecting his Bonsai tree and even missing some Saturday nights DJing at the Westy Disco. At weekends I had regular arguments with him about socialism and feminism and nationalism and religion. Every new concept I had come to terms with at university was challenged by my father at the weekends.

'Your father's a very clever man, you know,' my mother would say after he demolished one of my well-constructed intellectual arguments with a common sense retort. When I explained that the pop music he played at the Westy Disco was keeping working-class young people in a stupor of lowbrow culture and strangling their political awareness, he launched an unprovoked attack on the university intelligentsia.

'If any of them boys up there in their ivory towers had done a proper day's work in their life they wouldn't be teachin' you crap like that. For God's sake, tell them to catch themselves on!'

I was certain that the tower at university was made of concrete and not ivory, but it was at times like this that I wanted to bring my father to a seminar and set him loose on the most self-satisfied academics, because although they always sympathised with the poor workers of the proletariat, they appeared never to have actually met one.

On my trips home at weekends I noticed that my mother had taken on additional domestic duties with her parents. Granny and Granda were getting older and needed help to light the fire and make the dinner and wash up. I often accompanied my mother on a visit to my grandparents' house on a Sunday afternoon before catching the train back to Coleraine. Granda was usually out at the club for a wee stout and Granny was often in full flow about how Ian Paisley was saving us from being sold down the river and why Gerry Adams was a bad oul rip and why yer woman across the street thinks she is something.

'Our Tony's sharing a room with that wee Aaron Ward fella from BRA and his daddy's a dentist, you know,' explained my mother.

'Well, here, dear! Excuse me, I'm me and who's like me?' commented Granny, widening her eyes in my direction.

One Sunday afternoon I decided to introduce my grandmother to my theory that the reason she preferred *Coronation Street* to *Dynasty* was because British soap operas better represented strong matriarchal working-class women like Ena Sharples, whereas in American soap operas the women were decorative sex objects created by misogynistic script writers.

'Stop talkin' all swanky and stick thon kettle on for your granny, love,' she replied.

I dutifully obeyed, and when I returned from the working kitchen to serve Granny a mug of tea and a heavily-buttered iced finger, she was discussing my intellectual development with my mother.

'Our Tony's no dozer, so he's not,' she was saying proudly.

While my mother lit the fire and made the dinner and brushed the carpet and did the ironing, Big Isobel complained that nobody cared about her or did anything for her even though she was on her last legs. She also made regular enquiries about the state of my love life.

'Have you got yourself a nice wee girl up there yet, love? Ye know, one of your wee good livin' friends?'

She made me laugh even when she was describing the intimate details of her latest medical condition.

'My innards are ruined and my tubes are bluttered!'

Sometimes it seemed as if my granny and Orange Lil, the Belfast woman in a headscarf played by Jimmy Young on the TV, were the same person. Now that I was a grown man, I was beginning to understand why Granda spent so much time in the club having a wee stout. I could tell that all of this extra work was causing my mother a lot of stress, and when Auntie Emma called into our house for a wee cuppa tea and a chat she always started by asking Mammy about her nerves. It seemed as if my mother had to cope with almost as many family problems as Sheila Grant in *Brookside*, the gritty new soap opera on Channel 4, though I was obviously no bother.

Even the Westy Disco was changing. Uncle Henry had filled in an application form and got a grant to replace the old wooden floor, which was covered in spat-out chewing gum from thousands of Saturday nights. The new floor was made of a space-age material that was supposed to have been used on the Apollo spaceships, but the chewing gum still stuck to it just the same. A lot of the older members from the Bay City Rollers and *Saturday Night Fever* era had moved on to work or marriage or prison, and there was no sign of Titch McCracken. Lyn McQuiston said Titch had joined 'one of the organisations', but I refused to believe this. Yes, he would steal the eyes out of your head, but he wouldn't kill anyone. Irene Maxwell was still there on the rare Saturday nights I could make a visit to the Westy. She had moved on from her roller-disco phase and was now resplendent in knitted legwarmers like a Kid from Fame. When my da played a request for 'Starmaker' by The Kids From Fame everyone held hands in a circle and sang along. I joined in and found it strangely emotional. I hadn't witnessed such synchronized handholding in the Westy Disco since 'Seasons in the Sun' by Terry Jacks in 1974. It was strange to feel that I still belonged here while at the same time feeling like everything was changing and it was time to move on.

On one of my last visits to the Westy Disco I offered to act as assistant DJ to my father. As I filtered through piles of requests for Duran Duran, I was shocked to stumble upon a can of Carlsberg Special hidden behind a Madness LP. If it had not been for a request for 'Baggy Trousers' this secret would never have been revealed. I was shocked. This was not appropriate behaviour for a DJ. If Jimmy Saville had been caught doing anything bad like this on *Top of the Pops* he would have been sacked immediately! I advised my father that it was inappropriate for a youth leader to be drinking alcohol while performing DJ duties in a church hall, and though it was difficult to hear his response over the music, I could make out the words 'own business', 'sanctimonious' and 'wee bastard' between chants of 'Baggy Trousers.' I could tell from the expression on his face that my time as assistant DJ was at an end and I walked off, throwing down my headphones so hard that the record jumped and everyone booed and my father had to fade up Boy George prematurely.

The news on the portable TV in the tuck shop said that Mr Brezhnev with the eyebrows had died in Russia. I used this opportunity to introduce the first ever political debate on the Cold War in the Westy Disco. I explained to Philip Ferris that the capitalist Western media was feeding us propaganda about the Soviet Union and I assured him the Communists were actually dead on. I thought Philip would appreciate my socialist ideology because he had been a punk for years and punks loved anarchy in the UK. Philip loved U2, a new band from Dublin with a lead singer called Bono, which sounded like the name of a dog biscuit to me. Philip assured me that U2 were going to be even bigger than The Boomtown Rats but I wasn't convinced.

To everyone's surprise Philip had found a girlfriend. They had met at one of the regular gatherings of punk rockers outside the City Hall. She had spiky black hair and safety pins in all the same places as Philip apart from her deliberately ripped black tights. Philip never introduced her or said her name and she didn't speak, but she held onto Philip's arm and sneered at you as if every single word that came out of your mouth was completely stupid. In spite of this, I was certain that there would be some meeting of minds between anarchists and Christian socialists.

'Are you thinkin' of goin' to university yourself, Philip?' I enquired.

'Nah,' he replied.

At that moment my father put on 'Eye of the Tiger' and

Sammy Reeves jumped up on the dance floor doing a strange mixture of pogo dancing and shadow boxing. Sammy thought he was Rocky, but he looked more like Sylvester the Cat than Sylvester Stallone.

'I think you'd like university, so I do.' I told Philip. 'If you did the same course as me you'd learn all about how the media influences the working of major social institutions and brainwashes the masses ... except for punks and anarchists, like.'

Philip and his punk girlfriend looked at me thoughtfully for a few seconds.

'Well, what do you think?' I asked hopefully. 'Are yousens goin' to go to university too?'

'Ballicks!' they replied in unison.

Towards the end of my first semester at university I decided that I needed some new clothes. Now that I was an intellectual I felt the desire to transform my wardrobe as well – and besides, my old Wrangler jeans and bomber jacket now had so many holes they let the rain in. I was determined that my new wardrobe would reflect my personality and my individuality; my days of wearing the best-value clothes from the *Great Universal Club Book* were over. On a Saturday afternoon in Belfast I took a black taxi down the road and, for the benefit of the small animals on sale, managed to resist a visit to the pet shop in Gresham Street. I joined a long queue of shoppers at the security gates in Royal Avenue for a body search. This was to make sure I wasn't a terrorist planning carnage rather than a New Romantic on a fashion mission. After a disappointing visit to Man at C&A I ended up back in John Frazer's, the preferred fashion supplier of the men of the Shankill. This was where I had bought my Bay City Rollers platforms, my Harrington Jacket and my Peter Storm anorak. After nearly an hour perusing the bomb-damage-sale stock, I emerged with a brand new Wrangler jacket, a pair of combat trousers, a pair of leg warmers and a pair of Simon La Bon suede ankle boots. I couldn't wait to get home and try on my new clothes. While the rest of my family were out at the Westy Disco I stayed at home to try on my new outfit. I completed the look by using extra gel to make my hair look really big, like Bono from U2.

The next day, I decided to put on my new clothes before catching the train back to Coleraine. My father had agreed to give me a lift to Central Station in the green Simca and was waiting with my family in the living room where everyone's attention was on the snooker. When I walked into the room, my parents and brothers scanned me from head to toe. My hair was gelled up as big as Tina Turner's, with the longer bits at the back forming a mullet against the upturned collar of my new Wrangler jacket. Their eyes widened as they surveyed rest of my apparel, from my khaki combat trousers down to the black knitted leg warmers over my suede ankle boots. My wee brother started to giggle as if he had just heard a dirty joke on *The Young Ones* on BBC2.

'No son of mine is goin' out dressed like that!' said my father.

'Poof in Boots!' laughed my big brother.

'Och, don't you listen to themuns, you're a quare smasher, son,' said my mother.

But I didn't care what anyone thought. I was an adult now, and I could dress whatever way I wanted. I could express my individuality by wearing the same clothes as all the other students. I was a New Romantic, so I was.

8

DON'T YOU WANT ME, BABY

'Dum dum da dum-dum, dum dum dum dum!'

'Tickatickaticka.'

'Dum dum da dum-dum, dum dum dum dum!'

'Tickatickaticka.'

Aaron Ward was driving us the three miles to the university in his new car and we were singing along to the intro to Human League's greatest hit on Radio 1. We always performed this routine when 'Don't You Want Me' came on the radio, although we tended to stop when the female vocalist started singing about working as a waitress in a cocktail bar because that didn't sound very manly. Some mornings as we travelled to a 9.15 a.m. lecture, I imagined we were Bodie and Doyle in *The Professionals* acting on a tip off from Mr Hudson in CI5 and were on our way to stop international terrorists (or freedom fighters) from blowing up an oil refinery and killing the entire population of Coleraine. Since Aaron's parents had presented him with the gift of a Toyota my travels to and from the university had become much more bearable. The unremitting Atlantic wind and salty rain had been hard to bear while standing at the bus stop in the mornings and hitching a lift home in the evenings.

'When are you going to start givin' me some money for petrol, miser?' Aaron asked, not for the first time.

I had already had several arguments with Aaron since he accused me of not contributing to the petrol costs. Aaron and I argued quite a lot but we never fell out. Mrs Flood's daughter said we were like an old married couple.

'Oh, it's easy for you, so it is,' I said. 'We're not all loaded, ya know.'

I was broke most of the time, so I used my newly-acquired knowledge of class politics to accuse him of oppressing me with his middle-class values.

'Sometimes you are just *so* middle class!' I complained, aware that this was a particularly devastating put-down for any undergraduate.

Aaron said I was just jealous because I couldn't afford a car – which was true – but I denied this with all the fervour of Karl Marx himself.

I had been adept at the use of public transport in Belfast from an exceptionally young age; even when the buses were hijacked and burned in the middle of the road, I usually knew where to find a black taxi to take me up the Shankill. However, transport to and from university was turning out to be much more challenging even without the inconvenience of regular bomb scares. One Sunday night on the train, I was so engrossed in my Sony Walkman that I missed the stop for Coleraine. I was trying to figure out the meaning of the lyrics of Spandau Ballet's 'True', and when I casually opened my eyes I noticed the university campus on the far side of the River Bann. I ran to the conductor for help, and he stroked his chin and explained that we were now en route to Londonderry where I had never been before. The only person I knew up there was Marty Mullen, but he was in Coleraine and he still didn't like me even though I now wore a Wrangler jacket just like him. What if I ended up in the Bogside? What would happen to a wee Prod from up the Shankill if he inadvertently entered Free Derry? I would have as much chance as a Time Lord accidently landing his TARDIS on Skaro! The conductor sniffed deeply and attempted to reassure me by explaining that I had made an all-too-common mistake.

'Buck eejits do this all the time, son,' he said.

He clarified that the next stop was Castlerock, which was about five miles from Coleraine, and if I disembarked there I could catch a bus back into the town and everything would be grand, so it would. Little did he know that I had no money left after paying my train fare and buying a packet of Tayto cheese and onion and a Caramac in Central Station in Belfast. I jumped off the train in Castlerock and found myself standing alone, in darkness, on the station's single platform. It was like the video for 'The Day Before You Came' but with no Agnetha, which was as bad as watching 10 without Bo Derek. When I left the tiny station I spotted a public telephone box and wished it was a TARDIS even harder than I usually did, because I had no coins to make a call.

'If only I were The Doctor,' I thought. 'I could be transported back in time and arrive in Coleraine before I had even left Belfast – as long as I didn't press the wrong button and end up on the

Planet Skaro about to be exterminated by a million angry Daleks instead.'

I was jolted back by the realisation that I had no means of transport or communication, intergalactic or otherwise, and consequently I had no alternative but to walk and walk beside a long road that in some places didn't even have a footpath. It was freezing and murky and bucketing down as I began the long trek back to Coleraine. The rain quickly flattened my carefully constructed hairstyle, washing the gel right out of my hair, and the hailstones were stinging my cheeks. It was as if the sky was taunting me – 'Gormless wee crater from up the Shankill thinks he's something, but he's not!' I was completely scundered. It seemed very unfair that I was being punished so severely for the relatively minor offense of paying too much attention to a Spandau Ballet song. It was as if the universe was hackling on me.

I stuck out my thumb but not one car stopped to offer me a lift. I felt lost and alone in a strange and threatening environment. I was like Harrison Ford in *Blade Runner*, struggling alone against all the odds on an unforgiving post-apocalyptic earth. Some of the passing motorists sped through large puddles at the side of the road and splashed me. I was sure I could hear laughter after each drive-by soaking. After an eternity of plodding through puddles, I finally got back to the warmth of Mrs Flood's hearth in Portstewart. My suede ankle boots developed a white scum-mark as they dried out in front of the fire, and my leg warmers had to be wrung out like your trunks at the swimmers.

I struggled to acquire the vital skill of thumbing a lift. All day, every day, there was a queue of students outside the university sticking out their thumbs in the hope that a passing motorist would stop and provide a lift free of charge into Portstewart. This saved money on bus fares for more important expenses such as books, baked beans and the bar. I had never hitched a lift in my life because in Belfast everyone knew that such an activity carried the risk of being killed and dumped in a ditch for being Catholic or Protestant in the wrong place at the wrong time. Most people at university reassured me that it was safe to thumb a lift there, though the female students tended to hitch in pairs to avoid perverts. Unlike in Castlerock, the motorists of Coleraine were very generous and someone usually picked you up after about ten minutes. During the short journey they usually had a friendly chat with you about what course you were doing and where you were from and if you had asked the Lord Jesus Christ to be your own and personal Saviour. I had one rather disturbing experience when a souped-up XR3 with extra headlights and spoilers offered me a lift after a long, late-night session in the library on the use of propaganda in Soviet films. Within minutes of sitting down next to the furry dice hanging from the rear-view mirror I realised I had made an error of judgement. The driver introduced himself as 'Wee Davey from Ballymena' and explained that he was on his way to the disco in the basement of the Strand Hotel in Portstewart to 'eye up the talent, hey.' Wee Davey said he was young free and single but he looked about forty-something and I could see a bald patch through his attempted mullet. He was wearing a dated wide tie and an off-white shirt that didn't quite button at the neck, and he had clearly overdone it with Brut, an old-fashioned aftershave that brought back some painful adolescent memories for me. During the course of the short journey his speedometer reached 80 miles per hour while he explained to me the best way to 'pick up a wee bit of stuff' at the disco. As a newly-educated feminist I was tempted to start an argument with him regarding the derogatory terms he was using to describe women, but due to the speed we were travelling at I decided not to distract him. The faster he drove the more aware I was that I was clenching my buttocks against the sticky, red faux-leather upholstery and instinctively pressing my right foot to the floor.

'Hey, boy, that there brake pedal doesn't work, so it doesn't, hey,' he laughed.

When Wee Davey Knievel finally released me into the safety of the night, I was feeling nauseous from the combination of exhaust fumes, motion sickness and the details he had shared of an intimate encounter with 'a big blonde biddy from Ballymena' in the car park of the Strand Hotel.

Unlike Wee Davey, I had yet to achieve a proper intimate encounter with anybody. Yes, I had enjoyed many satisfactory snogs with a variety of girls from Glengormley to Millisle, and by all accounts I was a good kisser, but I was still a virgin like Cliff Richard and Queen Elizabeth I. The nearest I had ever come to sex was a particularly enthusiastic snog with Lorraine Dobson up an entry after the Westy Disco. It was the first night of our relationship, which had begun just an hour before during a slow dance to 'After the Love Has Gone' by Earth, Wind and Fire. I was shocked by the sudden passion of her kisses. Before I could even run my fingers through her hair and tell her she was very special, so she was, she started to eat the face off me. It was clear that Lorraine was much more experienced than me, and after a few minutes of the Frenchest kissing I had ever known I realised that if she didn't slow down there would be a stirring in the region of the jimmy joe, which could lead to great shame for a wee good livin' fella and an unplanned pregnancy for Lorraine. I knew such a disaster would give new meaning to the words, 'Don't you want me, baby?' My attempts to dampen her passion did not go down well. She became quite angry in a sexually-frustrated sort of way when I unlocked tongues and asked her if she thought *The Empire Strikes Back* was better than the original *Star Wars*. Lusty Lorraine chucked me within twenty-four hours, telling everybody that I was 'too quiet for her'. It was remarkable how quickly our relationship had moved to 'After the Love Has Gone'.

I definitely wasn't too quiet for the lovely girls in the Christian Union. The CU was good for meeting girls, but it was difficult to get to know them very well while praying for fellow students to get saved or clapping along to 'Our God Reigns'. Well, not everyone clapped – some members of the CU thought physical movement during praise songs was an inappropriate way of worshipping the Creator of the universe because you also moved your body during sex. I couldn't understand why sex was a sin, because if humans didn't do it we would all die out and God wouldn't like that. Several members of the CU also refused to sing 'Our God Reigns' because Catholics sang it when the Pope came to Ireland.

'I'll not be singin' "Our Pope Reigns",' Hamilton Johnston said with all the certainty of a Free Presbyterian.

Apart from these theological battle lines the CU was one big happy family, and it wasn't long before Aaron Ward and I were being invited to the Halls of Residence for supper with some of the lovely girls. The Heathers from Portadown made us nice cups of tea in Tweetie Pie mugs and Lesley from up the country made us toasted Veda and cheese and shared some of her mother's delicious tray bakes. We chatted about music and TV and who fancied who in the CU. Now and again we engaged in deep religious and philosophical debate about whether girls should wear hats in church and if Jesus would come again in the Rapture and leave all the unrepentant sinners on earth while we all got beamed up to heaven like when Mr Spock rescued Captain Kirk from the surface of an exploding planet controlled by an evil alien entity in *Star Trek*. When it became clear that I was the only truly committed socialist in the gang I felt compelled to challenge our sense of harmony, and I did this by interjecting with my most devastating put-down – 'That's just *so* middle class!' One evening, as we were tucking into the remains of a mountainous strawberry pavlova baked by a Heather's mummy, I became irritated with Aaron's enthusiasm for sport. After ten insufferable minutes of tales of rugger glory he began to enthuse about golf, and I remembered my father saying – 'No son of mine will ever be playing no middle-class golf.'

'Oh no, please no, not golf! Sometimes you are just *so* middle class,' I interrupted.

The group was supposed to bow to my socialist analysis, but on this occasion the lovely Lesley from up the country intervened, in a manner that suggested she fancied Aaron.

'You're obsessed with working class and middle class. It's all "class this and class that" with you. There's no such thing as class,' she asserted.

How dare she challenge my political analysis? I thought.

'But that's just a typical middle-class attitude,' I continued, but to my surprise, she didn't back down.

'Up the country we don't bother with class. I never heard of class until you boys from Belfast started chitterin' on about it.'

I had never been accused of chittering on about anything in my life. Although I was a feminist now and believed that girls were allowed to talk just as much as boys, this was going too far! I drew breath, preparing a detailed retaliation on how bourgeois elites fear class politics because it threatens their power, when Lesley decided she had clearly heard enough of my socialism and abruptly changed the subject.

'Anyway, enough of all that oul nonsense. Mummy's taking me to Anderson & McAuley's in Belfast on Saturday to buy me a new designer track-suit.'

Anderson & McAuley's was a swanky department store in Royal Avenue. It had an escalator and you could buy expensive perfume there from posh ladies wearing too much make-up.

'No way!' enthused a Heather from Portadown, and immediately the conversation veered away from politics to fashion. Aaron noticed this and chuckled as I huffed over my pavlova.

Most of the time, though, there was little discord in our gatherings. We told silly jokes and discussed whether Boy George was male or female or both and I did impersonations of Orville the Duck. The craic was mighty, and sometimes we laughed so much that we cried. On one occasion we went out at midnight looking for a telephone box to see how many of us could fit inside. Ten of us crammed in, giving the impression that it had TARDIS-like proportions, but an old woman came out in her slippers and gave off that we were noisy, lazy, good-for-nothing students and threatened to report us to British Telecom and the RUC. My social life was in sharp contrast with many of my peers. Before early morning lectures, Marty Mullen complained about his hangover and boasted about how many pints he had swallowed the night before and joked that he couldn't remember half of the hilarious antics he got up to while intoxicated. Everyone patted him on the back and said he was 'a wile boy' and 'some handlin', but I found all this talk very boring. I didn't dare to admit that I had been eating caramel squares with nice girls from the Christian Union, though, or my already questionable ideological and social credibility would have been irreparably damaged.

In spite of making good friends with lots of lovely girls from the CU, I found it difficult to secure an actual girlfriend. Praying and laughing and eating tray bakes together was all very well, but I was a man now and I had physical needs like Clint Eastwood on a late film on BBC2. Through an intermediary, I asked one of the girls from Portadown who wasn't called Heather to go out with me, but she turned me down with a 'no' as firm as any spoken by Rev. Ian Paisley. After that, I briefly pursued Martha from Gilnahirk who spoke in tongues and laid her hands on you to heal you. Unfortunately Jesus told her that, although I was nice enough, I was not the man for her. It was clear that Martha didn't want to lay a single finger on me. After a while, I started to worry that I had lost my touch. How could the same sex symbol that got fourteen – yes, *fourteen* – Valentine cards only a year earlier at Belfast Royal Academy have become so repulsive? I had never had a problem attracting girlfriends before. If I'd had looser morals I could have turned the Westy Disco into my personal harem, like Yul Brynner in *The King and I*, but with Belfast accents and more chewing gum. These months spent in the romantic wilderness required serious reflection, so I took my woes to the beach. As I walked along the sandy shore, praying for guidance and wondering what I should do, I decided that perhaps it was time for me to give up women for a while. I thought it would be unfair to the female sex for me to withdraw entirely, even for a short time, but that perhaps I should keep myself for a special relationship like Bobby and Pammy Ewing. I had bought a book at the Christian Union bookstall called *Growing Into Love* by Joyce Huggett. The book was all about a Christian approach to relationships and marriage and the benefits of waiting until you were married before having sex. I read it from cover to cover, though I read the chapter on sex first, and it all made good sense to me, because the more women JR had sex with in *Dallas* the less happy they all seemed to become. For many in the CU this became the handbook on how not to have sex. *Growing Into Love* was a sort of a reverse *Kama Sutra*. The book contained practical advice, such as always leaving the door open when you were alone in a room with your girlfriend so others could keep an eye on you and stop you getting up to something. Everyone thought it was hilarious that the author's name was Huggett, though not everyone approved when I joked that she should have been called Joyce Don't-Hug-It instead. I could tell that I had enjoyed more *Carry On* movies than most of the other members of the CU. When I called the book *Groping Into Love* I received a few disapproving tuts from some of the holier girls, who explained that vulgar humour was 'not a very good witness'. I resisted the temptation to rename the author Joyce Suck-It, as I suspected that a reference to oral sex would scupper any chance I had of one day becoming president of the Christian Union. Only Aaron and Lesley from up the country found my sarcasm hilarious. Of course, sex before marriage was a sin, but this was irrelevant, as I hadn't found anyone who wanted to have sex with me before, during or after marriage. It wasn't as if I was sexually frustrated or anything. In arguments about the morality of sex before marriage, Byron Drake accused me of 'repressing my animal nature'.

'You just need a good shag, Tone!' he said.

I argued that it was possible to have self-discipline and control your physical urges and that casual sex and promiscuity spread disease and caused people great emotional pain, and a good socialist and feminist shouldn't be sexually exploiting women anyway.

'Bet you wank as much as I do, Tone!' he replied.

Byron Drake could be very annoying. We got on well most of the time, and I was pleased that he approved of my new New Romantic clothes – even though they were obviously a cheap version of his – but how dare he accuse me of being sexually frustrated! It wasn't as if I was thinking about sex all the time. My mind didn't *once* wander to sex with Rita Hayworth in the library while I was trying to write an essay on sexual power and the femme fatale in film noir. When I was walking on the beach devising solutions to the world's problems my mind never *ever* wandered to sex; I was too absorbed in the waves churning in and out and in and out and caressing the moist sand. How could you even think about sex when the wonder of creation was all around you? The landscape was so thrilling I sometimes had the urge to run into the ocean and thrust myself into the surf. I was much too entranced by the power of nature to imagine Bo Derek coming out of the waves in her wet swimsuit like in *10*.

Next Byron would be suggesting that I imagined Bo inviting me up to the dunes, taking off her swimsuit and offering her beautiful body to me for hours of unrelenting passion. Joyce Huggett and Jesus would have disapproved of these sinful fantasies, if I'd had them, which I didn't. Of course, at night it was harder, but I had no control over my dreams. I may have been single and celibate, but when I was asleep the devil regularly tempted me with Debbie Harry in a bubble bath. But in spite of Byron's taunts, I was neither repressed nor denying my animal nature. I was definitely not sexually frustrated in any way, so I wasn't.

9

VIDEO KILLED THE RADIO STAR

'What is it with "so it is", Tone?'

Byron Drake was angry with me and I had no idea what I had done to upset him so much.

'What do you mean?' I asked innocently. 'All I said was that our media production assignment is going to be class, so it is. I'm going to make a radio documentary about …'

'You people finish every bloody sentence with "so I do" or "so it is" or "so a bloody something-or-other"!'

'We do not, so we …' I stumbled. 'We do not!'

'It's a nationwide speech impediment,' he said and slammed his *Guardian* newspaper down on the table so petulantly that he spilled coffee all over my revision notes on media, culture and society. I was ragin'!

'Well that's just a typical arrogant English attitude, isn't it?' I retorted, mopping my notes with a flimsy paper napkin.

'Why can't Irish people …'

'*Northern* Irish!' I interrupted.

'… just end a sentence with a full stop?'

'That's just the way we talk, so it is.'

Byron smacked his forehead with his palm. I had a sudden urge to assist him. 'There you go again! It's just so fucking irritating!'

Now I was just as angry as Byron. I needed a devastating put-down in response to this unprovoked attack on my people, and I needed one fast.

'Oh, that shows just how middle class you really are,' I said, as passionately as if I were a Spanish Inquisitor accusing someone of heresy.

This was not the first time I had heard educated people mock the Northern Irish vernacular. I was well aware that the intelligentsia did not approve of 'aye', 'yousens' and 'wise a bap'. It was strange, because English people were supposed to be on our side, but when criticism was levelled at us in the haughty tones of an English accent it hit a nerve of resentment within me that would have impressed a Provo. This was the same feeling I experienced when James Prior, the posh new English Secretary of State for Northern Ireland came on the news to talk down to the people of 'Naaawwwwthan Aaaaland'.

I could tell Byron was still smarting from the ultimate insult of being labelled middle class, but he regained composure sufficiently to continue his attack, albeit in a slightly more Cockney-sounding accent than before.

'Do me a favour, Tone. Try ending just one fucking sentence without "so it is".'

'Well isn't that just typical of youse …'

'Arrggh!' he seethed.

'Centuries of English oppression against the Irish …

'Oh, so *now* you're Irish, so you fucking are!'

'Now you and your snotty, middle-class, English twit accent are trying to censor the same people you oppressed for centuries so that we couldn't even speak in our native tongue ... SO YOU ARE!'

I was aware that I was starting to sound like Gerry Adams. If Granny had heard me speak like this she would have taken the poker to me.

'Idiot!'

'Eejit!'

'Retard!'

'Capitalist!'

Byron stormed off. He was so angry he forgot his *Guardian*. I hadn't seen him this angry since 'Shaddap You Face' kept 'Vienna' by Ultravox off the number one spot.

I was angry too. After months of learning not to say what I really wanted to say, now I had to learn not to speak the way I spoke. I understood that this was what becoming an intellectual was all about, but I was finding third-level education very demanding. I gathered up my soggy revision notes and got up to leave. Conor O'Neill was holding court with a group of first year sociologists at the table behind me. He was talking about politics and going very red in the face as per usual.

'Oooh, Thatchurr!' I heard him growl.

I swiftly escaped the debate chamber that was the university café to go play a game of *Frogger* in the Students' Union. I had been trying to communicate to Byron that I was excited about my first opportunity to make a proper radio programme. When I was younger I imagined I was a Radio 1 DJ counting down the Top 40 on a Sunday night and played each song in turn on my stylophone, but now I had the opportunity to become a real, bona fide broadcaster like Terry Wogan on the BBC and Big T on Downtown Radio. For the first time I was going to have the opportunity to be like Woodward and Bernstein, the American journalists who got Richard Nixon into trouble for all his oul fibs. I had been reading lots of books about Watergate and how these two heroes had persuaded 'Deep Throat' to tell them about all the secret shenanigans that went on in Washington. Everyone on my course was inspired by what these two talented journalists had achieved, and Marty Mullen kept boasting that he had seen a brilliant video called *Deep Throat*, but I got most of my information about Watergate from books in the university library.

Once the professor had informed his eager young hacks of our radio production task I got to work on my ideas immediately. How could I uncover a major political scandal, make a documentary about it and have it finished in time for the professor to mark it over the Christmas holidays? There were plenty of burglaries in Belfast, but I was fairly certain they were not politically motivated like Watergate. Killing tended to be more politically motivated than burglary in Belfast, and in any case, the paramilitaries would kneecap you if you were caught breaking into someone's living room to steal their TV or Betamax video recorder. Once, burglars broke into our house and stole my mother's wedding ring and engagement ring, which she had taken off to do the dishes and left on the windowsill beside the kitchen sink. Even though Daddy bought her a new ring she was heartbroken and cried buckets because she said the originals were irreplaceable. If I ever found out who stole my mother's rings I would have abandoned my pacifist principles, and although I would not have blown their knees off with a gun, I would certainly have kicked the burglars very hard in the kneecaps and possibly the goolies.

I simply didn't have enough time to conduct a major political exposé before the end of the Christmas semester, so I began to consider tackling a major social issue in my documentary instead. First of all, I considered a programme about starvation in the Third World. This was a very good subject for a socialist to tackle, because capitalists caused poverty and socialists helped poor people. After some initial planning, however, I realised that this subject would not work on radio because you couldn't see the starving children and I had neither the contacts nor the resources to interview anybody in Africa. My next idea was to tackle the controversial subject of abortion. My idea was to record a debate between people who were for abortion and people who were against abortion, and I would be the referee like Donahue on TV in America. However, I abandoned this idea as well when Marina with the Daisy Duke shorts told me that men weren't allowed to talk about abortion because it was a 'women's issue'. I was struggling to find a hard-hitting social issue on which to break new ground in broadcasting until an amazing idea presented itself to me when I was home in Belfast one weekend. I was walking home with a fish supper after 'The Last Waltz' in the Westy Disco when I noticed two wee lads up an entry beside the church, apparently blowing into Stewarts Supermarkets plastic bags. It was too dark to see exactly what was going on but they seemed to be very enthusiastic and I could hear the faint, crackly sound of plastic bags expanding and contracting like the respirator when JR was in hospital after Bing Crosby's daughter shot him in *Dallas*.

'I saw two wee lads blowin' somethin' up the entry beside the church,' I said when I got home.

'Fruits,' said my big brother.

'Oh my God, that's them there wee glue sniffers again,' exclaimed my startled mother.

'Glue sniffers?'

'Yes son, they squeeze a tube of glue into a wee bag and sniff it to get high,' she explained. 'Now don't you be tryin' it!'

'Wise up,' said my big brother, shooting me a look of incredulity that suggested I would have neither the capability nor the rebellious streak required to engage in the sniffing of any adhesive.

'No son of mine is gonna throw away his life sniffin' glue,' proclaimed my father.

This was the answer! Glue-sniffing was my hard-hitting social issue! I decided on the spot that I would make a groundbreaking documentary on the social problem of glue-sniffing in Belfast. Woodward and Bernstein would have been proud of me.

And so the work began. I searched through all the newspapers and magazines I could find in the library to learn more about the evils of glue-sniffing. I read up on the science of how sniffing adhesives makes you high and how it can kill you. I decided to take a personal risk for the sake of my investigation and experimented with inhaling an adhesive myself, just to help me understand what the attraction might be. I realised it was illegal, and I knew the consequences could potentially be fatal, so I waited until I was alone in my bedroom in Portstewart one evening when Aaron was out at a rugby something-or-other. I turned the lights out, sneaked into the bathroom, and sniffed the back of a strip of Sellotape. I had my big Merantz tape recorder with me to record my feelings during my first narcotic trip, but no matter how deeply I inhaled the adhesive it didn't make me feel happy at all. As I had never been high in my life I wasn't sure what I was looking for, so I decided to abandon this personal experiment and look for real live glue sniffers to interview instead. This was where I had an advantage over so many of my fellow academics at university. I had concluded very early in my university career that the job of an intellectual was to talk about social problems and explain who (in addition to Margaret Thatcher) was to blame, rather than actually do anything practical about the problem. I also learned that a good journalist reports only what they see and never brings their own bias to the subject. One lecturer explained that this sort of professional impartiality was essential to stop your own prejudices creeping in and this was why religious people didn't make good journalists. As usual, I nodded in agreement and kept my head down. I may have been regarded as the wrong sort for a job in the media, but I had contacts on the ground. I knew practically every entry where they sniffed glue in Belfast. My father was correct once again; all of these academics in their ivory tower blocks had no idea how the working man or his glue-sniffing offspring lived.

The university had a high-tech radio studio and production room. This was where you cut radio tape with a razor to take out the bits where you stuttered or people talked nonsense and then spliced it back together with sticky tape. I learned that this was where the phrase 'To end up on the cutting-room floor' came from.

I borrowed the big Merantz tape recorder and a microphone and headphones from the radio production room and carried it home on the train to Belfast. I felt like a proper reporter just carrying the recording equipment, and when I got home I practiced saying, 'Tony Macaulay, *News at Ten*, Belfast' in a dead serious journalist voice. I had arranged an interview with the owner of a model airplane shop in the city centre. One of my neighbours worked there and had kindly persuaded the owner to let this bright young investigative reporter interrogate him.

'Don't worry, he's harmless, so he is,' she told him reassuringly before I began my interview. Unfortunately I had to ask the questions twice because I forgot to press the record button on my Merantz the first time, but I explained that I was doing this on purpose to give him practice. I asked the shop owner if he was aware he might be selling glue to feed the habit of addicts rather than to build Airfix Spitfires. He categorically denied that he was a drug supplier, and I decided not to push him too hard because he sold the best *Star Wars* models in Belfast.

Next I had to find some real live glue sniffers who would agree to be interviewed and who wouldn't beat me up, so I went undercover. I left my suede ankle boots and legwarmers at home and wore my father's Columbo raincoat. I carried my recording equipment in my big brother's sports bag as I was concerned that if any wee hoods spotted me they would steal my Merantz, sell it in Smithfield market and buy drugs with the proceeds. I cruised around the Shankill in the green Simca, observing the street as keenly as a sectarian gunman looking for a victim. Eventually I spotted two teenagers with glue bags up an entry. They looked too small and intoxicated to be able to deck me. I didn't want to alarm the boys, because a stranger driving up beside you and winding the car window down at night in the dark was usually a sign you were about to be shot dead. So I parked the green Simca around the corner and walked back to the entry with my bag of recording equipment over my shoulder. As I approached the teenagers, I noticed they were wee mods of about thirteen with 'The Jam' and 'Madness' written in thick black marker on the backs of their parkas. I was aware that my manner of approach was crucial in securing an exclusive interview, so I drew upon my experience of giving out gospel tracts in the estate and approached the mods with a friendly smile without being too forward, in case they thought I was going to try to convert them.

'Bout ye? I'm doin' a project for college about glue sniffin',' I said, careful not to use a single 'ing' for fear of possible alienation.

The smell of glue was overpowering. It reminded me of the smell in our garage when my father tried to fix my chest of drawers with industrial glue he had borrowed from the foundry. The glue sniffers didn't seem to be bothered that I had joined them, and didn't attempt to hide their illegal plastic bags of glue.

'Are you at college, wee lad?' asked the older-looking boy. When he looked up at me I noticed that he had sad, innocent blue eyes and patches of hardened glue on his cheek. I felt sorry for him.

'Aye,' I replied.

'Fruit!' laughed his wee mate.

'I'm makin' a radio programme but I'm not usin' any names and I won't tell the RUC,' I explained.

'Yer man's at college,' said the older boy.

'Fruit!' repeated his wee mate, who looked as if he hadn't even failed his eleven-plus yet.

'So, can I interview yousens?' I asked again.

The two boys looked at each other and sniggered as if they had just heard a dirty joke.

'Aye, way you go, wee lad,' the older boy assented.

I pulled the Merantz from the sports bag, fumbling a bit as I plugged in the microphone. The boys' eyes were already open very wide, but they seemed to open even wider at the sight of professional broadcasting equipment.

'Welcome to the house of fun!' sang the older mod, grabbing the microphone and performing as if he was Suggs from Madness. His wee mate inhaled from his glue bag and giggled. After joining in with a good-natured laugh, I retrieved the microphone, wiped off some glue and attempted to begin the interview. The boys were intermittently inhaling from their Stewarts Supermarket bags, swaying slightly, and slapping each other on the back and laughing.

'Tell me, why do young men like you sniff glue?' I asked.

'Bricks, bricks, bricks!'

'Aye, bricks!'

'Are you aware of the health risks of glue sniffing?' I continued as professionally as possible.

'Did you see the pigeons?'

'Aye, pigeons!'

'Aye, bricks and pigeons!'

'Welcome to the house of fun ...'

'In a town called malice ...'

'Oh yeah-heh!'

I decided to try another approach.

'If the Thatcher government was doing more about your education, do you think that perhaps you wouldn't feel the need to get high? Because, as it stands and due to her uncaring capitalist government policies, you've no chance of ever getting a job?'

I was really getting into the flow of it now.

'Bricks, brick, bricks and fuckin' pigeons.'

'No surrender!'

'In a town called malice …'

'Oh yeaaaaah-heh!'

The boys collapsed into a heap of glue and laughter and then began to sing 'The Sash'. I decided that I had probably got enough on tape to give an insight into the thinking of the Belfast glue sniffer, so I quietly departed mid-Sash, just before the 'Kick the Pope' chant after the final line.

When I went home to review the material I had gathered, I was devastated to discover that I had recorded absolutely nothing. The tape was blank! In all the darkness and confusion I hadn't plugged the microphone in properly and all of my courageous undercover journalism had been a complete waste of time. Back at the university, after hours spent editing the small amount of material I had gathered, it came to pass that my first piece of major investigative journalism was marked a miserable C, and I was so upset I briefly considered an elicit sniff of glue myself.

To become a great broadcaster I would have to do better, and my next chance to excel came with the announcement of our first video production assignment. I gave considerable thought to my first television production, but once again, lack of time was a major barrier. I had to rule out my original idea for the pilot episode of a new, hard-hitting soap opera set in West Belfast. *Snugville Street* would have been just like *Coronation Street*, but with Belfast accents and the Troubles. It would have made *Brookside* look like *Sooty and Sweep*, but it was much too ambitious for a university assignment. I also had to give up on my proposal for a documentary about UFOs over Northern Ireland as there weren't enough sightings and most of those were British Army helicopters. In the end, I settled on the same idea as most of the students on my course – I decided that I would make a pop music video. Everyone was making music videos for a new station called MTV that played nothing but videos of Duran Duran all day long, like a 24-hour *Top of the Pops*. My first radio production may have been a major disappointment but this probably didn't matter because, as The Buggles said, 'Video Killed the Radio Star'. I realised that this new genre of music television provided me with an opportunity to shine as one of a new generation of radical young television producers. So I decided to make a Cliff Richard video.

Cliff was a Christian rock and roll singer who everyone said looked very young even though he was ancient. My granny said he was 'a lovely wee good livin' fella' which I could identify with. My decision to make a video for a Cliff Richard song was not just artistically ground-breaking, it was intellectually courageous as well. I decided that I would use this assignment to finally reveal to my fellow Media Studies students that I was one of those dreaded establishment-propping-up, capitalist-supporting, responsible-for-the-murder-of-millions, practicing Christians. It had taken me a full year to pluck up the courage to admit that I was a wee good livin' fella, but I had decided I couldn't live a double life any more. If I revealed my beliefs at the end-of-term presentation on a big screen in front of all my lecturers and classmates, then at least next year (if I passed this year) I wouldn't have to sneak in and out of Christian Union meetings as if I was going to secret meetings of the UDA. My big admission of faith would be like when homosexuals in America told everyone they were gay. This was known as 'coming out', and Diana Ross had released a brilliant disco song all about it. When someone 'came out' they told everyone who they really were, even if it meant people would hate them. When George Simpson came out in the Christian Union no one hated him, at least not out loud. Everyone prayed that God would heal him and make him heterosexual and this worked for a while, but then he became mentally ill and everyone had to pray for him to be healed again.

When I confided in Byron Drake that I was going to come out as a Christian using a Cliff Richard music video he said that this was deeply ironic because Cliff still hadn't come out himself. I chose a song called 'Thief in the Night' from one of Cliff's gospel albums. This song was all about Jesus suddenly coming back at the end of the world and people either going to heaven or going to hell, depending on whether or not they were saved. The lyrics created some artistic challenges, as I had to film the whole video in Portstewart and it was difficult to recreate the end of the world in a small seaside town with a nice beach. Of course, this was exactly the type of creative challenge that I would have to rise to if I were to become a great film director. My video needed to have all the horror of the *Omen* movies, combined with the optimism of *Little House on the Prairie*. My first brilliant concept was to make use of the wooden chess set I had bought from a Romanian peasant in Mamaia the previous summer. I shot the chess set in close-up as some of the pawns were lifted up to heaven by the hand of God and others got knocked over as a metaphor for eternal damnation. The first line of the song was 'I could talk for hours but you wouldn't hear a word', so I needed to shoot a close up of someone's mouth talking a lot. I thought Lesley from up the country would be ideal for this part and when I asked her she was most obliging. I had to recruit a larger team of actors to help me to shoot the end-of-the-world scene, as I needed to represent all of humanity running around in a panic during an earthquake on Judgment Day. Lesley helped me to recruit her small friend with the glasses, several Heathers from Portadown, and Aaron Ward and some of his rugby-playing mates who were good at running around. I also persuaded my cousin Paul from the Donegall Road to come up from Belfast as a visiting actor especially for the location shooting. This group of young people was too small to adequately represent everyone in the world, so I had to use clever camera angles to fool the viewer into thinking that there were thousands of them. The main locations for filming were the beach and the graveyard. I was aware that too many of my fellow students' videos were set on the beach so I decided to use the sand dunes rather than the seashore. I was concentrating much too intensely on the creative process to allow my mind to drift to thoughts of me and Bo Derek writhing naked in those dunes. I got to shout 'Action!' like a proper director and this was the cue for my troupe of amateur thespians to run around the sand dunes in a panic, imagining it was the end of the world and the devil was coming to get them. I cleverly shook the camera to simulate an apocalyptic earthquake, a technique that had been used for years to great effect whenever a Klingon missile hit the bridge of the Starship Enterprise. In the graveyard, I filmed my actors rising up from the graves and hoped that no one would call in to visit their dead relatives while we were filming. There was a real risk that mourners might mistake my actors for genuine zombies and I would get in trouble with the council. After many hours of takes and retakes my actors became a little tired and short-tempered, which I understood was behaviour that every great director had to deal with.

'Tony's all right, but half an hour's usually long enough,' I overheard Lesley from up the country tell a Heather from Portadown.

When the sun began to set and there was insufficient light to film any further scenes of death, destruction and resurrection, I announced 'It's a wrap!' with all the conviction of Alfred Hitchcock and treated my cast to 99s in Morelli's.

The next stage of the production process was to edit the action in time with the music. I spent many hours in front of a huge editing machine, working late into the night to make sure the action in the film matched the beat of the music and the message of the song. I edited the scenes on the beach with so many quick cuts in succession it looked like it really was the end of the world, and eventually my work of video art was complete. My message to my fellow students, announcing my faith and the second coming of Jesus, was ready to be premiered.

On the day of the screening, everyone gathered in Lecture Room 1 to see our finished productions premiered on the big screen. We applauded a Chris Rea music video set on a beach; a really, really dark horror movie set on a beach; and a really, really deep murder mystery set on a beach. There was a documentary about legalising marijuana with interviews on the beach and a documentary about the beach. At last, it was my turn. I was nervous, knowing that from now on I would be known as a wee good livin' media studies student. I prayed that I wouldn't be thrown off the course or stoned to death and that at least a few of the viewers would experience a religious conversion. After several other music videos featuring a beach, it was finally my turn. The lights dimmed and the audience waited with bated breath, apart from Marty Mullen who went outside for smoke. My video began quietly at first and slowly grew into a crescendo of religious rock, the music blasting all of Cliff's conviction over the speakers. The audience watched my visual masterpiece in silence. When Cliff had sung his final word and my concluding image froze on the screen there was a long silence. Perhaps people were praying? Finally, Marina with the Daisy Duke shorts broke the silence by whispering a solitary, incredulous, 'Fuck!'

I had come out, so I had.

10

COURTING IN COLERAINE

At first me and the Belle of Bellaghy were just friends, so we were. But providence put us in the same Bible study group, and this provided an opportunity for romance. In addition to the main weekly meeting in LT17, the more zealous members of the Christian Union met every Tuesday evening in someone's flat for Bible study. This was an opportunity to study God's Word and pray and get to know the girls in a more intimate environment.

'Dear Lord, we are thankful that we do not live in a country behind the Iron Curtain, Lord, where our persecuted brothers and sisters, Lord, fear a knock on the door ...' prayed a Heather from Portadown earnestly.

At that very moment there was a knock on the door! I could not contain my laughter, and this drew disapproving looks from Clive Ross, the holiest student in the university, and Tara Grace, an English charismatic with a nice bum and the gift of tongues. The lovely Lesley from up the country had arrived late with a Tupperware box of her mother's scones, left over from the Festival of Flowers organised by Bellaghy Presbyterian Women's Association. It was Lesley's knock on the door that we had momentarily mistaken for a visit from the KGB. Barbara Brown, a Ballymena Baptist and very good kisser (according to Aaron Ward, the spoofer) was leading the Bible study, and although her eyes twinkled a little at the incident, it was only me, Billy Barton from Bushmills and Lesley herself who found the coincidence truly amusing rather than sacrilegious. Barbara had a good sense of humour when it came to clean jokes like my hilarious 'Knock, Knock. *Who's there?* Doctor. *Doctor Who?*' joke, but this particular 'Knock Knock' joke seemed to be a step too far.

We were studying a passage from the Book of Malachi at the end of the Old Testament. It was generally accepted that it was much more intellectual to study an obscure passage from the Old Testament than anything from the New Testament because no one could understand it, except for Clive Ross who bought a big Bible commentary from the Faith Mission bookshop to explain it all to us at length and in great detail. The Old Testament was sometimes really, really dark and always really, really deep. It was almost Nietzschean. Clive brought his Bible commentary to these meetings along with a hugely conspicuous King James Bible. I preferred to arrive with a pocket-sized Good News Bible tucked away in my back pocket to avoid being persecuted or laughed at by fellow intellectuals in the street. The Good News Bible was regarded as slightly suspect by some of the more conservative members of the CU because it was written in everyday language that anyone could understand. Boyd Harrison often argued that the King James Bible was the only true and authorized version of the Bible and all the new-fangled, modern versions would put us on a slippery slope and make us backsliders. I wanted to tell him to catch himself on, but I didn't want to start an argument that might sully the fellowship of the Bible study. Sometimes Boyd reminded me of Mrs Piper in our street in Belfast, who regularly said 'If the King James Bible was good enough for the disciples, it's good enough for me!'

Once we had regained our composure after the knocking incident and consumed every last crumb of the leftover scones, the deep spiritual discussion of the Book of Malachi continued.

'When I read this passage I feel really just kinda encouraged,' gushed Tara with a charismatic smile. She went on to tell us how God had told her to walk down the longest bus shelter in the world between the main university buildings so she could bump into a non-Christian girl on her course and tell her about God at just the right moment, because the girl was very down in the dumps with her third in Social Psychology. God never spoke directly to me like this, and so I felt spiritually inferior to Tara. God told Tara when to get the bus and who to speak to and who needed healed. The nearest I had to a direct line to the Creator was when I sensed very strongly that he disapproved of my daydreams about Bo Derek in the sand dunes.

As the discussion continued, we moved on to a debate about whether it was possible to live for a whole day without sinning. I declined to participate because I had already sinned with Bo Derek in the sand dunes at least twice that day. However, Clive Ross was adamant that it was entirely possible to be a perfect Christian, implying that he was a good, living example. I wasn't so sure that he was as perfect as he obviously believed he was. The more he went on about being perfect the more I wanted to give him a good slap, and I was supposed to be a pacifist, so how could Clive have been perfect when he was tempting me to sin? Morality was complicated.

'Don't be stupid,' said Lesley. 'Sure even the Pope sins sometimes and he's the most famous Christian in the whole world.'

Silence.

It was as if someone had let off a particularly stinky fart but no one in the room dared mention it.

'You've no idea!' she added, inexplicably.

Lesley clearly had no idea that most people in the Bible study group had been taught in their church that the Pope was the Antichrist, rather than the best Christian in the world; and in the unlikely event that there was an actual Catholic quietly present, Lesley's view was not in tune with the doctrine of infallibility either. Byron Drake often pointed out to me that there were hardly any Catholics in the Christian Union.

'All the Catholics are in the GAA Club having a bit of your utterly hilarious Irish craic and all you Protestants are in a holy huddle in the CU. Even when you go to university you stick to your own sides,' he would say, offering his unsolicited observations on the divisions in Northern Irish society. I wanted to argue against Byron and accuse him of always taking sides with the Catholics even though some of the members of the GAA Club hated him for being an evil Brit, but I knew his analysis was basically correct.

I smiled at Lesley until Barbara Brown skillfully broke the uncomfortable silence by moving us onto the cutting-edge issue of whether we should be premillennialists or postmillennialists. No one openly disagreed with Lesley, but it was obvious that she had said the wrong thing. As the tiresome debate continued I had to control the urge to slam Clive Ross's Bible commentary closed on his perfect fingers. I was certain the lovely Lesley would laugh at my irreverence. I liked this girl. Sometimes when I missed the last bus from the university to Portstewart I would call over to the Halls of Residence and tell Lesley that I didn't want to impose, but could she give me a lift home? She was always smiling and animated, always accommodating and always offered me a lift home, even though she said I was just using her. Lesley got annoyed when I said that I was sorry for asking but I wasn't middle class like some people and I didn't have a daddy who could afford to buy me a pony or second-hand Ford Escort estate with headrests for my birthday. She told me to wise up and stop being so jealous, and turned up 'My Song' on her Elton John's *Greatest Hits* cassette to drown out my socialist arguments.

On these short trips in the car it seemed Lesley could not pass a field of animals without commenting on how much she loved them.

'Och, look at the lovely wee lambsies,' she whooped at the slightest glimpse of a sheep.

Her excitement was uncontainable when she spotted a horse in any field.

'Och, look at the gorgeous wee palamino!' she shrieked as we drove along the road from Coleraine to Portstewart. I was confused, thinking she had just spotted a new Fiat.

I soon discovered that Lesley enjoyed science fiction, which was very unusual for a girl, and like me she generally disliked sport, which was very unusual for a boy. We were becoming good friends, just like *Mork and Mindy*, though I only greeted her with 'Nanu, nanu' occasionally.

But at the beginning of our second year at university, something happened which would change everything. Every year before the first week of term, the Christian Union met up for a weekend in a bed and breakfast in Portrush to pray and plan for the year ahead, and to meet the new first year girls. While we were rehearsing a drama which would remind the freshers about the importance of justice for poor people in the Third World, one of the Heathers from Portadown burst into the room.

'Lesley's in hospital!' she cried.

'Is it her appendix, hey?' asked Billy Barton, who had just arrived on his motorbike from Bushmills where they made whiskey for my granny.

'No, she's had an asthma attack and she's on oxygen,' explained Heather. I had never seen this Heather get so upset about anything. She was even more upset than the time the bulb in the overhead projector exploded while she was leading a chorus of 'Majesty' at the CU Praise Night.

'Hey, tell Lesley I was askin' her what's the craic, hey?' Billy requested.

Tara Grace offered to organise a special prayer meeting and said she would go to the hospital and lay hands on Lesley to heal her, but only if Lesley had enough faith and no hidden sins.

I was upset. I was so upset that when the meeting began I couldn't concentrate on the Bible teaching from the Second Book of Chronicles even though it was really, really deep. But why did I feel upset? Lesley and I were good friends, of course, but this felt different. I always thought Lesley was attractive even though she was a big stout girl from up the country. She always made me smile when she shouted at me in her lilting country accent. I called this her 'Bellaghy Whoop'. I had no idea where Bellaghy was – I was vaguely aware that it was somewhere north of Glengormley – and I had never heard anyone else speak in such a unique accent. I was amazed when I discovered that the word 'floor' had four syllables in Bellaghy. I noticed this the day I spilled a cup of coffee in the Students' Union.

'Look at the mess you've made on the fa-loo-wer-ra!' Lesley had whooped.

Lesley had lovely big eyes that widened with every emotion and she expressed a wider range of emotions than any girl I had have ever met. Yes, she talked an awful lot, and some of it was nonsense about clothes and shopping, but as time went on I began to notice that when Lesley actually stopped talking she had the sort of mouth you really just wanted to kiss. After a while, and most inappropriately in the middle of a meeting as we were singing 'Bind Us Together, Lord', I realised that this was what people in America called 'having feelings' for someone. To my surprise, I was having feelings for the lovely Lesley from up the country.

Once I heard the patient was feeling a wee bit better, I decided to go and visit her in hospital. Coleraine Hospital was so small and old fashioned that I thought that Florence Nightingale might still have been the matron and would appear any moment with her lamp. When I found Lesley's ward, I waited until all her family visitors with tidy hair and nice clothes had departed and went in with a bottle of Lucozade and a book about faith healing from Tara. I had never seen Lesley in a nightie before. When she saw me, she pulled the bedclothes up to her chin and touched her oxygen mask demurely.

'You've … no idea,' she said weakly, removing the mask.

She was wheezing like Oul Mac the day he had tried to give up cigarettes. I had a sudden urge to rip off the mask and give her mouth-to-mouth resuscitation.

'Tara Grace wants to lay hands on your chest to heal you, but I thought I would offer first, so I did,' I said.

Lesley almost relapsed with laughter. Her wheezing laugh reminded me of Dick Dastardly's dog, Muttley, but Lesley was starting to look more like Penelope Pitstop to me.

In the weeks that followed, when I wasn't studying the impact of Marxism on *Coronation Street* or arguing with Byron Drake about the existence of God, I wrestled with the dilemma of how and when I could ask the lovely Lesley to be my girlfriend. If she said no it could mean the end of a beautiful friendship, just like the couples in ABBA. Lesley would be Agnetha, but with short, dark, curly hair and a Bellaghy accent, and I would be Björn, except with a chin. After much thought, prayer and a good few walks the length of the Strand beach in Portstewart, I came to the conclusion that is was worth taking the risk. Lesley was so good-natured it was possible that she would still want to be my friend even after I embarrassed her with an attempted snog. One weekend when I was visiting my granny in Belfast, she made the customary enquiry about my love life.

'Any sign of a nice wee girl for you son, now you're all growed up and all?' asked Big Isobel as I removed the ashes from her fireplace with the previous night's *Belfast Telegraph*.

I obviously hesitated long enough to indicate the possibility of romance.

'Oh, as sure as you're livin', I think our Tony's got himself a girl!'

I hit a beamer and spilled ash on my Wranglers. 'How do you know that, Granny?' I asked.

'Have a titter of wit, son, your oul granny's no dozer, so she's not,' she replied.

Back at the university I had a confidential chat with one of the Heathers from Portadown behind the reference books for nurses in the library. We agreed that the perfect venue for me to ask Lesley out was the Strand Hotel disco in Portstewart. This was the apex of the triangle of romance on the north coast of Northern Ireland. The Strand Disco was nothing like the Westy Disco; it had a bar with proper alcohol rather than vodka and Coke smuggled inside in a C&C lemonade bottle, and a proper dance floor with no discernible splodges of chewing gum. There was a proper DJ wearing a *Miami Vice* shirt who spoke in an American accent with only a hint of a Coleraine twang. I had noticed that people from Coleraine said 'man' at the end of every sentence just like the grooviest people in America. In America they said, 'Hey, man. What's happenin'?' In Coleraine they said, 'What's the craic, mawn?' The disco in the basement of the old hotel was so plush, with padded seats around the dance floors and toilet seats in the Gents, it made the Westy Disco look wick. There were more brightly-coloured flashing lights in the Strand Hotel Disco than at the scene of a bombscare in the Europa Hotel.

So I hatched a plan with a Heather from Portadown. We had to keep it a secret from Lesley in case she worked out what was going on, and it also had to be hidden from the holier members of the Christian Union who disapproved of dancing because it was like sex with clothes on. Heather would arrange for me and her and Lesley and Aaron to go to the Strand Disco, 'just to see what it was like'. Then at the appropriate moment, in between Spandau Ballet and a Duran Duran twelve-inch, Heather and Aaron would disappear to the toilet and I would pop the question to Lesley. I fretted about how I should ask her. In Belfast we usually said, 'Will you see me, wee girl?' but this seemed too unsophisticated for the lovely Lesley from up the country. I didn't want to be too formal, either, as it wasn't exactly a marriage proposal. So I decided I would try a much cleverer and subtler approach. When we arrived at the disco it was completely empty. Lesley's perfect teeth gleamed white in the ultraviolet light and she was wearing big, shiny red earrings like the girls in Human League. Her make-up was perfect as usual, and her red lipstick was as glossy as her cropped black hair. It was no wonder I had taken a shine to this girl. She was dressed from head to toe in a new denim outfit with shoulder pads and a frilly neck, which I assumed had until recently adorned a mannequin in the window of Anderson & McAuley's in Royal Avenue.

'Do you like my Gloria Vanderbilt?' she asked us one by one.

I bought everyone a Coke because we are all too good livin' to drink. The four of us got up on the dance floor and boogied to 'Billie Jean' and, although I failed to pull off any authentic Michael Jackson moves, I noted that Lesley really knew how to shake her body down to the ground. At the pre-arranged moment, Heather and Aaron departed loo-ward, and I invited Lesley to join me for another Coke in the privacy of the small bar beside the emergency exit.

'Do you like my Gloria Vanderbilt?' she asked.

'Yes, it's lovely on you, so it is.'

'A hundred and fifty pounds with twenty per cent off.'

'I bet you didn't get that in the *Club Book*.'

'What's a *Club Book*?'

There were a few moments of silence as the DJ introduced Spandau Ballet in a transatlantic accent. I took a deep breath.

'Do you know the way, er, when someone likes someone …' I spluttered, 'and they're already good friends, and they, you know, don't quite know how to ask them out, so they don't …'

Lesley nodded and her eyes widened in her lovely way, and I knew she understood.

'Well, what would you do if someone like that asked you out?' I continued, looking at her and nodding slowly, as if doing so would translate my bumbling into an intelligible request.

Lesley's eyes lit up and she smiled her beautiful smile. 'Oh, I know what you're gettin' at, Tony,' she whooped.

I nodded enthusiastically.

'You want me to ask Heather from Portadown to go out with you, don't you? I'll ask her when she comes back from the loo.'

'No! No, not Heather.'

'Oh, you mean the *other* Heather?'

'No,' I insisted. 'Not any of the Heathers!'

'Well then, who?'

I looked at Lesley and smiled. Spandau Ballet were singing 'True'. After a few seconds, her eyes opened even wider than usual.

'You mean *me?*' she asked, as if the possibility had never even crossed her mind.

'Yes, of course I mean you,' I said, and I took her hand.

'All right then,' said Lesley. 'But I thought you fancied one of the Heathers.'

'Nope. Sure I'd never be bored with you,' I said.

'This much is tru-who,' crooned Spandau Ballet.

'I'm thrilled,' said Lesley, and I think she really was thrilled, even though she knew I was just a wee lad from up the Shankill.

We got up on the dance floor but the DJ faded up 'Every Breath You Take' by The Police. We slow danced, even though it was a song all about breaking up and hating each other and it wasn't very romantic at all, really. But we didn't care. We had our first snog that night in Lesley's kitchen while the kettle boiled. I ran my fingers through her hair and knocked one of her red earrings across the room as if I was winning a snooker tournament in *Pot Black* on BBC2.

The following week we went on our first proper date as a couple to see *Octopussy* in the Coleraine Palladium. Unfortunately, the cinema had little in common with a James Bond movie, apart from the occasional bomb threat. The Coleraine Palladium was like the London Palladium, but without heating or customers. Lesley snuggled up to me in the freezing cinema and laughed at my Roger Moore impersonation when they stopped to change the reel in the middle of the movie. Our carry-on seemed to irritate a man in an anorak sitting on his own in the row behind us, and he tutted several times at my superb imitation of 007, but we didn't care because we only had eyes for each other. When the movie was over we went to the Carrig-na-Cule Hotel in Portstewart for a romantic meal and I bought Lesley a Chicken Maryland and profiteroles with my student grant. After that, we went for a walk along the promenade in Portstewart. I had borrowed Aaron's headphones so we could plug in both sets and listen to Cliff Richard's *Love Songs* cassette together. We strolled along hand in hand, ignoring the icy wind and listening to 'Constantly', and finally we popped into Morelli's for a poke.

'You'll have to come to Belfast,' I said.

'You'll have to come to Bellaghy,' replied Lesley.

When a couple visited one other's homes this meant they were serious and didn't care about their house being too small or their big brother embarrassing them.

Within weeks everyone at university was saying what a lovely couple we were. Several of the Heathers from Portadown said that we suited each other very well because we both had very dark black hair. Clive Ross commented that we looked almost like brother and sister, which worried me as this sounded slightly incestuous. Byron Drake congratulated me on finding a fellow virgin to do nothing with, and Aaron Ward said we were made for each other because 'she's nearly as big a header as you, wee lad'. We may have started out like Mork and Mindy but it was clear that Lesley and me were transforming into Pammy and Bobby Ewing. At last, I had a real live girlfriend. We were coortin', so we were.

11

WESTY DISCO ON TOUR

'It saves lives, so it does!'

This was how one RUC officer described the Westy disco – or the Ballygomartin Presbyterian Church Youth Club, to call it by its full name – and the police in Belfast knew a thing or two about life and death.

'Well, it certainly does that, so it does,' everybody agreed.

Every Saturday night for more than ten years, four hundred teenagers had crammed into an ageing Nissan hut at the corner of the West Circular Road to dance to the Bay City Rollers, boogie to 'Saturday Night Fever', and wave their arms in a New Romantic way to the Human League. The police had begged the church to keep the Westy open all year round to keep the kids of the Upper Shankill off the streets and safe from riots, shootings and paramilitary recruiting sergeants. But the youth-club leaders needed a wee break during the summer, and there were far too many other distractions in July and August. Our side built bonfires and paraded on the Twelfth of July and the other side banged bin lids and marched on the anniversary of Internment. Both sides supplemented the political and cultural celebrations with summer riots, when we hurled projectiles at our neighbours across the peace walls and called them various categories of bastards. It wasn't a proper summer in Belfast without a riot. Once you felt the warmth of the summer sun on your face you knew it was time once again to go out in your figure, get your nose sunburnt and hate the other side even more passionately than usual. In a Belfast heatwave, plastic bottles filled with suntan oil were often accompanied by glass milkbottles filled with petrol. Summer on the peace line was just like the battle between the Rebel Alliance and the Empire on the forest moon of Endor in *Return of the Jedi*, but with no cuddly Ewoks. Belfast didn't do cuddly in the summertime.

The Westy also held activities on Tuesday nights to complement the disco dancing, snogging and alcohol smuggling that took place on Saturday nights. While Saturday nights were reserved for dancing to Duran Duran and Michael Jackson, Tuesday evenings included a youth club choir and old-fashioned ballroom dancing lessons, like on *Come Dancing* on BBC2. On Tuesday evenings we were given the opportunity to learn first aid and some people got a chance to do the Duke of Edinburgh. Due to this busy programme during the winter months and the obvious competing activities in July and August, the annual Westy Disco summer holiday had been instituted. At first, the trips were modest enough, to Corrymeela and Edinburgh and London, and they were subsidised by nice Americans and Dutch people who loved peace and wanted to give us a break from war-torn Belfast. But after a few years the trips became more ambitious, and eventually we had to save up and fundraise to go to Europe, which was east of England.

Some of us had never been further afield than the caravan site in Millisle before embarking on the adventure of a Westy Disco summer holiday. Some of the members had never even been on a plane before, and there was a big difference between a Shankill black taxi and a jet plane.

First we went to Ostend in Belgium, where we spent the week on a beach with sand and Ambre Solaire and in Oncle Willy's Bistrot significantly reducing the Belgian beer supply. My cousin Mark and I went to disco bars and I danced to Chic and got 'Lost in Music'. I couldn't get a Belgian girl, but I got to sample some Belgian chocolates and chips with mayonnaise and snails in garlic instead. The snails tasted like rubbery whelks, but at least I didn't boke them back up. Everyone thought Belgium was brilliant, or nearly everyone.

'Belgium's ballicks!' said Philip Ferris.

The following year we travelled to Jersey with the cows and castles, where you could pick as many strawberries as you wanted for a pound. We spent the week on a beach with sand and Ambre Solaire and I got tickets for an Elvis Costello concert and he sang 'Oliver's Army' and it was class! I had a big row with my father in St Helier when I accused him of slabbering because he was drinking too much, and he gave me a good hiding and I huffed the whole way through the wartime tunnels of the German underground hospital.

The most ambitious and memorable trip so far, though, had been the previous year's trip to Romania, behind the Iron Curtain. When Irene Maxwell heard that we were going to Mamaia she got very excited because she thought we were going to Sweden to meet ABBA. I had to explain that there was no such place as Mama Mia, although I admitted to sharing her disappointment. When it was announced that we would be going to Romania some people were very unsure if it was safe to go to a country with soldiers everywhere, but my father explained that it would be just like Belfast but with more sunshine, earthquakes and communists. This did not reassure everybody, and a few of the regulars stayed behind in the relatively less totalitarian environment of West Belfast. We spent a week on the Black Sea coast in Mamaia on a beach with sand and Ambre Solaire and I had a go at waterskiing and bought a wooden chess set carved by peasants for practically nothing. However, Mamaia was very different to our previous holiday destinations. The tourist hotels were in a compound surrounded by a fence and guarded by policemen with guns. One night towards the end of the week I was not allowed to enter the compound. My overuse of Ambre Solaire coconut oil and many hours of sunbathing had darkened my skin to the extent that I must have appeared local, and the police assumed I was trying to sneak into the tourist hotel to ask someone to sell me a pair of Western jeans, which was strictly forbidden. The police spoke to me sternly in Romanian and I replied as best I could with a 'no comprende'. After a few tense moments, the police officers noticed that my big brother and cousin Mark had collapsed in fits of laughter at the prospect of my impending arrest and imprisonment in a communist state. In the end, they smiled as if I was a pitiful child and let me go. I declined all the offers from the locals to buy my jeans, but I smuggled an extra Bible into the atheistic country and gave it to my room maid with a wee tip and a smile. If the police that had almost arrested me were to find out about my illegal Bible smuggling I was certain I would be jailed for years for my faith, like Saint Paul and thousands of Christians in Russia and China. Romania was a very strange country. We could only buy proper Coca Cola and Mars Bars with dollars in 'dollar shops', and although these stores sold some Western goods there was no sign of any Tayto cheese and onion crisps anywhere and this caused a degree of cold turkey to set in among the members of the Westy Disco. None of us had survived this long without a packet of Tayto cheese and onion before and it made us all feel homesick. Irene Maxwell was the most homesick of all. Irene had an unfortunate Belfast habit of referring to anyone whose name she had forgotten as 'Thingy'. This habit became much worse when she travelled abroad because anyone whose name she couldn't pronounce ended up also being called 'Thingy'. One night, in a bar with real live palm trees beside the lagoon, Irene and Heather Mateer went on the prowl for Romanian boyfriends, but they soon fell out after they both attempted to seduce the same fella.

'Like, what's your problem, wee girl?' asked Heather. 'Sure the one with the friggin' turn in his eye was yours.'

'I wanted Thingy,' complained Irene. 'Thingy was yours!'

Irene's affliction only got worse when she had been drinking Vodka and Coke, which she did a lot when we were abroad and her mammy couldn't smell her breath. At times Irene would give up on whole sentences and just say 'thing'.

'Like, it's not my fault if you can't even say his fuckin' name, so it's not,' argued Heather.

Heather had a beautiful way with words.

'But Thingy was a boke,' complained Irene.

'Well yours had a face on him like a Lurgan spade.'

'I fancied Thingy!'

'What are you like, wee girl?' shouted Heather.

'I know,' wept Irene. 'But my nerves is bad over here and I'm sweltered and them bloody mosquitoes is eatin' me alive and I miss my mammy and all and … ya know, like … like … thing!'

We went on a bus tour to Transylvania to see Dracula's castle but Christopher Lee wasn't there, and the only bloodsucking I encountered was the love bites my big brother gave his girlfriend in the back seat of the bus on the way home. Once again, I had no success whatsoever in securing a foreign girlfriend, not even a vampiric one. The only Romanian women allowed into the tourist compound were big round grannies who worked very hard all day long. I learned that there was almost full employment in Romania, which was the opposite of Belfast where there was hardly any employment. This was real live communism in action – everyone had a job and they didn't even attempt to build a DeLorean Motor factory! So all of the grannies worked very hard, sweeping the streets, cleaning the toilets and carrying wood and rubbish.

I bought a very cheap transistor radio in one of the Romanian shops and tried to find a radio station that played ABBA and Blondie. This proved to be very difficult as the local radio station played only marching band music and the DJ kept saying how wonderful 'Our great leader and president, Nicolae Ceaușescu,' was. It was like Downtown Radio only playing flute bands all day long while Big T repeatedly said how great the queen was. There was no proper news on this radio station apart from updates on all the impressive things 'Our great leader and president, Nicolae Ceauşescu,' was doing every day. It was the most boring radio programme I had ever heard in my life. It was even worse than *The Archers* on Radio 4, where English farmers talked about the weather and sheep. No wonder all the hard working grannies looked so sad if this was all they had to listen to after a long day's work! I was certain it would have cheered everyone up if the great leader and president, Nicolae Ceauşescu, had broadcast *Big T's Country and Western Show* on Mamaia radio for just one night. I was convinced that all those Romanian grannies would love Philomena Begley singing 'Blanket on the Ground'.

One unforgettable day, my cousin Mark and I went to a fairground. During a ride on the Big Dipper, I noticed that the rails were making a very strange, metallic cracking noise as the cars reached the top of the ride. Ten minutes later, everyone was screaming as one of the cars broke free of the Big Dipper, flew backwards at great speed and landed in the crowd below. The car landed upside down and the crowd rushed over to see if the people inside were all right. They turned the crashed car over and there were six Romanian lads around my age inside and they were all unconscious. I thought they were probably dead, and I vowed never to go on a Big Dipper again. Later that night when I got back to the hotel room I turned on the radio to hear how the injured teenagers at the fairground were doing. If this had been Downtown Radio there would have been an update from the Royal Victoria Hospital every half hour, but the news on Radio Mamaia simply reported that 'Our great leader and president,

Nicolae Ceauşescu,' had visited Mamaia that day and that everyone loved him and how great he was for the people of Romania. It sounded like Nicolae Ceauşescu was going to be the president of Romania forever and no one cared if six teenagers were killed in a fairground accident. Romania was a beautiful place and the people we met were kind and friendly, but I sensed that there was something not quite right about this country that was probably related to politicans and violence and power. Even though it was the strangest place I had ever encountered, there was something very familiar about Romania.

'I don't know,' Irene Maxwell said in Constanta airport on our final day, 'they're all dead on here in Mama Mia, so they are, but it's just dead sort of, ya know … thing!'

Even though I was at university now and very rarely made it to the Westy Disco on a Saturday night any more, I still signed up for the annual summer holiday. Actually, I had no choice. As my parents ran the Westy Disco, the trip also served as our annual family holiday. As a result, my wee brother became our mascot on our trips around Europe. He was ten years younger than everyone else and was spoilt rotten with sweets and ice cream as we travelled across the continent of Europe. The trips were exclusive, members-only events, so the lovely Lesley would not be allowed to accompany me – though she never expressed any desire to do so.

According to *Growing Into Love* by Joyce Huggett, I had to be faithful to Lesley while I was abroad. I had to practice fidelity like Bobby Ewing with Pammy and not yield to temptation and betray Lesley like JR did with Sue Ellen. Given my previous difficulties in securing a holiday girlfriend – apart from Maria, a beautiful Italian girl I met in London during the summer of *Grease* – I doubted that I would be presented with any opportunities for infidelity. But I had never been to Torremolinos before. When Uncle Henry announced that the summer trip this year would be to Spain, everyone in the Westy Disco got very excited and began singing 'Oh this year I'm off to sunny Spain, *Y Viva España*'.

'Spain's class,' cried Irene Maxwell. 'It's dead sunny all the time and you can get fish and chips and a lovely tan and all!'

'Well they're ballicks at football,' interrupted Philip Ferris. 'Sure we bate them in the last World Cup!'

This was followed by several choruses of 'One nil, one nil, one nil, one nil …'

'All the wee girls in Spain sunbathe topless with their diddies out,' gushed a wide-eyed Sammy Reeves, clutching his crotch inappropriately.

There was no doubt that this was going to be a special holiday. It was the first time the Westy Disco summer holiday would be to a destination that you could book with Joe Walsh Tours.

'Join the JWT set,' sang Irene, mimicking the advert from Downtown Radio.

'Chasing the sunshine,' chimed Heather Mateer on backing vocals.

When we landed in Spain it was hotter than beside the boney on the Eleventh Night in Millisle in a heat wave. There were hundreds of blocks of flats beside the sea, as tall as the Divis flats, but with more balconies and fewer British Army installations on the roof. In Spain, flats were called apartments and hardly anybody vandalised the lifts or pissed on the stairwells. It seemed that hot weather made living in a flat a much more pleasant experience. Once we arrived at our resort, the Westy Disco crowd were paired off and assigned our own individual apartments. This was to be the first Westy Disco holiday without bunks! My cousin Mark and I shared an apartment with a bath, a shower, a balcony and a cockroach. We couldn't wait to go to explore the history and culture of Spain, so as soon as we arrived we unpacked our bags and went down to sit beside the swimming pool in the sunshine. Luckily for Mark, he was accompanied by a fluent Spanish speaker – I had got a B in my Spanish O level, so communication would be no problem for me.

'Buenath diath,' I said to the bar man at the pool. 'Qué tal?'

I could tell Mark was impressed.

'Yeah, all right mate,' replied the barman. 'What are you 'avin'?'

The barman was from Liverpool.

The next day, we met two beautiful English girls with skimpy bikinis and expensive sunglasses who lived in Spain and spoke Spanish fluently. Irene Maxwell and Heather Mateer made friends with the two girls after an initial spat over a sun lounger.

'Thingy and Thingy from England are dead on, so they are,' confirmed Irene.

Once again, I seized the opportunity to dazzle all around me with my language skills.

'Buenath diath, chicath guapath,' I said, quoting from page five of my Spanish textbook – with a little flirting thrown in for good measure.

'Vivo en Belfast, so I do.'

'Oh Belfast, with the bombs?'

'*Tengo loth ocoth athuleth,*' I continued, as it seemed to be important in O level Spanish to tell people the colour of your eyes when you met them for the first time. I wondered if there were a lot of colour-blind people in Spain.

The girls began to laugh.

'*No comprendo, senoritath,*' I said.

The laughter grew and one of the girls fell off her sun lounger and scratched her elbow on the crazy paving.

'*Qué patha?*' I enquired.

More laughter.

Before I could utter another word of Spanish, my cousin Mark rolled his eyes and intervened. 'He thinks he's Julio bloody Iglesias,' he said.

'Have I got my words mixed up?' I asked.

'No, it's just …' More laughter. 'It's just, you speak Spanish like a Chinese homosexual!'

Now my cousin Mark joined in the laughter.

'Do you have a lisp?' asked one of the girls.

'No, I do not have a lisp, so I don't,' I replied curtly. I was offended now. These girls knew nothing of my achievements on the stage in Belfast Royal Academy – how could I have triumphed as the leader of the Jets in *West Side Story* with a lisp?

'But you speak Spanish with a lisp,' she said.

'Well that's the way I was taught to speak Spanish at school and I got a B in my O level, so I did,' I replied with muchas indignation.

For the remainder of the conversation we spoke in English. At the swimming pool later that day, as I turned over onto my front to tan my back, it occurred to me that my O level Spanish teacher had a lisp when he spoke English. It had never before crossed my mind that he also had a lisp when he spoke Spanish. I had learned to speak Spanish with a lisp! This embarrassing incident ensured that I did not attempt a sentence of Spanish in public for the rest of the week. It also ruled out any possibility of romance even if I *had* wanted to be unfaithful to Lesley, because the two English girls were now convinced I was gay – a misapprehension that was only strengthened when they saw the collection of ABBA cassettes stacked next to my Sony Walkman.

However, real temptation was soon to arrive, naturally in Swedish form. We met Anna and Elsa the next day – they were hanging their bikini tops out to dry on the balcony above us when they spotted Mark and I below. We were attempting to throw the cockroach over the balcony having successfully captured it in a wet beach towel.

I was wearing my new denim blue swimming shorts from the *Great Universal Club Book*, and even though my chest was very sunburned the girls looked at me the same way form one girls at BRA had eyed me up in the playground after *West Side Story*.

'Hi, you guys,' said Anna, coquettishly.

'Hello, boys!' added Elsa with a cheeky wave.

'Where is it that you very cool guys be coming from?' asked Anna, rubbing her thighs together excitedly.

I couldn't believe it! Gorgeous girls with bikinis and thighs from another country thought I was 'a very cool guy'.

'We're from Northern Ireland, so we are,' said Mark, trying to keep his tongue inside his mouth.

'Belfast,' I explained.

'Oh, Belfast. Boom! Boom! Boom!' said Anna.

We all laughed knowingly at our international reputation for explosions.

'And where are yousens from?' I asked

'We are from Sweden,' Elsa replied.

I knew it! They had 'Swedish' written all over their beautiful, tanned bodies. Anna was blonde like Agnetha and Elsa was dark like Frida. We had been blessed with half of ABBA in bikinis living directly above us. This was too good to be true, and it was going to put my faithfulness to Lesley to the test.

'Can we be coming down and visiting with you guys?' asked Anna.

'Aye, dead on!' I replied.

'Do you mean yes?' she asked.

'Aye, as sure as you're livin', we do,' I answered.

'You speak like a crazy English,' Anna said, shaking her head, and the girls disappeared back into their apartment.

'Themuns is *dyin*' for it!' said Mark, excitedly.

Within a few minutes the two Swedish beauties were knocking on the door of our apartment. Mark ran to let them in, tripping over his plastic flip-flops in his excitement.

Anna and Elsa entered the room like Agnetha and Frida entering the stage at Wembley Arena, and both girls sat down on my bed. Yes, on my bed. I had barely met these two gorgeous Swedes and already they were sitting beside me, in the flesh, on my bed. It was unbelievable! We started to chat.

'Do the British invaders try to be killing you in Belfast?' asked Anna.

'Well, it's not really like that, so it's not,' I replied. 'Have you ever met ABBA doing their groceries?'

'Do you like sex?' asked Elsa.

This was a rather more direct question than we were used to. In Belfast, the equivalent would have been, 'Here, wee lad, d'ya fancy a lumber up the entry?' But only a minger would be quite so direct.

I was too shocked to answer. The truth was that I liked sex with Bo Derek in the sand dunes in Portstewart quite regularly, but that was just in my head.

'Enough talking!' Anna announced, removing her bra from beneath her see-through T-shirt. I could now see her real live Swedish breasts – right in front of me and on my bed!

The two girls stared at Mark and I as if they were expecting us to do something very important. Anna licked her lips, and I wondered if they were chapped with the sun and all.

'Okay, sure we'll chat again tomorrow at the pool,' I said innocently.

The two girls appeared a little confused. They spoke to one another in Swedish, rolled their eyes and giggled.

'Are you having a girlfriend at home?' asked Elsa.

'Yes, I do. I'm goin' out with Lesley from up the country,' I replied.

The girls looked at each other knowingly and got up to leave. Anna deliberately brushed her breast against my arm and I felt a distinct stirring in the region of my jimmy joe. I had to think very hard about Mrs Thatcher for a few moments to suppress it; this usually worked very well.

'If you don't want to do it all, I can do it for you with my hand,' Elsa offered.

'Do what?' I asked, stupidly.

Mark had hit a serious reddener and was now crossing his legs. 'No, sure you're all right, we'll see yousens again the marra.'

Within a few seconds the beauty, the perfume, the thighs, the breasts and the sexual tension had departed our apartment.

'Themuns were dying for it!' cried Mark as soon as the door was shut.

'Stop you coddin' me,' I replied. 'They were not, were they?'

'She even offered to give you, ya know, a wee futter with her hand,' he explained.

'No way! Sure they only just met us!'

'Yes, I'm tellin' you! Them two were dyin' for it.'

'But they don't look like mingers. They're both gorgeous!'

It seemed that my complete lack of sexual experience had blocked an attempted seduction by Swedish temptresses. This was fortunate for me, because Joyce Huggett did not mention such a scenario of great temptation and sin anywhere in *Growing Into Love*. My cousin Mark was not quite as innocent as me, but he clearly didn't know what to do either. I knew that if I were to be a good Christian I would have to wait until I was married to do it with Lesley – but if I were to be faithful, I would have to resist these promiscuous advances for the rest of the week. It wasn't fair. After years of not so much as a summer holiday snog, two Swedish vixens in bikinis had been sitting on my bed and I didn't even know what to do! Most fellas of my age would have managed to get at least one of these girls pregnant by now. I spent the rest of the week on a beach with sand and Ambre Solaire avoiding the advances of my own personal Agnetha, even though she touched my thigh ever higher on every subsequent encounter. I had fantasised for years about being with Swedish girls – blonde or dark-haired – and now that the opportunity had presented itself I didn't know what they wanted to do, I didn't know how to do it and I wasn't allowed to do it anyway! I was a sexually frustrated virgin, so I was.

12

WAR AND PEACE

'That wummin!'

Conor O'Neill was on his soapbox again in the Student Union café where I was having a cup of coffee and a Kit Kat.

'Oooh, Thatchurr! Oooh!'

He was going very red in the face as usual. I marvelled at Margaret Thatcher's ability to influence Conor's blood pressure. The very mention of her name set him off on a rant that usually concluded with a close comparison between Mrs Thatcher and Adolf Hitler.

'That wummin,' he fumed. 'They voted her in once, they voted her in again and they'll keep on voting the witch in forever!'

At the next table there were nods of agreement over paper plates of limp ham sandwiches.

Encouraged, Conor drew breath and issued the prophecy, 'We'll never get rid of that bloody wummin.'

'Well, is that not democracy?' I ventured.

I was almost confident now, and I was prepared to question the unquestionable. Conor turned around slowly and surveyed with me as much suspicion as Doctor McCoy scanning an alien life form with impossibly blonde hair in *Star Trek*.

'Oh, right, so you support her do you?'

This allegation was almost as bad as the accusation of being middle class. I didn't like Margaret Thatcher because she seemed to care more about always being right than always doing the right thing.

'I didn't say I supported her, I just said that's democracy. If most people vote for her then she gets elected as prime minister.'

Suddenly, Marty Mullen swivelled around on his plastic chair at a table across the room, scattering plastic cutlery and the remains of a rubbery sausage roll.

'Well, with the Armalite in one hand and the ballot box in the other, Thatcher will be thrown out of Ireland and we will be a nation once again. In a Free. Socialist. Republic!' Marty chimed triumphantly as he dipped a piece of Twix in his tea. Several of Marty's clones nodded solemnly.

'Violence achieves nothing,' I said, aware that I sounded like John Hume. 'It just hurts people and makes everything worse.'

Marty sighed aggressively. I was daring to contradict the most uncontradictable person I had ever met. I was surprised by how confident I had become.

'That's just your middle-class Protestant values,' Marty retorted.

In my first year at university I had been accused of being middle class so many times that during the summer break I decided to double check with my father if it was possible that we were, in fact, lower middle class rather than working class.

'There's nathin' middle class about us, son,' he'd reassured me.

'Are we not maybe upper working class?' I'd asked.

'If anything, we're lower working class, and don't you forget it.'

'Well, do you think we might be *upper* lower working class?'

'No son of mine is gonna think he's middle class when he's nat,' he'd replied firmly.

So I was ready for this argument.

'I'm not middle class. You're actually talking arrant nonsense!' I protested, instantly realising that what I had just said sounded very middle class indeed. 'I'm a socialist, so I am.'

'Belfast Royal Academy and not middle class,' Marty barked with a derisory laugh. 'Wise up, wee lad! There's nothin' socialist about ye. You're just wan more part'ee the capitalist war machine in the six counties. Just admit it, will ye?'

'Hold your horses, wee lad,' I argued back (for once). 'I'm a pacifist. I'm not part of no war machine, so I'm not. Killing people just breaks hearts. The families will never forgive, ya know.'

'Tell that to the fuckin' Brits,' Marty hissed.

'I said killing people breaks hearts – that's anyone killing people. As long as it's your side doin' the killin' you think it's all right, don't you?' If my confidence grew any further I might get myself into trouble and become a legitimate target.

'Pure airy-fairy middle-class shite!' Marty shouted.

I had never heard anyone say 'airy-fairy' in a Derry accent before and I almost ruined the argument by bursting out laughing.

'My da works in a foundry on the Springfield Road in West Belfast. There's nothin' middle class about that.' I protested.

'Oh aye, jobs for the boys,' replied Marty. 'Where's the jobs for all the Catholics west'ee the Bann, eh?'

Marty ended every argument by saying everything that happened in the world was unfair to the people who lived west of the River Bann. It was true that the worst unemployment was always in Strabane and Derry, so I couldn't really argue with him. I was certain there must be some good things west of the Bann, but Marty wasn't one of them. He seemed to resent me just for being me, and he disliked me for coming from where I came from, and I couldn't change any of that. But just as Marty was about to launch into another assault on my socialist credentials, Conor opened up an attack on another front.

'Speaking of democracy, I think your precious Christian Union should be banned from the Students' Union altogether!'

'Wha?'

'It's a completely undemocratic organisation. Union my arse!'

''Scuse me – wha'?'

'The Students' Union should only allow clubs that are open to everyone and youse exclude people who aren't the right type of super-Christian,' argued Conor.

'Wise up, wee lad.' I said. 'Sure the Women's Group have to be women and the Socialist Group have to be socialists, so why can't the Christian Union be for Christians?'

'Ah, but them other groups are not part of the capitalist patriarchy headed by that wummin!'

Now I was in my second year at university I was getting really tired of all these arguments over politics and ideology. We said the same things over and over again and no one ever changed their mind and I always ended up feeling crap. I understood that this type of intellectual debate was expected of us as students, but sometimes I just wanted to forget about sorting out the world's problems. I wanted to leave my books in the university library and go home to Belfast and watch a good episode of *Doctor Who*, like the one where The Doctor had to decide whether or not to go back in time and commit genocide on the Daleks by blowing them all up before they could ever exterminate anyone. The Doctor himself had regenerated as a vet who liked cricket and celery and the long scarf was gone forever. The new, younger Doctor ran up and down spaceship corridors and climbed through ventilation shafts with renewed vigour and he seemed to hate violence as much as I did.

'Right, I'm away to meet my girlfriend,' I said, getting up to leave the debate.

No one said so much as a 'goodbye' or 'see you later'. There was no interest whatsoever in my new relationship. Even though I had known them for over a year now, Conor and Marty simply ignored me and Conor started ranting again about how 'that wummin' was out to destroy the unions and the National Health Service and the world. Sometimes I felt very lonely at university with my fellow socialists.

As I walked along the longest bus shelter in the world the now-familiar gusts of wind blew icy rain into my face. I had walked along this passageway hundreds of times in the past year.

'Hey, boy, what's the craic, hey?' said Billy Barton as he passed me en route to the library.

There was very little craic so I replied curtly with my customary greeting, 'Right?', and then felt wick because Billy looked offended and he was a right fella.

Now that I was in second year I knew my way around the

university and I knew lots of people, but on days like this I still didn't feel as if I truly belonged there.

To prove our maturity now that we were second year students, Aaron and I had decided to move out of Mrs Flood's bed and breakfast and into a rented house at the harbour with three other lads and no heating. My tiny bedroom was in the attic, but on stormy nights the salt-water spray from the waves crashing over the harbour wall still reached my Dorma window at the very top of the house. I sometimes opened the window during a storm and stuck my tongue out just to taste the saltwater. It was very grown-up to have our own place with other students who didn't want to do the dishes either, but after a few months I longed for a return to the warmth of Mrs Flood's house with her cute dogs and her friendly daughter and a chicken dinner in the evening.

When I reached the central buildings, there was a poster on the noticeboard advertising auditions for a new student production of *Hamlet*. This momentarily lifted my spirits – maybe if I joined the drama society and got the part of Hamlet I would feel more like a part of this place. I bumped into Tara Grace on the stairs and she asked me to pray for a girl on her course to be healed from her migraines, as this would be 'really just kinda beautiful'. When I agreed to add my supplications to her prayers she shrieked 'Praise Jesus!' just a little too loudly for comfort outside the confines of LT17.

When I arrived at the model there was no sign of Lesley yet, but Byron Drake and Aaron Ward were sitting under the stairs with their eyes closed and their headphones on, listening to their Sony Walkmans. I knew not to disturb Aaron because he had just bought the new Dire Straits album and got very grumpy if you interrupted him during 'Private Investigations', and this particular song went on forever. So I lifted Byron's *Guardian* and confidently slapped him across the back of the head.

'Hey Tone, leave it out,' he said.

'What are you listenin' to now?' I enquired.

'The greatest band of all time,' Byron answered.

'ABBA? Really?'

'Very droll, Tone, very droll.'

'It's yer man with the gladiola in his back pocket, isn't it?'

I was correct, of course.

'Listen, Tone. This man Morrissey is pure genius. His music is really, really dark, and really, really deep. It's almost Nietzschean.'

'But it's dead depressin' and you can't sing along to it!' I dared to disagree.

'Listen, Tone, The Smiths are not like all that pretentious New Romantic crap you listen to. There's nothing pretentious about Morrissey.'

Byron had spoken on a matter of art and culture and I dared not dispute any further.

'What are you reading these days, Tone?'

I was reading a *Doctor Who* novel called the *The Tomb of the Cybermen* and *Basic Christianity* by John Stott.

'Oh I'm still reading *War and Peace*, so I am,' I replied. 'It's really, really … long.'

I had given up trying to finish the book and it was costing me a fortune in fines at the Shankill Library.

'Until you've read *The Catcher in the Rye* you haven't read anything,' said Byron.

Some days Byron carried this slim book alongside his *Guardian* so I decided perhaps I should give it a wee read at some stage.

'I'm going to audition for *Hamlet* with the drama society,' I announced.

'Good for you, Tone. Nothing like a good bit of Billy Shakey.'

'Aye, dead on!'

'But you do know you have to be able to act to perform the Bard?'

At this point I felt compelled to explain to Byron that I was an accomplished actor in the mould of Roger Moore, having studied Roger's onscreen techniques in *Octopussy* at the Coleraine Palladium. I informed Byron that I had triumphed on the stage in Belfast Royal Academy's ground-breaking production of *West Side Story* and that I would take the transition from *West Side Story* to *Hamlet* in my stride. Byron opened up his *Guardian* and turned up the volume on The Smiths.

'Anyway, I'm meeting my new girlfriend here and we're going for lunch in the canteen,' I explained.

'Are you going for a virgin tea party, then?' asked Byron, throwing one end of his Yasser Arafat scarf over his shoulder.

'Very funny. When I was in Torremolinos all the Swedish girls were throwin' themselves at me, ya know. When was the last time you had a girlfriend?'

'Listen, Tone. I know how to pleasure a woman. I can bring a woman to pure ecstasy within minutes.'

'Oh, do you take her shoppin' to Anderson & McAuley's in Royal Avenue?' interrupted Lesley in her familiar Bellaghy whoop.

If Byron was expecting my girlfriend to be a wee mousey good livin' girl, he was in for surprise.

'Well, are we going for lunch or not?' asked Lesley, who was resplendent in her bright blue Dash tracksuit from Anderson & McAuley's itself.

'Are you Tony's girlfriend?' asked Byron.

'*He's* Lesley's boyfriend,' Lesley answered. 'You've no idea!'

'Good luck with that, Tone!' said Byron.

We left Byron and Aaron (still entranced by an endless Mark Knopfler guitar solo) to their music and made our way past the model of the university, along the corridor with the shop and the oversized pot plants and past the bank. As we walked hand in hand towards the canteen, I noticed that Lesley and I were wearing matching legwarmers like a couple from The Kids From Fame.

'I was in the port on Sunday night drivin' up and down the prom in my car and you've no idea! I saw these boys with a brand new XR3 and alloys, and I was ragin' because I've wanted one of them cars for years, and when they drove past me and tooted the horn it just made me even more worse!' Lesley effused.

'Cars are for capitalists, you know,' I interjected.

'I know, but the XR3 is lovely. It's gorgeous! When you drive a good car it becomes a part of your body.'

I had never thought of a car in this way before and I wasn't sure if I wanted my father's green Simca to become a part of my body.

'So, when are you taking me down to Belfast?' asked Lesley.

'Soon, I just have to arrange it with my mammy because my

granny hasn't been too well with her pains and her nerves and all.'

'Will you show me all the wee red brick houses where youse all live?'

'We don't *all* live in those wee streets you know. Sometimes you can be so middle class!'

'What's wrong with that?' asked Lesley.

'Well, you know I'm a socialist don't you?'

'What does that mean anyway?'

Lesley knew very well what socialists were because her degree was in Social Administration. I had a feeling that my girlfriend was secretly trying to test me.

'It means … well, it means that I believe in the redistribution of wealth so that resources are shared equally and not kept by the richest people like the bourgeoisie in Thatcher's Britain.'

Lesley yawned.

'You see. You're not even interested!' I said.

'Oh my nerves! While I'm in the library writing essays on prison reform you're saving the world by watching movies.'

Lesley was good at irony.

'If you really believe in socialism why don't you redistribute your own wealth?' she challenged.

'Well … I have fifty pounds in my Abbey National savings account, but I was saving that to buy a bike for uni.'

'So you're not going to redistribute your wealth to anybody then?' asked Lesley. 'Some socialist you are.'

'You just don't like socialism because of your pony and your middle class values.' I said, drawing upon my recent exchanges with Conor and Marty. 'What about the people west of the Bann?'

Lesley stopped walking and looked at me in disbelief.

'I've lived west of the Bann all my life! You've no idea,' said Lesley.

'Wha'?'

'Bellaghy is west of the Bann, you know,' she explained.

'But you don't complain all the time,' I said.

Lesley rolled her eyes and moved us on to more important matters. 'Do you like my new red lipstick?' she asked.

The next weekend when I was at home in Belfast I withdrew the £50 from my Abbey National Savings account and bought a second-hand bike in Smithfield market. I had never owned a brand new bike in my life. Even Santa Claus had brought me a second-hand bicycle down the chimney when I was a wee boy, and there was nothing middle class about that! The bike itself cost £45, and with the remaining £5 I bought a puncture repair kit and a brand-new innovation called a bicycle radio. This was basically a battery-operated transistor radio that you attached to your handlebars. The gadget worked very well in the shop, but when I switched on Radio 1 while cycling the sound of the wind and the traffic drowned out 'Karma Chameleon'. This made it frustratingly difficult to sing-along to Culture Club, which you would never do on the Ballygomartin Road anyway in case any wee hoods spotted you and beat you up for being gay. Then, one day in heavy rain, the radio short-circuited half way through 'Kajagoogoo' and that was the end of it.

One Sunday night I put the bike on board the train at Central

Station to convey my new mode of transport to Coleraine. Now that I was in second year I would be a fully independent traveller with my own set of wheels. I no longer depended on Aaron for lifts to and from the university so he could no longer complain about me not giving him petrol money because I was as tight as a duck's arse. When the train arrived in Coleraine that night, though, I realised that I would have to cycle home in the dark and I had not made provision for the unrelenting Atlantic wind and rain. I thought the three-mile journey would be easy on my new wheels, but when I set out I discovered that there were more hills to climb than I had previously realised. The bike had three gears, but this didn't help, and I had a sports bag full of tinned, baked beans on my back to feed me for the week. I was no athlete but I was shocked that I had neither the endurance nor the leg power to sustain me on this short journey. I had forgotten to buy a pair of bicycle clips and when I noticed the oil from the chain was rubbing onto my legwarmers I had to stop to take them off and tuck my combat trousers down my socks. Sheets of icy rain were blowing into my face as if the universe was giving me another good slap, and I couldn't help but wonder why I couldn't have my own wee car like Lesley and Aaron did. I would have been quite happy to be called middle class if it meant I could drive my own wee Mini Metro to and from university and play ABBA's *Greatest Hits Volume 2* on the cassette machine on my very own dashboard. As I made my way up the steepest hill of the journey I began to shed unexpected tears of frustration. I was trying to do my best with the resources I had, so how come my best was never enough? Why did everything have to be such a struggle?

When I finally arrived at my freezing house, soaked to the skin and upset, I collapsed straight into my sleeping bag and pulled the blankets over my head to keep out the cold and the world. I wanted to escape from reality, and within minutes I was in a deep sleep and dreaming that I was Luke Skywalker rescuing Han Solo from Jabba the Hutt.

A few weeks later, Lesley came to visit me in Belfast for the first time. I provided her with a detailed set of directions to guide her from the motorway to the Upper Shankill via the streets with the fewest bricked-up properties. Lesley arrived exactly on time and parked her Ford Escort estate outside our house, dwarfing the green Simca in the process. As it was a Saturday morning my brothers were both out playing sports and overachieving with balls, so only my parents were at chez Macaulay to greet Lesley from up the country. I was very nervous. What if Lesley thought our house wasn't swanky enough? What if Lesley didn't like my parents? What if Betty and Eric didn't like Lesley? What if Lesley told my father about winning trophies at gymkhanas? What if my father told Lesley that Christianity was just a load of oul fairy stories? What if Lesley realised that I was just a wee fella from up the Shankill and decided to chuck me?

My father decided to welcome our guest from up the country with his signature Ulster fry, complete with extra potato bread from the Ormo Mini Shop. My mother put a tablecloth and placemats on the formica table in the living room for this special occasion. Mammy welcomed Lesley in her Gloria Hunniford telephone voice, but when she heard that Lesley had a pronounced country accent she relaxed and spoke normally. Lesley was wearing a teal designer tracksuit from Anderson & McAuley's that my mother said was lovely on her. My father told Lesley that he used to go fishing for eels near Bellaghy. Lesley explained that her mother was a primary school headmistress, which impressed my mother, and her father was a building contractor, which impressed my father. When it emerged that Lesley was a good Presbyterian even though she was from Bellaghy there was a sense of relief all round. The meal proceeded without incident, even though Lesley declined the offer of an extra sausage and a Paris bun. I was relieved that everyone got on so well together in spite of the dangerous class divide between us.

After our Ulster fry, I took Lesley out in the green Simca for a grand tour of Belfast. I showed her the Nissan hut where the Westy Disco took place on a Saturday night.

'That there's the Westy Disco,' I said excitedly, as if I was a London tour guide pointing out Buckingham Palace.

'Is that it?' she asked.

Then I took her to Woodvale Park and the Shankill graveyard and, as promised, showed her a proper Belfast entry behind the red brick terrace houses with the bins out. I took her to Tommy and Peggy Lusty's fish and chip shop for an authentic Shankill Road pastie supper, though she declined the offer of a pickled egg. Outside the chippy we bumped into Irene Maxwell and her mammy who had been shopping in the very few shops still left on the nearby Crumlin Road.

'Hiya, Irene!' I said.

Irene was a ska girl now and was wearing a Madness T-shirt and too much eyeliner.

'Hiya, wee lad,' she replied, chewing her Wrigley's gum.

Irene looked Lesley up and down as if she was a judge inspecting a poodle in the *Crufts* final on BBC2.

'Oh, you must be …Thingy?' she said to Lesley.

'This is Lesley, from up the country. She's my girlfriend,' I said indignantly.

'God love ya, Lesley,' Irene replied, still looking at me.

'You've no idea!' said Lesley.

Following this encounter I led Lesley over to the peace wall between the Falls and the Shankill and she could hardly believe that people could live like this. We drove up the Falls Road to Andersonstown where the IRA lived, and I showed her the massive fortified army barracks overlooking the city and the huge housing estates that could swallow all of Bellaghy. I was certain Lesley was impressed by my lack of fear of being on the other side, but she seemed to take it in her stride as if this was quite normal. On the way back we had to casually drive around a burning car because there had been trouble the night before, and once we had checked that the Simca's doors were locked she barely even flinched.

Then I brought her up the steep incline of the Glencairn Road for a panoramic view of the city. We passed the Glen where I used to catch tadpoles and where the paramilitaries dumped bodies. From this vantage point you could see the dome of the City Hall; Samson and Goliath, the big yellow cranes of the shipyard; the Belfast-Liverpool ferry, Belfast Lough, and some shops that were still smouldering from the latest firebomb in the city centre. I was very proud of Belfast and I could tell that Lesley was impressed by the city and my big city ways. As we toured the streets of Belfast, Billy Joel came on the car radio singing 'Uptown Girl'. This was very appropriate because Lesley was like my 'uptown girl' except she was from up the country, which meant she was my 'up the country girl', but I was definitely her 'downtown man'.

Finally, we went to visit my granny off the Donegall Road and I was mightily relieved when the matriarch and my new girl got on famously.

'God love him, we never knew what our Tony would end up bringin' home with him,' Granny said.

I was slightly offended by this.

'Och, look at you, son,' she said. 'You're all growed up now with a lovely big girl from up the country and all.'

I could tell from the size of Lesley's eyes that she had never been inside such a small house in her life. Granny's terraced house was what Belfast people called a 'wee kitchen house', with just one main room downstairs with a working kitchen.

'Look at the two of youse together,' said Granny, looking us up and down. 'You're a quare couple of smashers, just like our Charles and Diana.'

I looked at the various plates and mugs featuring Charles and Diana on the mantelpiece, and although I was convinced we looked nothing like the Royal couple I appreciated the sentiment and decided it would not be an appropriate moment to engage in a socialist argument against the monarchy. I was praying that Lesley would refrain from asking Granny if she liked her Gloria Vanderbilt.

Granny allowed Lesley to help me clean out the hearth and light the fire and sent us round to the shop to get her some messages, including a ham shank for her dinner and a prescription from the chemist for ointment.

'Och, you're a lovely big girl, so you are!' Big Isobel told Lesley.

When we said our farewells to Granny, I knew it was time to broach a sensitive issue with Lesley.

'Remember I showed you that proper Belfast entry with the bins and all this morning?'

'Aye, behind all the wee two-up, two-down houses,' answered Lesley correctly.

'Well, you're not a proper girlfriend and boyfriend where I come from unless you've had a snog up an entry on the Shankill Road.'

'No way!' Lesley answered coquettishly. 'Do you really want to kiss me up a boggin' entry?'

'Yes, you promised you'd do it if I brought you to Belfast!'

The frisson of young love was in the air of the Simca as Lesley nodded and I turned on the ignition.

'I'm going to take you boldly where no wee girl from Bellaghy has gone before,' I said in my best James T Kirk accent.

'Well, we'd better hurry up. I'm meetin' Mummy in Ballymena at three o'clock for the big sale in Go Gay.'

We parked the car near the Chinese take-away that had been closed down for rats and I led my lover to an entry opposite the Shankill graveyard. With my back to the bins and her lovely hair brushing against the red bricks I kissed Lesley gently on the neck. We were briefly interrupted by some familiar-looking mods who passed by whistling 'The Sash' and smelling of glue.

'Yeeeeooo!' they jeered suggestively.

Alone once more, we kissed and maintained a passionate embrace for ten perfect minutes. Just as the entry was beginning to steam up slightly, a woman in a housecoat and hair rollers appeared through her back door. She had a droopy feg hanging from one side of her mouth and her hands on her hips. After briefly surveying our activities she began shaking her fist and shouting at us.

'Away a that with ye, ye dirty bastes, youse!' she yelled.

We were a proper couple now, so we were.

⟨13⟩

TO BE OR NOT TO BE

To be or not to be – that was the question, so it was. I was well aware that the role of Hamlet would be a far cry from the role of Riff, the leader of the Jets in *West Side Story* but every great actor had to prove his versatility. Mr Hudson had proved this when he retired from being a butler in *Upstairs, Downstairs* to become the head of CI5 in *The Professionals*. Peter Davidson had made the interstellar leap from a vet from the Yorkshire dales in *All Creatures Great and Small* to a Time Lord from the Planet Gallifrey and there was no better acting role in the whole universe. The only problem I anticipated was learning all my lines. I had studied *Hamlet* for my English A level and there was no doubt that Hamlet had an awful lot of words to say. Remembering all of these lines would be a major challenge, but with my experience of previous productions of Shakespeare at BRA and learning the answers to the questions in the Presbyterian catechism I was certain I was up to the task. Of course, I wasn't so presumptuous as to be certain I would land the part of Hamlet himself, but there were lots of other good parts in the play – such as Hamlet's best mate, Horatio, as well as Rosencrantz and Guildenstern. When I arrived for the auditions in the drama studio I looked around the unlit room and didn't recognise a single one of the faces in the shadows. I sat down beside a tall student in training shoes who introduced himself in an English accent as Mark Broder. He liked football and Kate Bush but he was dead on. One by one, all the aspiring Hamlets and Ophelias were invited forward to read a short extract from the play. The director was a suitably eccentric-looking English lecturer with an English accent, long hair, a beard and the compulsory corduroy trousers. He called out the names of each hopeful actor in turn and we all had to come forward and read a few lines on the darkened stage. I was feeling slightly nervous, but I was determined to draw on my newfound confidence and take the audition in my stride. However, as the aspiring thespians got up in front of me to audition, I noticed to my dismay that nearly all of them had posh English accents. Most of the students auditioning were from England and spoke proper all the time, but even the students who were from Northern Ireland invented posh English accents to read their lines. Everyone was trying to sound like Lord Olivier and Sir Ralph Thingummy. The only exception was a short, thin and prematurely bald student called Alex who dispensed with the script and just performed the gist of it in an American accent.

'He's a method actor,' explained Mark.

I had no idea what a method actor was. I did know a few Methody actors who had performed in the school play in Methodist College in Belfast, but this was very different and I was intrigued.

'Is Roger Moore a method actor?' I asked Mark.

'No, Tone. Roger Moore is not a method actor.'

I was amazed at how quickly English people transformed me into 'Tone'.

'Jack Nicholson is a method actor. They imagine themselves completely into the role and stay in character even off stage.'

I knew instantly that I wanted to become a method actor, but as my turn approached I wondered whether or not I should put on an English accent for the audition. I was quite capable of doing a good English accent. Everyone said I could do wonderful impersonations of Frank Spencer, Roger Moore and Orville the Duck. But as a committed socialist from Northern Ireland, I decided that if I were to be Hamlet I would bring an authentic, working-class Belfast accent to the part. After all, Hamlet was the Prince of Denmark; if anything he would have spoken English with a Scandinavian accent, like Agnetha from ABBA but not quite so sexy. Hamlet wasn't from the south of England any more than he was from West Belfast. So I decided to make a statement by auditioning in my normal Norn Iron accent, resisting the temptation to turn my 'eights' into 'ates' and my 'nows' into 'naows'.

'Good luck!' Mark Broder said as I got up on the stage. I was wearing my New Romantic suede ankle boots and knitted leg warmers. I hoped I looked arty enough and that this would assist me in getting the part – or any part for that matter. I took a deep breath.

'"To be, or not to be, that is the question:
Whether 'tis nobler in the mind to suffer
The slings and arrows of outrageous fortune,
Or to take arms against a sea of troubles,

And by opposing end them? To die: to sleep –'"

'Okay, that's enough, thank you.' The director stopped me before I had even begun to emote.

I couldn't tell whether I had impressed him so much that he didn't need to hear any more or whether he had quickly decided that I was wick. His long hair covered his eyes, so I couldn't tell what he was thinking. He scribbled down a few notes about my performance and invited Mark forward to audition next. I sat down and listened as Mark read the same lines, only more confidently and in a proper English accent, and I immediately began to feel inferior. Maybe it was because the news headlines on the BBC were always read in this accent, or perhaps it was because the queen and Mrs Thatcher talked this way and they represented authority and always being right. I realised then that I was not destined to play Hamlet with a Belfast accent. What was I doing there, anyway? Why was a wee lad from up the Shankill auditioning for Shakespeare? Maybe I just needed to catch myself on a bit. If my big brother had been there to see me I knew he would say 'Wise a bap, ya big fruit!' My only real experience of Hamlet was the cigars my father used to chain smoke. However, my hopes were kept alive by the fact that it was a very long play with lots of speaking parts and it would probably be okay for some of the less-important words to be spoken in a Northern Ireland accent. Maybe I would be awarded a lesser role and I could use it to experiment with method acting.

At the same time the following week, the aspiring cast members gathered once more to hear the cast list. I hadn't given the audition a great deal of thought during the seven-day wait as

I was distracted by an essay on sexuality and the femme fatale in film noir and an argument in the Christian Union over whether it was okay to fundraise for the Third World on a Sunday. I had been in this nerve-wracking position many times before, but, as famous actors always told Terry Wogan on BBC1, 'It's all just a part of the industry.' During my schooldays I had been given the devastating news that I had not been cast as either Tom or Huck in *The Adventures of Tom Sawyer*, and I still recalled the occasion when the part of Tony in *West Side Story* was not given to me, despite my name *and* talent. I had experienced disappointment before, so I had learned to lower my expectations. I clearly wasn't English enough to play Hamlet, but perhaps, in this groundbreaking new production, Horatio at least could hail from West Belfast? As Hamlet and Ophelia and Gertrude and Claudius were announced I could feel my heart pounding with excitement, but once we got past Rosencrantz and Guildenstern I realised that there was little need for excitement. When it was announced that Mark Broder had been given the part of Horatio I was disappointed, but I had to admit that Mark was more confident and English than me and would probably do a better job. I began to fear the ultimate humiliation of a non-speaking apart. Was I destined to become an extra in *Hamlet*? I hadn't been given a lowly non-speaking part since I was a sheep in the nativity play at Springhill Primary School. I could never become a proper method actor if I had no words to say! This was going to be embarrassing; everyone would assume I lacked talent rather than an English accent, my big brother would slag me desperately and say I should play a tree because my acting was wooden, and Lesley would be left wondering if my previous triumph in *West Side Story* had been nothing short of miscasting.

'Don't worry, Tone, you'll get a part. You weren't that bad,' said Mark.

'Now the sentries,' said the director, flicking his unkempt hair and pausing dramatically, as if anyone cared at this stage. 'Marcellus – Tom Macaulay.'

I looked around the room for a Tom before raising my hand shyly. 'Do you mean Tony?' I asked.

'Yes, you!' the director replied, as if I should be ecstatic.

Not only was I a mere sentry, nobody even knew my bloody name!

As soon as the last parts had been handed out I fled to the library with my copy of *Hamlet* and I looked up the part of Marcellus to discover how many – if any – lines I had to speak.

To my delight I discovered that I had quite a lot to say in act 1 scene 1. I may have been a lowly sentry, but I actually got to spot King Hamlet's ghost and offer to 'strike at it with my partisan'. This was similar to Luke Skywalker striking at Darth Vader with a lightsaber. Over the page and there I was again – albeit to a much lesser extent – in scene 2, helping Horatio to tell Hamlet about the ghost. Was I really going to appear in every single scene of the play? I was absent from scene 3, but there I was again in scene 4 and I got to say one of the most famous lines of the whole play! I had even quoted this line in my English A level exam.

'"Something is rotten in the state of Denmark",' I practised, being careful not to pronounce 'rotten' as 'ratten' in my Belfast accent.

It may have been just one line but this was as crucial to *Hamlet* as a honk from Chewbacca in *Star Wars*. The role of Marcellus definitely had potential for method acting – I could imagine I was a real sentry for weeks and really get into the part. I would have to imagine that, rather than being a Protestant pacifist from West Belfast, I was a weapon-carrying soldier from Denmark. I turned the pages excitedly. There I was again in scene 5! In act 2 it seemed that Shakespeare was giving me a wee rest. However, when I got to act 3 I was devastated to discover that Marcellus did not make another appearance for the rest of the play. The sentry's job was done, and my final line was to be spoken in act 1 scene 5, 'We have sworn, my lord, already.' My heart sank like a badly skimmed stone in Lough Neagh. I wanted to swear already, my lord! If I had been Shakespeare I would have brought Marcellus back to say, 'There's *still* something rotten in the state of Denmark' at least once later on in the play just to remind the audience of the importance of these words for A level English exams. Just because William Shakespeare was the greatest writer ever didn't mean he wasn't capable of the odd mistake. The writers of *Dallas* used this technique all the time to remind you that Lucy Ewing was still out there somewhere plotting against JR, even though she hadn't been in an episode for ages. As it turned out, our wonderful director decided that, contrary to the script, the sentries should return to the stage to emote at all the blood and guts and wonderful acting by Hamlet and Co. in act 5. Although this directorial innovation brought me back on stage for an extra twenty minutes at the end, it also meant I had to hang around for nearly two hours between my on-stage appearances and this was far too long for a method-acting novice to stay in character. The result was that I couldn't just go home for a fish supper after delivering 'something is rotten in the state of Denmark' in act 1! The director pointed out that, 'if people like Tom do a good job this year, they will get a better part next year.' So I decided I would just have to persevere, and if I learned all my lines and performed well and the director learned my name at some stage, there was still hope for a leading part in next year's production of Shakespeare.

The director explained his vision for reinventing Hamlet for the 1980s with a great deal of passion and hair-flicking. Our new, visionary production would introduce Shakespeare to the *Dynasty* generation. The stage would be specially built in the design of a chessboard, and this modern set design would contrast with plush, traditional costumes with good shoulder pads. As it turned out, 'plush' didn't stretch to the attire of the sentries. I wore wellington boots and a helmet so you couldn't see my face and carried a pike made from a broom handle.

'Something is rotten in the state of my costume!' I said to Mark Broder at the first dress rehearsal, as he entered stage left in tights and velvet finery.

The rehearsals continued for weeks. Poor Hamlet had so many lines to learn I'm sure he had to give up studying for his degree, and our director displayed all the pain and anguish of a tortured artist as he strove to draw finely-honed performances from his young troupe. Only the elfin beauty of sweet Ophelia and an exchange of sarcastic jokes between Horatio and myself lightened the most tragic scenes and the most difficult rehearsals. I found some of my fellow actors to be rather self-satisfied, and this always sounded worse in an English accent. The banter between Rosencrantz and

Guildenstern in-between scenes was almost Shakespearian in its ribald cleverness. This gave me the opportunity to introduce Mark Broder to some Northern Ireland terminology when I had to explain to him what the term 'a pair of bokes' meant. He laughed so hard his plastic sword rattled in its scabbard.

Finally we were ready for our first performance. Lesley, Aaron and several Heathers from Portadown came to watch the premiere in the Riverside Theatre, which was beautifully situated overlooking the River Bann – albeit on the east. I was able to change out of my costume to talk to the audience during the interval, as it would be several hours before I was required back on stage for the bloodbath. The critical analysis of the performance provided by my friends was enlightening.

'Not quite *West Side Story*, is it?' smirked Aaron.

'It's a wee bit boring, Tony, so it is,' commented a Heather from Portadown.

'You don't suit them there welly boots and I can't see your face,' complained Lesley.

Some of the other comments I overheard during the interval were less encouraging, including one man who made it clear that he would not be staying for the second half.

'The most pretentious crap I have ever seen in my whole life,' he remarked as he ran for the door.

I was strangely reassured by this insult. If only the director had been brave enough to cast an Upper Shankill Shakespearian method actor in the role of Hamlet, this could have been a much more successful and gritty production. There was nothing pretentious about a Hamlet with a Belfast accent! I tried to convince Mark Broder that a socialist interpretation of Shakespeare would have made a West Belfast Hamlet a real possibility. In fact, I argued, there was no reason why Hamlet had to be white or male either for that matter! *Cagney and Lacey* had already proved that women could be heroes too.

'Yeah, so in socialist Shakespeare, the prince of Denmark would be a Chinese lesbian in a wheelchair!' mocked Mark.

After the initial run at the New University of Ulster I assumed that *Hamlet* was over, but to my surprise we began to receive invitations to perform internationally. The drama society was asked to visit universities in La Roche-sur-Yon in France and then in Erlangen in Germany. This was even more impressive than when the Westy Disco choir had been invited to sing in a church in Edinburgh. And so off we went as travelling artistes, performing all around Europe with our chessboard stage and my wellington boots and helmet. Our success overseas was stunning. It seemed that the fewer words of English an audience could speak the more they appreciated our performances. And I knew they weren't just feeling sorry for us because we were from war-torn Northern Ireland, because most of the cast were actually from England!

I got to tell people in France and Germany that something was rotten in the state of Denmark. If this trend continued, I would soon be telling people in the state of Denmark itself that something was rotten in it. The travelling was tiring, though, and our schedule was gruelling. It wasn't easy being an actor on the road for a world tour. I finally understood what life was like for Roger Moore when a new Bond movie came out. But I held my pike erect through every performance and bowed graciously at the multilingual plaudits.

Unfortunately Mark Broder decided not to go on the overseas tours, and they replaced him with a different English Horatio who wouldn't speak to me. Few of the other principal actors deigned to speak to me either, even when travelling and living together for weeks at a time, so I understood the loneliness of the travelling artiste. This was so different from my trips abroad with the Westy Disco where you knew everyone and the craic was ninety. It was true that none of my fellow actors ever got sent home for drinking too much and starting a fight in the street or assaulting a foreign police officer, but at least the Westy Disco crowd was warm and friendly.

I did eventually get to know some of the other supporting actors a little better on the boats and buses we took and in the hostels we stayed in. I learned things on this tour that a thousand Christian Union trips to the Greystones Conference Centre down south couldn't have taught me. I learned from one actor that it probably wasn't a good idea to go with a prostitute in Paris after you'd had too much to drink, as you would feel completely minging for the next week and possibly even longer. Benny and Björn had been writing an exciting new musical about playing chess and the first song they released said that 'one night in Bangkok makes a hard man humble'. It was clear that one night in Paris could have a similar effect. Another fellow thespian who was very happy and relaxed all the time explained to me that the odd-smelling cigarettes he liked to smoke so much were not, in fact, regular Benson & Hedges. I decided to have a serious conversation with Byron Drake about him smoking marijuana in the toilet of my flat and telling me that he was smoking menthol cigarettes to help with his sinuses.

I went to the cinema in France where they watched films entirely in French without any subtitles. I saw an award winning film called *La Balance* that everyone said was hard hitting and gritty and *très bien*. The movie was all about racketeers and police informers and gang leaders and murder – it was just like Belfast in French.

By the end of term, our production of *Hamlet* was judged a masterpiece of theatre and a Europe-wide success. It was decided that the drama society would build on this success with *The Comedy of Errors*, a Shakespearean comedy full of farce, slapstick and mistaken identity. I knew that I had paid my dues as a sentry in *Hamlet*. Now the director would give me my big break as he had promised, and I could finally have a wee go at method acting. All those hours of standing in my wellies with pike in hand, emoting at Hamlet's every word and tolerating smug sarcastic asides had surely earned me a leading part in this next production. But when the time for casting arrived, to my great disappointment I was cast once again as an officer. It was deeply ironic that the only teenage pacifist in West Belfast should be repeatedly cast as a soldier in arms, or at least in wellington boots. This time when I searched through the text I discovered that I had even fewer lines than Marcellus. Once again, all of the clever English students had got all the good parts, and the director had failed to recognise the bright light of talent shining before him. Either that or I was just a wick actor. I concluded that something was rotten in the state of the drama society. I retained my dignity and declined the part. The director told several of the principals that he was disappointed that Tom had given up.

In spite of all my efforts, my acting career had come to an end. I abandoned my ambitions to be the next Roger Moore and gave up my hope of becoming a great method actor like Jack Nicholson. Of course, I was aware that I could have a successful future after acting, like Ronald Reagan did in America, but I knew then that I would never replace Peter Davidson as The Doctor. I had once again tried my very best, and once again it simply wasn't good enough. It was not to be, so it wasn't.

NEW ROMANTIC

I was a New Romantic, so I was. When I first started out at university I was only pretending. Simon Le Bon would have laughed at my feeble efforts. Now that I was more than half-way through my second year, though, I was completely mature and free to buy and wear whatever clothes I wanted without my mother's approval. I was no longer dependent on the limited availability of pilot jumpsuits or East German army jackets paid over 20 weeks from the *Great Universal Club Book*. It was the 1980s and my tablecloth scarf, combat trousers, suede ankle boots and legwarmers were the height of cool. Of course, I didn't go to the extremes of frilly shirts, eyeliner and lipstick, as this was too expensive to achieve on a student grant and too androgynous to avoid the risk of getting your head kicked in. I had plenty of hair, though, and I decided to make the most of it with the assistance of many tubes of hair gel from Boot's Chemist. After many hours of practice in front of the mirror I managed to construct a hairstyle of Duran Duran proportions. I didn't care for the sort of floppy fringe sported by Byron Drake, even though it made him look like the lead singer in the Human League, so I concentrated on height and volume on the top of my head and length at the back. To achieve this I limited my visits to His and Hers hairdressers on the Shankill road so my locks would grow long and thick enough to support a hairdo worthy of an appearance on *Top of the Pops*. Some days my hair was as impressive as one of the 'wild boys' in the Duran Duran video where Simon Le Bon was strapped to a spinning windmill and his head got dunked beneath the water with each revolution. This was a brilliant video with fire and trampolines and dancing and monsters. I wished I had the resources to make a video like this on my course, even if it had to be set on a beach. When I raved about this post-apocalyptic mini movie to my big brother, he made it clear that he did not approve of my newfound New Romanticism.

'Pity they didn't stop turnin' the windmill when that big fruit's head was under the water,' he remarked.

When I boasted to Billy Barton that my hair looked as trendy as one of the 'wild boys' from the Duran Duran video he was not impressed, either.

'Sure that's nothin',' he said. 'There's been a quare lot of wile boys runnin' round Bushmills for years!'

Of course, New Romanticism wasn't just about clothes and hair – it was also a brilliant new form of pop music. I bought cassettes by great new bands such as the Thompson Twins, who had three members – one black, one female and one ginger – none of whom were actually related. I bought a cassette by Tears for Fears who sang a really, really dark and really, really deep song about living in a very, very 'Mad World'. Tears for Fears were so cool and big haired that I tried very hard to appreciate the album tracks that I didn't really like. I had come to realise that an intellectual has to make an effort to appreciate art that most people don't instantly enjoy, like Bob Dylan songs and modern art paintings that were almost Nietzschean.

Never before in the history of pop music had there been so many bands using synthesizers and electric drums. It used to be just Kraftwerk and Gary Numan and Jean Michel Jarre, but now everybody was playing electro-pop. I sometimes played along on my stylophone until the batteries went dead. My father had once again kept up to date with the latest technology by purchasing a shiny new, portable radio-and-cassette stereo with speakers built into the front and extra buttons to turn up the bass. Apparently the nickname for this new type of stereo player was a 'ghetto-blaster', but to me this sounded more like the name for a petrol bomb (in America they called it a 'boom box', but that still sounded much too explosive to me). This latest technological innovation was suitably silver and space age and looked just like the one yer woman used when she couldn't stop dancing in *Flashdance*. I borrowed the ghettoblaster one Sunday night and after that it remained with me in Coleraine. I bought the new Howard Jones cassette with my student grant and played 'What is Love?' with the volume turned up full in an attempt to lessen the pain of having to do the dishes in our student flat every two months. I played my Howard Jones cassette so many times that it got stuck when I tried to rewind it, and I had to take it out of the ghettoblaster and rewind it with a pencil. As the 1980s gathered pace, the make-up and the clothes became more and more outrageous, just like the shoulder pads and plotlines in *Dynasty* and *Dallas*. It was definitely the era of the shoulder pad soap opera. Margaret Thatcher and Nancy Reagan even had a friendly shoulder pad competition when Maggie visited Ronald Reagan in America to build their 'special relationship' and give the Soviets a hard time. Conor O'Neill said that New Romanticism was a 'disgusting display of excess and indulgence typical of Thatcher's Britain' and naturally blamed it all on 'that wummin!'

Of course, now that I had a real live girlfriend I had to learn to be a true romantic as well as a New Romantic. I discovered that girls loved to receive nice, romantic presents from their boyfriends rather than anything too utilitarian such as oven gloves or a duster. Of course, as a feminist I would never have insulted Lesley with such stereotypically gendered gifts, so I bought her a pink cuddly dog for Valentine's Day which she loved and put on top of the wardrobe in her bedroom. For Christmas I gave her the gift of a Panda rug from the British Home Stores, although for some reason this present elicited less enthusiasm. When I decided to buy Lesley jewellery for the first time, I saved money by skimping on beans on toast for weeks. A gift of jewellery was an indication of true love, so it was very important to get it right. I secretly researched what type of jewellery Lesley liked the most by asking a Heather or two about her preference of precious metals. They told me that she preferred three colour gold, which was the latest big thing, and I decided to buy Lesley an expensive three colour gold locket in the shape of a heart. The locket opened so you could put a photograph of yourself inside for your girlfriend to gaze upon at any time, day or night. This exclusive gift would have to be sourced in one of the finest jewellers in Belfast, so one weekend I travelled home, made my way into Belfast city centre and, after a full-body search at the security gates, proceeded to Argos. I had to queue for ages, but when I eventually got to the front of the line I was able to look up the jewellery section in the catalogue and fill in an order form with the wee biro on a chain, like my big brother when he put a bet on in the bookies. Then I made my way to the cash desk.

'Where's your wee slip, love?' enquired the purveyor of fine jewellery at the cash register. She pressed some buttons on an amazing new kind of computer that instantly checked if the product was available. Argos was like an instant *Great Universal Club Book*!

'You're in luck, love. It's in stock,' she announced.

I wrote my biggest cheque since paying the deposit on my student flat and handed it over.

'You can collect it over there in a wee minute, son,' the cashier advised, pointing to a long counter lined with cardboard boxes. I waited as a small man collected a new strimmer to tidy up his lawn, a fat woman picked up her *Jane Fonda's Workout* video, and a mother with two noisy children waited impatiently for a My Little Pony doll with a unicorn horn. After everyone else's boxes had been delivered from the warehouse upstairs, I stood alone and began to fret that the necklace had been out of stock after all.

'Are you gettin'?' enquired the lady at the collection desk.

'No,' I replied.

'Where's your wee slip, love?'

I presented her with the copy of my order and she disappeared into the warehouse, returning with a small plastic bag containing the exquisite locket, and a stainless steel toilet brush for the customer behind me.

'The bog brush and the wee necklace,' she announced.

I rushed forward to claim the precious gift.

'You're dead lucky, wee fella,' she explained. 'They're goin' that cheap this is the last one, so it is.'

The Coleraine Palladium became a regular romantic rendezvous for me and Lesley. I held her hands to keep them warm when the Superser at the front of the cinema flickered and ran out of gas before the interval and the staff had to change the gas tank as well as the film reel. My gold-adorned lover and I cuddled through the most romantic classics of the year, such as *Psycho II* (which was really, really dark), *Jaws 3D* (which was really, really deep) and *Breakdance 2: Electric Boogaloo* (which was really, really crap). We were as happy as Charles and Diana on tour in Australia, except I had no money and Lesley's dresses were from Anderson & McAuley's in Royal Avenue rather than Harvey Nicholls in Kensington.

However the colossal class divide between me and Lesley was never far from my mind. Our backgrounds were so different. When I had been delivering newspapers for Oul Mac up the Shankill, Lesley had been riding ponies for a stud farm in Kildare. Only a few years ago while I was working as a breadboy on the Ormo Mini Shop on the peace line in Belfast, Lesley had been preparing triangular cheese and tomato sandwiches for supper at the Presbyterian Women's Flower Festival in Bellaghy. These social and cultural differences threatened to come between us on more than one occasion. When Lesley arrived at university one Sunday night driving a new, blue Renault 5, which she named 'Rocky' after Sylvester Stallone, I was shocked at the extent of her wealth and resources. All I had was a rickety bike with a broken radio. Even my father's green Simca looked pathetic compared to Lesley's Renault 5. It was like comparing Gary Ewing's house in *Knot's Landing* to Southfork Ranch where JR lived in *Dallas*.

'Well, whad'ya think of my new car? Isn't it gooorgeous?' she asked with the proudest of Bellaghy whoops.

I paused, swallowed, and put on what Lesley called my 'self-righteous bake'.

'Have you ever thought about how many starving children you could feed for the cost of that car?' I replied sullenly.

'Och, stop you bein' jealous, wee fella, and c'mon with me and we'll give it a good hoke down the Agherton Road. You've no idea!' she continued, completely unassailed by my socialist critique.

Clive Ross made it clear that he too disapproved of Lesley's worldly materialism, although his reproach was less direct and came in the form of a prayer at the Bible study meeting in his freezing flat.

'Dear Lord, we humbly beseech you to challenge us to give up our material possessions for the sake of others and for the sake of the Gospel,' he prayed.

'Yes, Lord!' Tara Grace agreed, raising both hands heavenward with pure serenity.

I gave Lesley a dig in the arm.

'Forgive us for putting money and clothes and new cars before you, Lord,' he prayed.

'Yes, Lord!' repeated Tara, on the brink of breaking into tongues.

There was only one person in the room with a new car. I gave Lesley another dig in the arm. We both opened our eyes before the 'Amen's and shared a wee wink.

My first trip in the new Renault 5 was across the border to Dublin for a student leadership training conference. It was a long drive – down the M1 past the Maze (which was Protestant for Long Kesh) where the IRA escaped; through the army checkpoint at the border where you worried you might get blown up; across the border into bandit country where you worried you might get shot by a sniper; on into Dundalk and across the River Boyne where King Billy won; down through all the wee towns with colourful shops in the main streets; through Drogheda with the bridge and the big chapels, until finally we reached the traffic jams in Dublin. It was a long journey, so we stopped in one of the wee towns to change our pounds into punts to buy petrol and Love Hearts and a bag of Chocolate Éclair sweeties and several packets of Tayto crisps. We both agreed that Tayto in the south never tasted as nice as in the north, despite the fact that the bags looked almost the same.

Every time we passed a field of animals Lesley whooped. 'Och, look at the lovely wee lambsies! … Oh, look, I bet you that wee donkey's a character! … Oh. My. Nerves – that stallion is gorgeous!'

'Why, thank you,' I replied.

The whole way down to Dublin we played cassettes, or listened to the radio, turning up the volume for all the best songs. Going down the Dublin Road wasn't half as bad as Ian Paisley always made it out to be! I wound down the car window and sang along to Wham!'s 'Bad Boys' as we sped through the hills of Newry. When we crossed the border I switched to RTÉ Radio 2 which was a sort of Catholic BBC Radio 1. Larry Gogan played 'Sunday Bloody Sunday' by U2 and we sang along even though we were Protestants, because I had heard Bono was a proper pacifist like me. I played drums on the dashboard to 'The Eye of the Tiger' the whole way down O'Connell Street, past a real McDonald's that wasn't allowed up north and the old Post Office with all the bullet holes. Lesley put on her James Taylor's *Greatest Hits* and held my hand during 'You Got a Friend' like a true New Romantic. Of course, Lesley did most of the driving because she said I didn't know what to do with a car. I agreed that she should drive as a feminist statement because it was normally the man who was supposed to drive the woman and I wanted to challenge gender stereotypes and I didn't want to crash her new car. My limited driving skills were often a point of discussion among my fellow students who all agreed that I was probably safer on my bike. On the way home from the Fair City I fell asleep. I dreamt that I was Michael Knight driving a brand new Knightrider, an artificially intelligent computerised car that spoke to me in an American accent, and Lesley was Dr Bonnie Barstow with the dark hair and lovely eyes. However, just as I was about to stop an evil Russian from setting off an atomic bomb in California, I was woken by the sound of Lesley speaking.

'Do you wanna stop for a wee see?' she said seductively.

I required no further encouragement. Within minutes Lesley had pulled into a layby for changing your flat tyres and we were locked in a passionate embrace, our bodies separated only by the gear stick and the handbrake. But just as we were really getting into it, Lesley backed away from me suddenly.

'Oh. My. Nerves!' she shrieked.

'What's wrong?'

'You've ruined my good Gloria Vanderbilt!'

'Wha?'

'What are you like, wee boy?'

'*Wha?*'

'We're friggin' plastered!'

I looked down to discover that I'd been lying on the bag of Chocolate Éclair sweeties as I slept and they had melted all over my brand new white T-shirt. There were unpleasant-looking brown stains across where it said 'Choose Life' on the front (the same as George Michael's in Wham!). I had opted for a T-shirt with a nice, clean message this time instead of 'Frankie Says Relax'. Radio 1 had banned Frankie Goes to Hollywood because apparently 'Relax' was about sex or being gay or something. A George Michael T-shirt seemed much more sensible and heterosexual to me. But now my trendy T-shirt was minging! At some stage mid-snog the melted chocolate on my T-shirt had transferred onto Lesley's good white Princess Diana blouse from Anderson & McAuley's, and now she too was covered in unsightly brown stains. Her blouse had a designer label in the shape of swan, which now looked as if it was pooping inappropriately.

'You've no idea!' Lesley shrieked. We drove another mile or two down the road and stopped in a car park near Banbridge, a town with a proper nightclub called The Coach. We got out at the side of the road and used tissue paper and Lesley's make-up remover to wipe the brown stains off my George Michael and her Gloria Vanderbilt. A British Army landrover sped past, splashing water from a puddle all over my good jeans and I was sure I heard someone with an English accent shout, 'Shat yourself, mate?'

'Brits!' I thought. Marty Mullen would have been proud of me.

I continued to use my second-hand bike from Smithfield market as my main mode of transport in the final weeks of my second year. When the sun came out and the exams began I studied hard to keep up my 2:1, which was like a B at A level. I cycled to and from the university for all of my exams, rhythmically reciting facts about the history of mass communication with every push of the pedals. The summer holidays were on the way and I was enjoying living by the seaside and beside Morelli's. On sunny days the students flocked to the beach. My fellow virgins had a Christian barbecue with hamburgers and sausages and sang 'Majesty' on one sand dune, while my fellow Shakespearean actors opted for marijuana, Morrissey and nookie on a neighbouring sand dune. I had managed to make my student grant last until the end of term and I was looking forward to signing on the dole with everyone else in Snugville Street and having some money for my summer holidays. I was also looking forward to volunteering for a charitable summer scheme on the Antrim Road led by Rev. Patrick Traynor, a ginger minister who had radical views on the church helping poor people in the inner city. But on the day of my Feminism exam, all of my positive end-of-term feelings were shattered. I had just left The Diamond where I had written several excellent essays about the media being unfair to women, blaming the BBC and Margaret Thatcher. I was looking forward to a pleasant cycle back to Portstewart in the sunshine and I was planning to meet Lesley, some Heathers and a few other friends for an end-of-term poke on the prom. My bicycle was locked safely in the bicycle shed underneath the Central Building and once I hopped on my saddle I would be heading for the seaside within minutes. I was not prepared for the crime scene that awaited me in the bike shed. I couldn't believe my eyes – my rickety bicycle was still locked securely to a pole, but the wheels were gone! The saddle was gone! The light was gone! Even the wee basket I used for carrying my books was gone! It had all been stolen by some wee tea leaf from Coleraine. All that remained was the frame, the pedals and the oily chain that fell off every two miles. My shock turned to anger, and I kicked the wall of the bike shed so hard that I stubbed my toe and had to limp to the bus stop to try to hitch a lift. It wasn't fair. This bike had been my most expensive possession in the whole world, apart from my collection of ABBA albums. What use would anyone have for a saddle and a couple of wheels from a second-hand bike from Smithfield market? I had been as much a victim of spite as of theft, I decided. When I arrived in Portstewart

Lesley was most understanding, and she gave me hug and bought me a knickerbocker glory in Morelli's.

'Hey, boy, what's the craic, hey?' asked Billy Barton.

I ignored Billy's question as this was a situation devoid of craic.

'I locked my bike in the bike shed and some hallions stole the wheels off it,' I fumed.

Tara Grace offered to pray that the thieves would repent and return my wheels under the conviction of the Holy Spirit and Clive Ross explained that this was God's way of teaching me to be less dependent on material goods and more dependent on the Lord.

'It was desperate, so it was,' I lamented. 'It was just sittin' there with no wheels nor nathin'. It was just a shell … like one of them there DeLoreans in the closed-down factory in Belfast.'

Aaron Ward was somewhat less sympathetic and burst into laughter at this description of my forlorn, wheel-less bicycle.

'Oh, aye, but if it was your middle-class car that got nicked you'd be laughin' on the other side of your face, wouldn't ye?' I barked.

This just made him laugh more. Lesley said that Aaron and I argued like an old married couple even though we had only lived together for two years now.

The trauma of losing my bicycle triggered an impulse that I had kept under control for several years. As a teenager I had developed a habit of purchasing pets that inevitably lived very short lives. As a result, there was a substantial pet cemetery in our back garden beside the greenhouse where my father grew tomatoes and killed greenfly. Up until this point I had resisted the urge to buy any of the helpless creatures in the Coleraine pet shop, even though I was a regular visitor and often tempted, but the distress of losing my bike had driven me over the edge. I should have known better. After all, I was nearly twenty years old and not a gormless teenager anymore. I had lost so many previous pets to premature death, I sometimes imagined that when I walked into the pet shop the parrots would squawk in a Scottish accent like yer man in *Dad's Army* on BBC1, 'We're all doomed, Captain Mainwaring! We're all doomed!'

So the next day I went into Coleraine and bought a hamster and a cage with a squeaky wheel and a wee bottle for him to drink from. I named my new pet Buffy, and everyone said he was dead cute even though he bit a Heather from Portadown on the finger. I used the remainder of my student grant to stock up on straw and sunflower seeds to feed him and a huge plastic bag of sawdust to line the bottom of his cage. Deep down I knew all of this was a mistake and certain to end in tragedy. Previous experience suggested that the poor wee crater was condemned. We lived together happily for the last few weeks of term, our relationship blighted only by the incessant squeaking of his exercise wheel during the night, which continued even after I applied Flora margarine to the mechanics of the wheel. However, history was determined to repeat itself like an election in Northern Ireland. Poor Buffy developed a sore ear and began to fall over as he tried to run around his cage. At first it seemed that he had merely developed a mild case of hamster vertigo, possibly caused by the over-enthusiastic use of his wheel through the wee small hours of every single night. But when I noticed that his condition had deteriorated to the extent that he could no longer stand up, I ran to the telephone box to call Lesley. She responded immediately, turning the Renault 5 into an animal ambulance and transporting me and my patient to the vet in Coleraine.

'Don't worry, Tony,' Lesley said reassuringly. 'Sure you've been lookin' after the wee crater really well. He'll be all right, so he will.'

Lesley loved animals and talked about her ponies and dogs and wee banties – which I thought meant 'birds' – with great affection, so I knew she would be horrified to learn that nearly every pet I had ever owned had come to a premature end. If she found out I was an animal assassin she would chuck me for sure, so I had no choice but to keep this dark secret to myself.

Lesley held my hand in the waiting room and joined Buffy and me in the consultation cubicle as if she was one of the family. The vet looked most concerned over his half-rimmed glasses. I had the urge to ask him the question Captain James T. Kirk always asked Doctor McCoy in such dire circumstances, 'What are his chances, Bones?' but I didn't need to. The vet shook his head and explained that Buffy had a terminal tick. As Lesley gripped my hand the vet gave the devastating verdict that it would be kinder to put Buffy to sleep. I was shocked, not so much that yet another one of my pets lacked longevity, but that for the first time I had to decide to end the animal's life. At least all the others had simply died of natural causes or unfortunate accidents – apart from the gerbil and the snake who had died together in a fight to the death. This was euthanasia! We had discussed this moral dilemma in tutorials, but this was real. As a pacifist I could not possibly countenance the termination of a life.

Lesley could tell that I was struggling with the ethics of this dilemma. 'It would be cruel to keep the wee crater alive,' she said gently.

I nodded and the vet took this as assent. Buffy was gassed and I was upset and I vowed never to buy another pet for as long as I lived.

As I considered the prospect of moving into my third and final year at university I was amazed that time had passed so quickly. The university bosses had decided to change the name from 'The New University of Ulster' to simply 'The University of Ulster'. Just like my student career, the university officially wasn't going to be new anymore. It seemed like only yesterday when I had gone to my first lecture, played my first game of *Frogger* and watched my first film noir. For my final year, I had agreed to move into a new house in Millbank Avenue with Aaron and two new friends – Peter from Holywood who liked U2 and prayer, and Colm from Scotland who liked Robbie Burns and rugby. Our new accommodation was the same rent but about one degree warmer than the fridge I had shivered in for the past year, and it had an open fire like my granny's which you could light with newspaper, sticks and wet coal. Once the summer was over we would be moving into our new digs. I would be studying for finals and starting to look for a job and thinking about life after university. I was going to be a proper mature student, so I was.

SPIELBERG BEWARE

I was a final year student, so I was. I could hardly believe it. I was twenty-one years old and finally shaving daily. Somehow, in the midst of all the intellectual, romantic and spiritual excitement of the past two years I had failed to notice when exactly I finally began to need a daily scrape of the razor. Ironically, now that it was an essential part of my morning ablutions, I no longer had the desire to shave every day. After many years of longing for any sign of facial hair, now that I had them I simply took my bristles for granted. I rebelliously went several days without shaving, as having masculine designer stubble like George Michael had become very fashionable. I resisted the urge to grow a full beard, however, as this was considered very old-fashioned, and I certainly did not want to look like Grizzly or Gerry Adams. Clive Ross grew a full beard to make him look more like Jesus.

As I moved into my final year of Media Studies, I realised that I needed to start preparing for my future career. The only proper paid employment I had secured to date had been as a paperboy and a breadboy, and although I had acquired exceptional customer service skills this was not enough to sustain my career now that

I was an adult. I still dreamed of becoming a great investigative journalist in the tradition of Woodward and Bernstein, although now I was also open to the idea of becoming a consumer champion, like Esther Rantzen with the teeth who exposed corrupt companies and penis-shaped vegetables on *That's Life*. I still harboured a desire to be the next Terry Wogan, using my Northern Irish charm to dazzle live television audiences with witty repartee and persuading famous actresess like Shirley MacLaine from *Terms of Endearment* to tell me secrets they had never revealed to any interviewer before. The technical term for this was 'a scoop', like when that journalist found out that Cecil Parkinson had a mistress and a love child and he was forced to resign from Mrs Thatcher's government. The journalist who discovered *The Hitler Diaries* in East Germany had the greatest scoop of all time, until another journalist came up with the scoop that the diaries were a forgery.

However, as my degree also included practical modules on photography, radio, television and film production, I realised that I could also pursue a career in Hollywood in the USA, which was very different from Holywood in County Down. I could be a great director, following in the footsteps of Michael Winner and Stephen Spielberg. All I needed was a wee bit of practice. Stephen Spielberg was a genius, which made it okay for him to have a proper beard. My two-day stubble indicated that my filmmaking genius was still in its early stages. Stephen Spielberg had directed all the best movies I had ever seen – apart from the *Star Wars* movies and *Doctor Who and the Daleks* with Peter Cushing – and he was widely regarded as science fiction royalty. He directed *Close Encounters of the Third Kind* where the aliens were intelligent life forms that could play a great wee tune on a synthesizer like Depeche Mode. Spielberg also directed *E.T.*, about an alien who flew a bike across the moon and phoned home and made me cry even though I was far too old and cool to be weeping at a movie. Spielberg's movies were so brilliant that millions of people went to see them over and over again and they earned so many millions of dollars that the first movie was always followed up with a sequel. But cinema had been in decline for a long time, even outside Belfast where the cinemas weren't being burned down. This was because video had taken over. Video hadn't just killed the radio star – it had stopped people going to the movies as well, because now we could watch everything on video in our own homes. My Uncle Freddie got videos of the *Rocky* movies before the films even came out! Some of my media studies books said cinema was finished, but I thought that Spielberg might just save it. I was looking forward to the sequel to *Raiders of the Lost Ark* with Indiana Jones, though I wasn't sure how the first film could possibly be bettered, and I couldn't wait for *E.T. 2*.

In my final year of university I had to create another video of my own to show off all the film production skills I had acquired over the past three years. I had learned a great deal about genre and screenplay, plot and narrative, I had studied everything from *Citizen Kane* to *Dial M for Murder*, and I knew how to create a really, really dark and brooding screenplay using ambivalent imagery and angular camera perspectives. This was my last chance to showcase my talents for the whole world to see, so I decided to put all of this learning into practice in one final, artistically complex and sophisticated production. I decided to make a pop video of an ABBA song. However, as ABBA had more or less split up and were no longer considered cool (Byron Drake argued they had never been cool to begin with) I cleverly found a cover version of one of their best songs by a genuinely hip New Romantic band called Blancmange. This band had achieved a huge hit with 'Living on the Ceiling' and everyone thought they were a serious and credible part of the New Romantic movement with their synthesizers and space age clothes and implausibly large shoulder pads. The lead singer's hair was as big as his collars were small. So it came as a great surprise to many of their fans when Blancmange recorded a cover version of 'The Day Before You Came'. This was one of the Super Swedes' final hits before Benny and Björn started writing songs about chess and Agnetha and Frida released solo albums which I alone purchased. 'The Day Before You Came' was a melancholy song about how life for Agnetha was routine and boring and very sad right up until the day before she met me. Although this song had been one of ABBA's least-greatest hits it was a groundbreaking composition. In fact, it was the only love song I knew which referred to the gritty, everyday reality of having your dinner and watching TV – 'I'm sure I had my dinner watching something on TV / There's not, I think, a single episode of *Dallas* that I didn't see.'

I knew it wouldn't be easy to create a video worthy of the lyrics of this classic song that was good enough to be shown on MTV, but I was up for the challenge. After all, I had managed to simulate Armageddon on the beach and cemetery in Portstewart for my Cliff Richard video.

ABBA's original video for 'The Day Before You Came' wasn't one of their best ones. It featured Agnetha in a raincoat with good shoulder pads, waiting at a train station in Stockholm and looking very sad because it was 'the day before I came'. She was oozing Scandinavian beauty and melancholy, but it was still just a video on a train. The official Blancmange video didn't do the song justice either because there were far too many scenes on a more dirty-looking train in London. Blancmange even had the audacity to use parts of the original video to suggest that Agnetha was flirting with the lead singer (as if he had a chance with his bad teeth). So it was my responsibility to create a new music video worthy of the song, as a tribute to the genius of Benny and Björn and the beauty of Agnetha (Frida just sang a few 'oohs' with a new spiky hairdo in the background as she was busy moving onto serious rock with Phil Collins). I persuaded a few of my fellow students to play the lead romantic parts. My housemate Colm agreed to be the leading man, going through the motions of life without love on a dull and ordinary day. I persuaded a Heather with long hair to be the girl who hadn't come yet (Byron Drake laughed and said there were many girls like this in the Christian Union). Colm looked good on camera because he was dark and handsome, like me, and my chosen Heather looked amazing when she shook her big hair like a member of Bananarama and I transformed her into sexy slow motion. I considered setting the video in California or Barcelona but my budget wouldn't stretch that far. In fact, as I hadn't enough money to buy train tickets to transport my principle actors to Belfast I made the artistically innovative decision to set the video in a university in Coleraine.

My premise was that it was the day before the girl got transferred into an easier course at Coleraine after failing her first year of Law at Queen's University in Belfast. As nearly every video production in the Media Studies department contained at least one scene set on the beach in Portstewart I decided to shatter convention and film my video entirely in the stark urban landscape that was the university campus. I wanted it to be really, really dark and really, really deep. Behind the superficial narrative of a love story brooded the suggestion of socialist revolution with a hint of impending apocalyptic disaster. When I explained to the professor that I wanted to create a *Mad Max* tone blended with New Romantic sensibilities and a hint of Swedish kitsch, he said he was relieved that I wasn't going to do anything too pretentious.

'I must have gone to lunch at half past twelve or so, the usual place, the usual bunch,' sang Blancmange.

I persuaded all my friends to meet up with Colm and me in the university canteen so that I could film them having sausages and chips with baked beans. I gathered all of the necessary equipment, including a microphone with a very professional-looking feather duster on the end, and as I walked across the longest bus shelter in the world I could tell from the admiring glances I received that my fellow students were impressed to see a film crew on campus. When I arrived in the canteen and explained my vision for the piece, everyone was surprised that on this occasion there was no religious or socialist message. I explained that sometimes it was important to create art for art's sake and simply to tell a story that people might relate to and enjoy. It was also important that no one called you a wanker at the end of term screening.

'Hurry up, Tony Spielberg,' Aaron Ward said impatiently after five takes of Colm eating sausage and chips. 'I've rugby training to go to!'

I informed Aaron that although he thought he was being funny and sarcastic by calling me 'Tony Spielberg', Spielberg's mates probably mocked him and called him 'Stephen Hitchcock' when he was in college. I said I would remind him of this incident when the world premier of my first science fiction blockbuster was on in Leicester Square in London, and then he'd be laughing on the other side of his face.

'You'll be lucky to direct a crap episode of Doctor Who,' he taunted, and on hearing this the rest of the gang felt compelled to impersonate Daleks with their knives and forks and shout 'Exterminate!'

'How can the Daleks be masters of the universe when they can't even climb stairs?' asked Aaron predictably.

Intellectuals always pointed out this particular weakness in the Doctor Who universe.

'Oh, you think you've found my Achilles heel, don't you, rugger boy? I'll have you know that some Doctor Who is almost Nietzschean, so it is!'

'Well if you don't hurry up and get this over with there'll be ructions and you won't have any actors left for your wee fillum,' answered Aaron.

As a committed pacifist I once again needed to resist the urge to knock Aaron's lamp in. Instead, I quietly decided that most shots of Aaron would end up on the cutting room floor, and that would harden him. Of course, all of this unnecessary mockery wasted more time, and we had to do yet another take of Colm and his friends eating their sausages and chips the day before a Heather came. The baked beans were getting cold now, which stretched the acting skills of my volunteers because everyone complained that cold beans were disgusting. Even the lovely Lesley complained. I could tell from her uncharacteristic silence that she was not happy.

'What's wrong with you?' I barked.

'Ach, ya know,' she replied.

'What?'

'This isn't too much craic,' she finally whooped.

'Will youse all stop your gurnin' or I'll give youse something to gurn about,' I grunted.

I regretted not asking some of my fellow thespians from the drama society to contribute serious acting to my video production. Hamlet and Ophelia would have consumed cold baked beans with grace and gravitas no matter how many takes it took. They may not have spoken to me, and they still didn't know my name, but they would certainly not have allowed any hardship as minor as cold baked beans to distract them from their art. Where was a troupe of semi-professional actors when you needed one?

In spite of the tensions on set – which I knew were probably an everyday occurrence for Spielberg too – I eventually had sufficient footage to realise my artistic vision. After many hours of editing to ensure the scenes shifted in line with the narrative of the lyrics and the images changed on the most appropriate electric drumbeat, my latest pop music video was complete. I showed the final edit to Lesley and asked for her critical feedback.

'Well, is it really, really deep?' I asked. 'I want it to be almost Nietzschean.'

'It's brilliant, so it is, but my hair wasn't right in the canteen and my earrings look all wrong,' she replied.

I brought a copy home but I couldn't show it on my father's Betamax video recorder because my video was recorded on VHS. My father insisted that Betamax was better than VHS and my mother said that he was a very clever man, so he was, who knew a thing or two about gadgets. So we borrowed the Westy Disco VHS recorder to debut my video in Belfast.

'Ach, that's a lovely wee story, love,' was my mother's critique. 'I can hardly believe my wee son is able to do all that by himself.'

'Well, it's really, really, dark and really, really deep as well, ya know, Mammy,' I explained. 'It works on many different levels, so it does.'

'You're doin' rightly son,' my father said warmly, in spite of his disapproval of the VHS tape.

'Loadacrap,' said my big brother, laughing heartily. 'I'm keekin' myself!'

'Class!' my wee brother said finally, before unplugging the video recorder because *The A-Team* was about to start on UTV.

I was starting to get seriously worried about what lay ahead for me after university. There were no jobs in Belfast. You used to be able to rely on someone you knew in the foundry or the shipyard to get you 'a start', but now those days were gone, as Bucks Fizz would say. Every time I travelled from Belfast to Coleraine on the train, I looked out the window of my freezing carriage at the forlorn sight of the abandoned DeLorean Motor factory. The shells of space-age, stainless steel cars languishing in the rain seemed to sum up the Northern Ireland economy. Belfast was like one of these DeLoreans – plenty of potential, but scuppered by selfishness and stupidity. I tended to agree with my granny's assessment of John DeLorean.

'That DeLorean fella's nathin' but a bad oul rip!'

Belfast was like John DeLorean, seemingly full of promise, but ultimately full of shite.

If I was to get a job in the media I would need to gain some experience and apply for lots of jobs. First I applied to be a presenter on a new music programme called *The Tube* on Channel 4, but I didn't even get an interview. In the end they gave the job to yer man who played the piano in Squeeze, and he kept making mistakes! I was certain Jools Holland's presenting career would be over soon and this might just leave an opening for the likes of me. I applied to do a journalism course at the College of Business Studies in Belfast because that's where Eamonn Holmes went and he had taken over from Gloria Hunniford presenting *Good Evening Ulster* on UTV. I also applied to a journalism school in Dublin even though this decision might hasten a united Ireland, and I wrote to BBC Northern Ireland to ask if I could read the news like Rose Neill because she was also very young and attractive like myself. What would be the point of becoming the first person in my family to get a university degree if I couldn't get a job? If I couldn't secure employment when I graduated I would have to join the queue in Snugville Street to sign on with all the other unemployed people on the Shankill, and most of them hadn't even passed their eleven-plus. I often wondered why so few people from the Shankill went to grammar school and university compared to other parts of the city, but nobody else seemed to care. All the politicians cared about was getting re-elected so they could keep us British and make sure the IRA never got their united Ireland. After the IRA tried to kill Margaret Thatcher in the Brighton bomb I was sure Maggie would never allow a united Ireland. The IRA said they 'only had to be lucky once' to kill Mrs Thatcher, and Marty Mullen said the bomb was 'a legitimate act of war against an imperialist force of occupation'. I tried to argue with Marty's militarism – I explained that for a pacifist there was no such thing as a legitimate act of war, but Marty said I was just being middle class. I asked Marty if he didn't feel sorry for Norman Tebitt when they were digging him out of the debris of the hotel in his jammies on the news.

'Wise up, wee lad!' he replied.

I was sick and tired of all the hatred. I dreamed of a future Northern Ireland free from hatred, where all children could live and learn and play together.

'Wise up, wee lad!' I thought to myself.

The possibility of peace seemed more distant than ever. The longer the Troubles went on, the more bitter and divided everyone became. Now that I was educated, I understood that there were many very different and very clever ways to justify killing people to get your way. I had wrongly assumed that when people became more educated they would naturally become pacifists, but I discovered that intellectuals had lots of ingenious vindications for war. I was weary of all the excuses for killing people in Northern Ireland, but as I learned more about conflict in other countries it was reassuring to know that other people killed each other to get their way too. I began to read books about war and peace in the conflict section of the university library near where Marina with the Daisy Duke shorts sat. I discovered that Jews and Muslims hated each other just as much as Catholics and Protestants did, and Beirut made Belfast look like a Sunday School picnic at Pickie Pool. I learned that sectarianism hadn't been invented in Belfast. People in other countries also blamed everything on the other side while making excuses for the atrocities of their own side, and killing for the sake of national identity seemed to be a pretty normal part of being a human being. I was soon as fascinated by the subject of conflict resolution as I was by Tina Turner's thighs on *Top of the Pops*. If I could get a job as a journalist I could start out reporting on the price of cows in Ballymena or reading warnings about fog on the M2 on a Monday morning, but I could eventually become a courageous war correspondent in a white suit and bullet-proof jacket, shining new light on the inhumanity of war around the world. The media was becoming more and more powerful, and soon audiences would be so appalled by the graphic brutality on their television screens that they would all choose peace over war. This was my vocation. I just needed to persuade someone, somewhere, to give me a wee start. Deep down I was still a dreamer, so I was.

16

FAREWELL TO BIG ISOBEL

Life, the universe and everything were just as complex as in the *Hitchhiker's Guide to the Galaxy*, so they were. I found that late night debates over Yellow Pack coffee in student digs were a good place to increase my understanding of the big issues of life, death, world hunger and the possibility of intergalactic travel. Students proposed very sensible solutions to the world's problems between midnight and 2 a.m., though after this time the discussions usually deteriorated into stupid arguments or just plain slabbering. Byron Drake knew everything about everything, especially late at night when I suspected he had been smoking marijuana again.

'No offence, Tone, but I can't believe that in the twentieth century someone like you could reach the age of twenty and have so little experience of life,' said Byron, breathing heavily into his Yasser Arafat scarf in an attempt to create some heat in his freezing flat.

'Twenty one,' I said, cupping my hands around a tepid CND mug. 'And you haven't had sex yet either!'

'Don't comment on things you know nothing about, Tone.'

'Well, I've yet to see you even going out with a wee girl. At least

I can snog Lesley any day of the week, apart from weekends when I go home to get my washing done.'

'Listen, Tone. I date women from England, not "wee girls" from Ireland, and what happens in the sack in Essex, stays in Essex,' Byron said cryptically.

I was confused. Why would anyone want to have sex in a sack? I remembered doing sack races on sports days at school and the sack was always dead itchy on your skin, so it was bound to wreak havoc with your jimmy joe.

'Okay, then tell me about the last time you had sex,' I said.

Byron tapped his nose sagely. 'I know how to please a woman in every conceivable direction.'

I wanted to repeat the words of Duran Duran, 'Please, please tell me now, is there something I should know?' but I wasn't prepared to give Byron the pleasure of knowing he knew more than me, even though he already knew he knew more.

'Every direction? Like, do you need to use a compass?'

'Ha, ha. Very droll, Tone, very droll. Let's just say the women I make love to have no complaints.'

'Aye, in your dreams, big lad!' I said, noticing once again how working class I sounded when I had an argument with Byron.

I accepted that I had lived a very sheltered life growing up on the Shankill Road in the 1970s, but I wasn't as naive as Byron thought. It was true that I had no significant personal experience of sex, but I was certain I would get a chance at some stage in the next decade.

'Life is not an episode of *Doctor*-fucking-*Who*, you know, Tone,' Byron said, letting his ginger fringe flop over one eye.

I was appalled that anyone would dare to use the F-word when referring to *Doctor Who*. This was just as bad as the time my big brother said 'shite' during one of his increasingly rare appearances at church. He used the offending adjective during a solo of 'How Great Thou Art', and while I agreed with his critique of the soprano's performance, this sort of language was completely unacceptable.

Byron went on to suggest that I needed to listen to The Smith's latest album because Morrissey had something really, really dark and really, really deep to say to our generation that would awaken me both intellectually and sexually. While he was explaining how Morrissey's songs were almost Nietzschean, I fell asleep.

Benny and Björn had awakened me to the fact that 'the history book on the shelf is always repeating itself' but apart from this it was becoming clear how little I really knew about life. I wasn't too familiar with death either. Apart from the normal day-to-day deaths of the Troubles, I had very little personal experience of it. Our neighbour, Mr Oliver, had been murdered by cheering gunmen in our street, and apparently I had a twin brother and sister who were stillborn, but I didn't know them personally so, apart from the nightmares I had about them, these deaths had very little impact on me.

Of course, I had extensive experience of animal death due to my inability to keep alive any of the pets I had purchased to date, but my primary understanding of human death came from the news and the horror movies I saw on TV. These sources provided plenty of good advice on how to avoid death; I learned not to walk past an empty car with its headlights on in Belfast city centre, and I knew that it was unwise to walk across the peace line after dark. I knew that whenever I was stopped by wee hoods and asked if I was a Protestant or a Catholic it was best to answer according to which side I thought they were from, rather than give a truthful and potentially fatal answer. I also understood the dangers of having a shower in a motel room in America and that it was unwise to explore a deserted castle in Transylvania when you're far from the nearest town and your car has run out of petrol. Furthermore, thanks to the work of Ridley Scott, I was fully aware of the potential dangers lurking on derelict alien spacecraft, *especially* when you were about to go into stasis. I knew how to avoid death, all right; but I had no idea how to deal with grief. I was as upset as everyone else when Captain Mainwaring and Sergeant Wilson and Grace Kelly died in quick succession. I was upset for months after Adric died helping The Doctor to stop a freighter controlled by the Cybermen from crashing into the Planet Earth. However, I had not experienced proper grief until my grandparents started to die.

My father's father had died when I was too young to remember. Everyone said he was a real gentleman. He'd played cricket for Woodvale Cricket Club and Ireland; my Auntie Hetty still had his international cricket cap in her roof-space and my brothers had both inherited his cricketing genes. My father's mother was known as Nanny, and she was a proper granny with kisses and presents and nice blue cardigans and false teeth and knitting. When she died everyone was very sad and I had never seen so many adults cry, but Nanny was old and tired and her passing seemed natural. When my Great-auntie Doris with the pearls and proper accent died it was very sad too, but she was even older than Nanny. Everyone said she had been a real lady and very glamorous in her youth but that she had been away with the birds for a few years. On her deathbed she kept repeating a verse from Psalm 23, 'And I will dwell in the house of the Lord forever', which didn't sound like being away with the birds to me.

When my mother's father died it was traumatic for my mother and the whole family. Wee Francey had worked in the bookies for most of his life and loved a wee stout. He retired to be a security man on the door of the local pub, and my mother always worried what would happen to him if the IRA decided to blow up the pub. Granda was also very old and seemed quite fed up, but he died after his bed caught fire while he was having a wee smoke and everyone was just as upset about the way he had gone as the fact that he had gone. I was late for the funeral because I had misjudged how long it would take me to drive to Brown's Funeral Parlour on the Lisburn Road.

'You'll be late for your own bloody funeral!' my mother had said through her tears.

The passing of my first three grandparents was very sad. Waking up and remembering that Nanny and Granda were gone forever was my first taste of grief, and when I saw my parents' obvious distress I couldn't help but wonder how I would cope without them when it was their turn in forty years' time.

'That's us movin' up into the first division now!' my Uncle Sammy said to my father at Nanny's funeral.

In many ways Big Isobel was the biggest grandparent in my life, aside from her vast physical proportions. She was the family matriarch, an enormous personality, and an important part of my life for as long as I could remember. My earliest memories were of getting the bus down the Springfield Road to visit her and holding my mother's hand as we walked up Roden Street, long before they built the Westlink motorway through the middle of it to make a peace line. I must have been only four years old when Granny gave me a shilling to go around to Mrs Adair's wee sweetie shop for a Lucky Bag and Sherbet Dip. Every time I visited Granny's house I would check if the tiny toy soldier I had found in my Lucky Bag was still irretrievably stuck between the paving stones in her minuscule front garden. I remembered the days we arrived while Granny was out at the shops buying a nice ham shank for Granda's dinner. I was amazed when my mother simply reached into the letterbox to find the front door key dangling on a piece of dirty string and let us in. Big Isobel knew everything about me and I knew nearly everything about her, including some of her more intimate medical conditions, which I didn't want to know about. Granny spoke of mysterious ailments like 'the change', 'trouble with the waterworks' and 'problems in the back entry', and she swore by the healing properties of Valium when you were 'bad with your nerves' or 'your head was turned'.

The thought of Big Isobel passing away was difficult to contemplate, in spite of the fact that, for as long as I could remember, she had been saying, 'I'm in my coffin already, love. They just can't get the lid on!' Every time I had been to visit her since I started university she remarked that I was 'all growed up nigh', and ever since meeting Lesley she always made sure to enquire about the state of our relationship.

'How's the big Lesley girl, love?' she would ask.

'Aye, dead on, Granny,' I would reply briefly.

'In the name of God, don't you go havin' a wee notion of none of them other wee hussies up there in Coleraine and breakin' that wee girl's heart!' was her sage advice. I was shocked at Granny's doubts regarding my loyalty to Lesley, and she could read this in my face.

'Don't be lookin' at me with the face trippin' ye! You wouldn't be the first Holy Joe to run off with some wee whouer!'

I wasn't sure whether to use my spiritual or feminist credentials to argue that I was not a 'Holy Joe', but I decided not to bother as Big Isobel would just accuse me of getting all swanky on her again. Since the age of four, she had distinguished me from the other grandchildren by describing me as 'the wee swanky one'.

'Ach, wise up, Granny, you're scunderin' me!' I said, prompting an enormous hug from Big Isobel and a typically hearty laugh that made her sofa shake.

'And don't you be gettin' that wee girl into trouble neither,' she warned.

I was astounded at how she could move from suspicions of infidelity to concerns of unplanned pregnancy in a matter of seconds!

Given her volatile temperament, this was a good outcome from an exchange with my granny. She was not averse to shouting at you to 'get out of the house and never darken my door again!' because you had questioned the morality of hiding behind the sofa and pretending no one was in when the tick man called. She would often threaten violence when upset. On more than one occasion she offended my pacifist sensibilities by threatening to 'draw my hand across your bake, ya cheeky wee hallion,' simply because I refused to 'run the wee brush over the carpet, love – this place is startin' to look like a real dunderin' in!'

Big Isobel was quite outspoken on political and constitutional matters too. 'Well if it wasn't for the Big Fella we'd a been sold down the river long ago,' was her analysis of the achievements of Rev. Ian Paisley. According to her, the Secretary of State for Northern Ireland, James Prior had 'a face on him like a scalped arse' – and of course, Gerry Adams had 'the sorta bake you'd never get tired kickin'!'

Granny also had her own distinctive views on art and culture. She was a dedicated viewer of *Crossroads*, and she was completely intolerant of any talking in the room during an episode of *Coronation Street*, frequently telling us to 'shut yer bakes while Carnation Street's on or I'll warm the ears of the whole bloody lotta youse!' Big Isobel was also very excited about a new Irish country and western singer from Donegal called Daniel O'Donnell, who she said was 'a lovely wee fella, and he's good to his mammy.' Though her less-favourable musical reviews could be quite cutting.

'Look at the neb on yer man on the piano,' was her description of Barry Manilow; and as for Boy George – 'For the love and honour of pig's gravy, what is the world comin' til? Would ya look at the cut of thon wee lad all dressed up like some wee doll!'

Big Isobel was so full of life it was hard to imagine her life coming to an end until that unhappy day finally arrived. It was Lesley's birthday, and we had been on another trip to Dublin for student leadership training in her Renault 5. As a special treat we had gone to McDonalds in Dublin because you couldn't get a Big Mac in Northern Ireland. I presented Lesley with a padded pink birthday card and a fine gold bracelet from Argos. It had been a truly happy day, but when we arrived back at my house in Belfast I noticed that the venetian blinds in every window were closed even though it was still daylight. This was usually a sign that someone had died in our street, so I wondered immediately if something was seriously wrong. I didn't say anything to Lesley in case I was just catastrophising, but as soon as we entered the house I sensed the gloom. I could hear my mother and my Auntie Doris, who was a lovely singer from Lambeg, weeping in the sitting room. My father came out and delivered the bad news.

'Your granny died this morning, son,' he said.

I gave my mother the longest hug I had ever given her, and she sobbed on my shoulder the same way I used to cry on her shoulder when I was a wee boy. There was a steady stream of visitors to our house and plenty of cups of tea and triangular egg and onion sandwiches served by Auntie Emma and Auntie Mabel. Lesley helped with the dishes like she was one of the family, and Auntie Doris took the time to admire Lesley's lovely gold bracelet even though she was grieving the loss of her mother.

It was strange that Granny had died on Lesley's birthday, because I had been born on Big Isobel's birthday. She always said I was her best birthday present ever, and when I thought about this I had to go hide in my room to cry for a while because men weren't supposed to cry. Neighbours and distant relatives I didn't see very often called at the house and everyone said that Big Isobel was a character, so she was, and she's in a better place now, God love her. Rev. Lowe called in to shake everyone's hand firmly and say a prayer. He seemed genuinely upset, even though he buried people every day. He always had great craic with Big Isobel, even though her faith was a little unorthodox for a Presbyterian. I didn't know anyone else who said they loved the Lord as much as Granny, but in the next breath she would call her neighbour – who you were supposed to love – 'a sleeked wee bastard'. It was hard to believe that Big Isobel was really gone, but within a few hours we had visited the funeral home on the Lisburn Road to pay our final respects and the awful truth began to finally sink in. My parents and my brothers and I took turns to say our own personal goodbyes to Granny. She was laid out in a small dark room that smelled of death and lilies, with stained glass windows and wooden panelling on the walls. After all those years of hearing her say the words, Big Isobel really was in her coffin but they hadn't put the lid on yet.

When it was my turn I hesitated at the door and approached the coffin very slowly, half-expecting Big Isobel to shout, 'C'mere over here and see me, son, and stop all that oul futterin' about over there!' Granny looked so still, so quiet and peaceful, but her spirit was not there in that room with me. Her body was just a shell. I felt an overwhelming sadness I had never felt before, and I realised she was gone. Big Isobel was gone. In her own words, she had 'gone to the happy huntin' ground'. My tears dripped onto one of the shiny brass handles on the casket, and when I wiped them away I caught the reflection of my own sad face, twisted like in one of the crazy mirrors at Barry's Amusements in Portrush. I kissed Granny on the forehead and talked to her as if I was four years old again, thanking her for all the birthday cards, the Christmas presents, the hugs, and even the shouting matches. I told her I loved her very much and that she had been a good granny to me, so she had, in spite of all her oul shenanigans. Finally, I said farewell to Big Isobel.

'So this is grief,' I thought.

The funeral was not without incident. The church was overflowing with Granny's relatives, friends and neighbours from the Donegall Road, as well as many family friends who all turned out to pay their respects and offer their condolences. There was even a group of mourners from the Westy Disco. There were lots of flowers and handshaking and everyone said they were awful sorry for our loss, even old men I had never met before. Lesley sat beside me and held my hand during the prayers. Rev. Lowe led the service, and he spoke warmly and personally about Isobel Taylor. It was obvious that he really knew her and really cared about our family's loss. Some ministers just saw burials as a chance to tell a crowd of non-churchgoers to get born again, before it was their turn to go to hell.

When it came to doing a lift of the coffin I was one of the first.

'You're in the second lift, son,' said Uncle Freddie.

What if I drop her? I thought, panicking. What if I fall over and cause a commotion and let the whole family down?

No one had ever explained to me what a lift was or how to do it properly, but I just took the lead from the other men and the undertakers and I managed it all right. Big Isobel weighed over twenty stone, and as the edge of the coffin dug into my shoulder I understood the term 'dead weight' for the first time. I had to put one arm around my big brother's shoulder, something I had never done before, and hold one of the brass handles with my other hand. As we walked slowly along the wet tarmac road behind the hearse my right cheek touched the cold, polished wood, and it felt as though Granny was kissing me on the cheek one last time.

It was at the graveside that Big Isobel made her final mark. The cemetery smelled of freshly dug earth and freshly cut lilies, mixed with the musk of death. After the saddest part of 'ashes to ashes and dust to dust', the undertakers began lowering the heavy coffin into the grave using large grey straps attached to the brass handles. Suddenly, there was a crack, and one of the brass handles detached from the coffin. There was a collective gasp from the mourners. The coffin lurched to one side and threatened to topple over. I imagined the casket flipping over, the lid falling off under Big Isobel's immense weight and Granny diving out of her coffin and into her grave in one final grand gesture. Fortunately, the undertakers imagined a similar disaster and moved swiftly to steady the swaying casket. For years Granny had told me she was in her coffin already, they just couldn't get the lid on – today it seemed as if she was saying, 'Look! Even when I'm in my coffin they can hardly keep the lid on!' I was sure Big Isobel was watching this from somewhere in her happy hunting ground, laughing one of her great big laughs that made her sofa shake.

I was back at university the day after the funeral, getting to grips with an essay on the promotion of capitalism in television game shows. For weeks, my first thought every morning was that Granny was dead. I felt an empty, gnawing feeling in my stomach, and I understood this was loss and grief and all part of being an adult. It was only when my first thoughts of the morning returned to Lesley and my final exams and *Doctor Who* that I realised I had emerged from a period of mourning for my dear granny. Dealing with death was a major part of growing up but, ironically, now that Big Isobel was gone, no one would ever again tell me that I was 'all growed up now', so they wouldn't.

17

GO WILD IN THE COUNTRY

Bellaghy sounded like a fascinating place, so it did. Of course, it wasn't Monte Carlo or Gallifrey, but I was enthralled by detailed accounts of Girls' Brigade displays and IRA marches, Church of Ireland flower festivals and an ancient haunted bawn. There was talk of Seamus Heaney, Mad Dog, ponies, and a deserted church in the middle of a lough accessible only at the height of summer. On top of all that, there was the exciting goings on in Mrs Steen's drapery shop and the juicy gossip from Greens' grocers, which made the ups and downs of the Sugdens in *Emmerdale Farm* sound positively boring! The more I listened to Lesley talking about the wonders of Bellaghy the more I wanted to go on an adventure up the country.

I received an official invitation to visit Bellaghy one weekend when I needed a break from my rigorous film production schedule. This wasn't simply my first experience of the intriguing south Derry village – it was to be my first introduction to Lesley's parents (or Mummy and Daddy, as she called them). Lesley was an only child, so she talked about her parents and her extended family a lot. Even though we had yet to meet, I already felt as if I knew all her cousins in Maghera and Magherafelt, right down to the price tag on the latest outfit they'd bought in Go Gay in Ballymena. Bellaghy sounded so different from Belfast and so far away from my native Upper Shankill that when we arranged the date for my first visit I felt like I was Alan Whicker from *Whicker's World* on UTV, about to go on a great adventure to see fascinating people and exotic places hidden from the rest of the world. Geographically, I was aware only that Bellaghy was somewhere north of Glengormley until Lesley pointed it out to me on a map.

'Sure you boys from Belfast think the world ends at Glengormley. You've no idea!' she said.

Bellaghy was near the top of Lough Neagh and close to Toomebridge, where my father used to fish for eels in green waders before the Troubles. My big brother had begsied the green Simca for some football, rugby or cricket match where he could show off his brilliance with balls, and although I was sure he had done this deliberately just to sicken me, I was not altogether disappointed at being unable to display our humble family car to Lesley's folks. They had three cars between them – one for Mummy, one for Daddy and one for Lesley – and every single one of their cars was bigger, more expensive and less rusty than the Green Dream Machine. Although Lesley was largely unfamiliar with the concept of public transport she phoned the bus station in Belfast to find out the details of the journey for me. She provided me with clear instructions on where to catch the blue and white Ulsterbus to Bellaghy, how much the ticket would cost and where to disembark on the Toome Road. There she would pick me up in the Renault 5 and transport me the final few miles to the enchanted village itself. Alan Whicker usually travelled on a Concorde but I was happy enough to get an Ulsterbus to Bellaghy. My main experience of this particular mode of public transport had been watching Ulsterbuses burning on *Good Evening Ulster.* For as long as I could remember the paramilitaries had been burning buses to free Ireland or keep Ulster British, or simply to show how upset they were by the latest political development. I felt sorry for all the bus drivers who must have been very bad with their nerves after so many hijackings.

When the day of my journey arrived I made sure I was on time for the bus and bought a one-way ticket to Bellaghy. I had learned from my mistake on 12 February 1982 when I missed the train to Coleraine and almost ruined my life. This was a similarly important appointment, though I hoped Lesley's parents weren't going to subject me to a formal interview. As Lesley was an only child, I knew her mother and father would have very high standards for her. What did they think about their only daughter going out with a wee lad from up the Shankill? Of course, there were plenty of people from the Shankill who had come up in the world, such as Norman Whiteside who played for Manchester United. Nonetheless, I was certain Lesley's parents would have been much happier if Lesley had been doing a line with someone like Aaron Ward whose father was a dentist, and there was no way in a million years that I would ever play for Manchester United because, to quote my big brother, 'Our Tony couldn't kick back doors!' I knew the Evanses were good Presbyterians, so I clung to the hope that being a good livin' Sunday School teacher in Whiterock Orange

Hall might compensate for my humble origins. As I travelled up the motorway into lands well beyond Glengormley, I fretted that Lesley's wider family might not accept me, as I had never once bought an outfit in Anderson & McAuley's in my life. Lesley's budget for one Gloria Vanderbilt outfit was equal to my annual budget for John Frazer's. I contemplated pretending that my father was actually Mr McAuley himself and that he worked with Mr Anderson in the shop in Royal Avenue, but I knew my lie would be exposed if anyone took the time to compare the spelling of our surnames.

The Ulsterbus crossed the bridge with the Irish tricolour flags and IRA graffiti at Toome and then passed the enormous, fortified police station with scorch marks on the security gates from the rocket attacks. As I admired the lovely scenery I worried about all the stupid things I might say in front of Lesley's parents that would deem me an inappropriate boyfriend. Finally, I reminded myself to say all my 'pleases' and 'thank yous' and 'sorrys' to prove that I was dead well brought-up and educated and all.

As the bus approached what I believed to be the correct bus stop I spotted the blue Renault 5 parked at the side of the road and I could see Lesley using her rearview mirror to fix her hair and apply fresh red lipstick. I appreciated that she wanted to look nice for me, although the lipstick was a bit of nuisance when it rubbed off on my lips and I had to wipe it off with a hankie or the sleeve of my best Simon Le Bon blouse. I leapt up from my seat, wobbling slightly with the weight of the sports bag containing my jammies, wash bag and Good News Bible, and pressed the button to inform the driver that I wished to disembark. Being an inexperienced passenger I had left this quite late and the bus driver scowled at me and shook his head, but I forgave him because he was probably bad with his nerves due to all the hijackings. I jumped out of the bus and landed in a shuck, splashing mud all over my suede ankle boots which I had brushed especially for the occasion. I inhaled the scent of cow's clap and slurry, and as I exhaled I knew I had finally arrived up the country.

Lesley welcomed me with a red lipstick kiss and one of her perfect smiles. She was obviously very excited. Lesley was excited most of the time, but today she was even more excited than usual as she talked me through her detailed plans for the day. After I met her parents and her cousins we would visit the historic Bellaghy Bawn which was across the road from her house, and Cuddy's Department Store in Magherafelt, which had been bombed a few times and sold lovely clothes. Lesley drove us slightly too fast down a winding country road snugly framed by shucks and hedges.

'Look at all the gorgeous wee lambsies,' she said as we passed fields full of sheep. Within five minutes I could see the sign announcing our arrival in the beguiling village of Bellaghy.

'That's our church – there's the hall for the GB and there's the church for the services. The railings need painted and you've no idea … Mummy's in the choir and she's the captain of the GB and sometimes plays the organ and counts the money and she never stops and you've no idea … and that's the RUC station, it used to be a big manor house until the police took it over, and there's Mrs Steen's shop and down there is Greenses and the Masonic Hall on the corner …'

I thought it strange that in spite of the fact that everything around me was quaint, rural, and slightly run-down, the RUC station for this wee village was nearly as big and as heavily fortified as the police station at Springmartin near where I lived, and that was situated on the West Belfast peace line.

'Is this the peace line?' I asked.

'Och, don't be stupid, we don't have peace lines up the country. We all live together in the one village here.'

'That's great!' I said. 'So everyone gets on well up here in spite of the Troubles and all.'

'Well, I wouldn't say that now. We've had more than our fair share of bombs and shootings. The Troubles isn't all about the Falls and the Shankill, ya know. One night they blew up half of Bellaghy. There was hardly a window left in the village. Our greenhouse was shattered. You've no idea!'

'But how can the two sides live together in the same village if all that's goin' on? That would be like the Falls and the Shankill being all mixed with no peace walls.'

'Bellaghy's a republican village and we're the minority. And it's not just IRA republicans, it's the real extreme ones round here – the INLA. They kill each other when they're not killing soldiers and policemen and Protestants.'

It had never occurred to me that Catholics and Protestants could live together in such close proximity, apart from up the Malone Road where they were too posh to fight.

'Sure, Mad Dog grew up in the house next door to us,' Lesley said casually.

'What? Mad Dog that shot all those poor people in that wee church in Darkley?'

'Yes, his sister was my best friend when we were growing up.'

'What?'

'I was an only child and they were a big family, so I played with all the kids next door.'

This was a revelation. Lesley lived beside real live republicans and spoke to them and was even friends with some of them. It seemed that in Bellaghy it was normal for Presbyterians to live right next door to the INLA. This brought new meaning to the phrase 'love thy neighbour.'

'Everyone knows who tried to shoot who and who blew up the village and who killed who,' she said. 'You've no idea!'

On this occasion Lesley's catchphrase was true – I had absolutely no idea what this would be like. I was friends with Marty Mullen and I was certain he was a republican but I didn't think he'd actually killed anyone – at least not yet.

'How could you even look at your neighbours if you knew your side had tried to kill them or they had tried to kill you?' I asked.

Lesley shrugged her shoulders. 'That's Bellaghy,' she said, as if this was the most natural behaviour in the world.

'Did you ever try to argue with the republicans or ask them to stop killing us?' I asked.

'Yes, I had a big debate with Boomer one day.'

'Boomer?'

'I understand them you know. I've seen the way the army treat them. Anyway, they're a bit brainwashed, everything's black and white, so I don't think Boomer listened to me. He just sees me as the wee privileged Protestant girl next door that hasn't a clue about the armed struggle.'

Now we were in her natural habitat my views of Lesley were changing with every passing minute. I had always thought she was just a lovely big girl from up the country with nice clothes from Anderson & McAuley's and her own car, but now I was discovering that she had actually argued with terrorists and asked them to lay down their weapons! I had been a committed pacifist all my life and I had never done anything remotely as brave as this, though I did once manage to persuade Titch McCracken to stop throwing shoplifted marleys from the Mace over the peace wall.

'This is our house here,' Lesley said, turning off the main street and driving down a long lane with trees and bushes and more heathers than Portadown. We arrived at the rear of a large, detached house with a patio on one side, and stables, outhouses and an orchard on the other. A door opened and a middle-aged couple emerged. The man was very tall and thin with dark, slicked-back hair, and the lady was well-dressed with big glasses, a lovely hairdo and a friendly smile.

'That's Mummy!' Lesley said excitedly.

'Well, welcome to Bellaghy,' said Mummy.

I walked forward and shook Mummy's hand and then shook Daddy's hand, which was so big it made mine feel like the hand of a child.

'Thank you, thank you,' I said politely.

'C'mon into the kitchen. The kettle's on,' Mummy said, leading us into one of the biggest kitchens I had ever seen in my life. There were hundreds of red cabinets and still room for a table and chairs in the middle.

'You sit yourself there, Tony,' said Mummy.

Lesley, Daddy and I sat around the smoked glass table – which was as impressive as any I had ever seen in the window of Gillespie & Wilson's on the Shankill Road – while Mummy moved around the kitchen like a bee buzzing from flower to flower, preparing our wee cuppa tea. She placed one of her Himalayan pavlovas in the centre of the table and my mouth began to water instantly. Then she surrounded the pavlova with a series of smaller plates containing geometrically perfect caramel squares; freshly baked fruit scones with butter, jam and a dollop of fresh cream; and a plate of chocolate biscuits from a good tin, rather than Yellow Pack chocolate digestives which students lived on.

'I just thought I'd make you a wee snack before dinner,' Mummy explained as she poured the tea into proper china cups with saucers, which rested on proper place mats with pictures of fox hunting.

'Would you like a piece of pavlova?' she asked.

'Yes, please, thank you,' I replied.

Once we began eating and drinking everyone relaxed into conversation. We talked about how long it took to get here on the bus, when the bawn across the road was built, how I was getting on in university, what a lovely kitchen this was and it's terrible all that's going on in Northern Ireland, so it is, and sure it's a minority on both sides causing all the trouble, so it is.

'Have another scone,' said Mummy.

'Yes please, thank you,' I replied, filling myself up nicely after my long bus journey.

'I'm going to take Tony out for a wee run in the car to show him round before dinner,' Lesley said.

'Have another caramel square,' said Mummy.

'Yes please, thank you,' I replied, still thoroughly enjoying the sweet Presbyterian feast.

Lesley had told me that Daddy was a quiet man, like John Wayne in the movie, and so if he didn't talk much it didn't necessarily mean that he didn't like me. He was very friendly but once he had finished his cuppa tea he went and sat in the corner beside the radiator and began to read a Western paperback.

'Remember to show Tony the school now, won't you, Lessley,' Mummy said, pronouncing 'Lesley' very politely, with an extended 's'. 'Have another chocolate biscuit, they're Marks & Spencer,' she added.

'Yes please, thank you,' I replied, though I was starting to feel quite full.

We chatted for another while about the school up the mountain where Mummy had been headmistress for years and where they got very good results in the eleven-plus.

'Have another piece of pavlova,' said Mummy.

'No, thank you, I think I'm full up now,' I replied.

Silence.

'Och, sure go on, you would, you could, you should,' said Mummy.

'Okay, sorry, thanks, you've persuaded me, yes please,' I responded with the utmost courtesy.

Lesley talked uninterrupted for several minutes about going to the wee school and how it got the best eleven-plus results in mid Ulster and Mummy joined in with a few stories about some of her more errant pupils.

'Now, have another scone, Tony,' Mummy commanded.

'Oh no, sorry, thank you, really I couldn't, I'm full up now. It's all so lovely, thank you.'

'Och, none of that, you will, you can, you should, sure you're a growing boy!' said Mummy, clearly not prepared to take 'no' for an answer.

The food was all delicious and I enjoyed being spoilt in this way, but I had to wonder if I would be permitted to stop eating before all the plates were empty.

'We need to go now,' said Lesley, 'or we'll not be back in time for dinner.'

'Och, Lessley,' Mummy tutted.

The possibility of missing dinner rescued me from any further force-feeding and off we went in the Renault 5 to explore the wonders of south Derry. First of all, Lesley showed me the GAA pitch, which was a completely new experience for me as there were no GAA pitches on the Shankill. Then Lesley pointed out a neighbour's farm across the road.

'That's where Albert artificially inseminates the pigs, over there,' said Lesley.

"Scuse me, wha?'

'Bellaghy's very big for artificial insemination of pigs, you know,' she said proudly.

I was speechless.

Thankfully, before I could begin to picture pigs being artificially inseminated by Albert, Lesley drove us down a narrow, winding lane opposite the GAA pitch. She explained that this was where she went for long pony rides in the summer holidays, to an island called Church on a beautiful lough called Beg. I had always thought a 'beg' was what you carried your shopping in.

Lesley provided me with a running commentary.

'And that's a wee cottage with no electric and the wee man always sits there and has a wee chat with you, and Mummy collects for the lifeboats round here and everybody gives even though it's the 'Royal Lifeboats' and we're nowhere near the sea, so we're not … and Seamus Heaney's from over there and Daddy knows him and they're an awful nice family, and all the swans land here from Iceland in the same fields every year and the Orange Hall gets paint bombed all the time, and there's a brilliant Garden Centre in Maghera …'

We stopped at the edge of the lough. The scenery was breathtaking. I was fascinated by the giant dragonflies hovering over the water, which reminded me of the *Doctor Who* episode, 'The Green Death' where an enormous fly hatched from a giant maggot and squirted poisonous slime at the UNIT soldiers until the third Doctor swatted it with his cape. It was so peaceful and picturesque on the shores of Lough Beg, it was hard to imagine people wanting to kill each other round here. I told Lesley that the closest thing I had to somewhere special like this when I was growing up was up the fields where I picked blackberries or up the Glen where I caught tadpoles and the paramilitaries dumped bodies. We stopped for a while to gaze at the mysterious Church Island. Lesley pointed out rags hanging from an old tree beside the ruins of the church, where Catholic pilgrims prayed once a year in summer when the lough was low enough to walk out to the island. It sounded magical – albeit not very Presbyterian –

and Lesley's excitement about the place was infectious. After this idyllic sojourn the Renault 5 transported us to Magherafelt. Lionel Richie sang 'Stuck on You' on the cassette radio as we drove up a very broad street in the centre of the town.

'What's this street called?' I asked.

'Broad Street,' said Lesley.

Country people are very straightforward, I thought.

Once we had seen both the streets in Magherafelt, we moved on to a wee village called Tobermore with only one street, where Lesley pointed out her auntie's bungalow beside the Orange Hall. After that we drove towards the Sperrin Mountains, taking a winding country road in the middle of nowhere to Kilross Primary School where Lesley had been a pupil and Mummy was headmistress. I hadn't experienced so many country roads since playing Olivia Newton John's *Greatest Hits* on repeat.

When we returned to Bellaghy for dinner, the table was all set out with a tablecloth and placemats and napkins like for a Christmas dinner. There was soup for starters with proper soup spoons, roast beef with roast potatoes and proper mash (rather than Smash) and the tastiest peas I had ever tasted. This was followed by a freshly baked chocolate cake with ice cream and fresh cream for dessert and then a wee cuppa tea and some traybakes in the living room. As Lesley and I settled down to watch *Dallas* on the biggest television I had ever seen – with wooden doors and a brass lock and key on the front and everything – Mummy offered me some more of her sweet delights.

'Och, now don't be sayin' no, have another wee caramel square. You would, you could, you should!'

'Okay, yes please, thank you,' I replied, wondering how I could possibly consume another crumb.

I accepted further sustenance, even though at this stage it felt like the chocolate was clogging my throat. This rich cuisine was so different from my normal student diet of sausages and baked beans and a few Jammie Dodgers that I began to feel a little ill. I feel asleep on Lesley's shoulder while Sue Ellen was mid lip quiver. That night, after a subtle snog in the good room, Mummy arrived with supper which included a slice – or two or three if you weren't assertive enough to refuse (which I wasn't) – of apple tart and fresh cream. Finally I was ushered to the guest room, with thick walls, a huge double bed and a hot water bottle. Mummy showed me to the bathroom and I marvelled at the plush curtains, the millions of bath cubes (which I presumed were Christmas presents from all the children at the school), the expensive aftershaves you couldn't buy in Boots and the posh beige bathroom suite, which included a separate shower unit and a bidet. This finally confirmed to me that Lesley was middle class, because working-class houses had their showers attached to the taps in the bath and only middle-class people had bidets, though these were usually of an avocado hue. I thought it odd that middle-class people needed a separate facility to wash their feet in, because working-class people got by just fine washing their feet in the bath or with a face cloth in the wash basin. Once I had completed my ablutions (including washing my feet in the bidet, for the experience rather than for hygiene purposes) I returned to the guest bedroom. The bed was festooned with more eiderdowns, cushions and pillows than I had previously thought it possible for one mattress to support.

When I removed the restraining silk tassles and pulled the heavy curtains I was amazed at how dark and quiet it was up the country, even though the house was right beside the road. As I lay in bed, swamped in soft furnishings and with my stomach fuller than it had ever been, I considered all the new experiences of my first day in Bellaghy. I drifted off and dreamt that I was The Doctor being chased by a Caramel Square, and though I made it to the TARDIS in time and hid behind the console, an army of Caramel Squares descended upon me and not even my sonic screwdriver could stop them from overwhelming me.

'Breakfast!' Lesley said, popping her head round the door. She didn't enter, of course, as Joyce Huggett forbade this.

I glanced at my watch. It was 8 a.m., and already I could smell streaky bacon sizzling in Mummy's gigantic frying pan downstairs. There was no food as welcome in my digestive system on a weekend than an Ulster fry, but it was very early and it seemed like only a few hours since my last feed.

'Hurry up, you. Mummy says it nearly ready!'

'Lessley,' I heard Mummy call from downstairs. 'Is he never up yet?'

I climbed quickly into the shower cubicle, which was somewhat like getting into a TARDIS only to discover it was smaller on the inside and contained a beige soap-on-a-rope which matched the bathroom suite.

'Hurry you up, it's nearly out!' called Lesley.

I decided that I didn't have time to use the beige bidet and patted myself down quickly with an enormous brown towel the same colour as the carpet and the bathroom suite. Colour co-ordination was clearly very important in Bellaghy. As I got dressed I began to feel slightly nauseous from the combination of the sudden awakening, the early morning rush and my huge feed the day before.

What if Mummy and Daddy think I'm a lazy wee shite from the city who can't get up early to do manual labour like a proper countryman? I fretted.

I dashed downstairs, almost toppling a glass cabinet of Limoges porcelain crockery en route. The kitchen was a hive of frenetic activity. Daddy, who had obviously been up since 6 a.m. building a greenhouse and fixing several cars, was assisting with the sausages, bacon and black pudding while Mummy perfected the eggs and the soda and potato farls. Lesley was boiling the kettle and making the tea and all three were contributing to the setting of the table, complete with a toast holder, china butter dish, butter knives, and place mats and coasters imprinted with scenes of rural eighteenth-century England.

'Sorry, can I help, please?' I enquired.

'Not at all. You're the guest,' Mummy smiled, cracking a brown egg into the pan. 'You sit there.' She directed me to the specified guest chair. Mummy clearly enjoyed the challenge of hosting and I was somewhat overwhelmed by all the attention.

'Your beige bathroom suite's lovely, so it is,' I ventured.

'It's Sahara Gold,' said Lesley.

I sat down amid all the activity and the delicious smells, but all of a sudden I began to feel very sick. I was surrounded by the makings of the perfect Ulster fry – a massive feast of meat and enough fried bread to empty a shelf in the Ormo Mini Shop – but due, more than likely, to my over-indulgence the day before I was feeling increasingly queasy.

'I feel a bit sick,' I whispered to Lesley, who looked most concerned.

'You have to eat Mummy's fry, she's been preparing for it all week,' she whispered back, our conversation masked only by the sudden sizzling of mushrooms being added to the frying pan.

I started taking deep breaths in an attempt subdue the nausea, but with every breath I inhaled the odour of fried meat and mushrooms and by this stage the smell was sickening rather than appetising. Lesley observed me closely, aware of the potential disaster unfolding in her kitchen. My face had turned a whiter shade of pale and she quickly realised that an intervention was going to be necessary.

'Tony's not feeling well,' she said, much to my relief.

Mummy looked over her bifocals with a mixture of shock and disappointment as the frying fat spat at me from beneath the eggs.

'Och, sure you're all right now. You just need a good fry and you'll be fine.'

'Sorry, I think I need to lie down,' I confessed. 'Then I'll be all right, if that's okay. Thanks for the fry, please, sorry.'

Mummy, Daddy and Lesley cast glances at each other from their various workstations across the kitchen. I was embarrassed – if I had farted explosively at the kitchen table it could not have been worse. Mummy looked hurt, as if her cooking was so horrible it was making me sick, Lesley looked concerned about Mummy, and Daddy went outside for a smoke.

'Sure, you would, you could, you should just try a wee plate,' Mummy persisted, and she proceeded to set a plate of sausage, bacon and egg in front of me. Normally the smell would have overwhelmed my taste buds but in my current condition it only made me wretch. If I didn't move quickly I was going to be sick all over the kitchen table, and there would be undigested sweetcorn and diced carrots all over the antique placemats depicting scenes of pastoral England.

'Sorry, excuse me, please, thank you …' I rapidly left the table and darted upstairs to the bathroom. As I departed I caught a glimpse of the shocked expression on Mummy's face and I could tell that Lesley was embarrassed to have a boyfriend who was made sick by her Mummy's Ulster fry. I made it into the bathroom just in time. I fell to my knees onto the brown shag-pile and boked into the beige bidet. I boked again and again, completely evacuating the richness of the previous day's cuisine from my convulsing stomach. Such was the volume of my vomiting that Lesley shouted upstairs, 'Are you all right? It can't be that bad!'

I had always been a noisy boker, and this was not a problem in the privacy of my own home, but in my girlfriend's house, on my first visit to meet her parents, on the first offer of her mother's monumental Ulster fry, it was definitely adding insult to injury to be vomiting so loudly into their beige bidet. After a few minutes of cold sweat and further evacuations, I began to feel well enough to start cleaning up.

'I'm all right now,' I said to Lesley through the locked bathroom door, meticulously removing all traces of boke from the beige bidet so Mummy wouldn't get any between her toes the next time she used it. 'I just need to lie down for a wee minute.'

When I emerged from the bathroom Lesley mopped my brow like a nurse. It seemed like she still cared for me even though I was an utter embarrassment. I lay down for fifteen minutes, and eventually I felt well enough to return to the crestfallen kitchen scene where I slowly consumed a mini Ulster fry under Mummy's watchful eye.

'Sorry, that was lovely, thanks,' I said as I cautiously set my knife and fork down vertically across the plate in a polite but firm indication that I could eat no more.

'Sure you need a nice cuppa tea to calm your stomach now,' said Mummy.

'Sorry, thanks, I'm all …' I attempted, but the cup was poured and set before me and to my surprise it did ease my nausea, though I did have to firmly decline the offer of two Rice Krispie buns and a slice of fruit cake from Ditty's Bakery in Castledawson even though it was 'the best fruit cake in Mid Ulster' and I was 'a growing boy' and all.

Later that day as Lesley gave me a lift back to the bus stop we discussed the success of my first meeting with her family. By all accounts everyone thought I was a lovely fella, although the breakfast table incident had certainly raised eyebrows.

'You'd better not be sick the next time,' Lesley said.

I took this as her way of saying that her family liked me and accepted me because there *would* be a next time, on the condition that it be a vomit-free visit. As we waited at the bus stop Lesley drew back from a goodbye kiss, leading me to fear that I had let her down and nobody liked me and she was going to chuck me.

Reading the concern on my face she explained, 'I'm not kissin' a bake that's just boked!'

'Have you got your return ticket?' she asked.

I searched in my pockets and found only a 50p, a stick of Wrigley's and a Greenpeace badge.

'You were supposed to buy a return ticket, ya eejit ye!' said my love.

'But I've no money left,' I explained.

'Typical!' said Lesley.

'Oh, that's so middle class,' I retorted.

'Change the record,' she shouted.

Lionel Richie was singing 'Dancing on the Ceiling' on the cassette radio.

'Well I've no money with me, either,' Lesley explained, 'We'll have to go back to the house and borrow your bus fare from Mummy!'

She was ragin'.

'I'm sorry,' I said

'Wee lad!' sighed Lesley.

We returned to the house in Bellaghy. Fortunately Daddy was not home, having escaped to the pub after doing all the dishes. I was too sheepish to leave the car, so Lesley made a brief visit to the kitchen to obtain the required finances. When Mummy came to the back door she appeared to be laughing as if she was taking my silly mistake in a good-natured manner. But what if she thought I was irresponsible with money? This, combined with my weak stomach, might just be enough of a reason for Lesley's parents to deem me an unsuitable suitor. Lesley was kind, and even gave me a kiss on the cheek when she left me back to the bus stop. It seemed as if my mistakes might be forgiven. But what if she thought I was nothing but an embarrassment that she couldn't even bring home to her parents and decided to chuck me for some boy from Ballymoney with an XR3? I was insecure, so I was.

18

MR PRESIDENT

It was election time again, so it was. As a mature, intellectual adult with a socialist ideology I understood the importance of democracy. This latest election would have a major impact on the lives of many people around me for years to come, so it was vital that the right representatives were elected to the key leadership positions.

The election for the committee of the Christian Union was an annual event and as a responsible final-year student I decided to throw myself wholeheartedly into the democratic process. This was unlike any government election I had ever participated in at home. In my few short years as a voter in West Belfast, no one I backed had ever been elected. I had queued up for my ballot paper, marked my 'X' and posted my voting slip in the black box as a member of the population of West Belfast. Most people in my constituency voted for Gerry Adams, even though he supported killing people for a united Ireland, which was an affront to my pacifist convictions. Subsequently, Gerry Adams was elected as my new MP and he refused to go to London to sit in the House of Commons because he hated the evil Brits for all the hundreds of years of oppression and everything. At least in the Christian Union elections there was no suggestion of an armed struggle, no one tried to shoot anyone and there was a chance I could actually have an influence. Of course, as this was not a secular election it was carried out without any of the untoward competitiveness or rancor of a political poll in Northern Ireland. In the CU elections you didn't have to promise to smash or kill anyone to become prayer secretary and none of the candidates for missionary secretary pledged to drive anyone out of the country. All proceedings were carried out with due spiritual reflection and prayer. It is true that Clive Ross privately advised voters that, until George Simpson had proved for certain that God had healed him from his gayness, it was unwise to cast a vote for him. I thought this was unfair and unnecessary, as George himself had said he wasn't ready to take on a leadership role as he was still suffering from the depression that set in shortly after he got healed straight.

This year I decided, after much humble thought and prayer, to allow my name to go forward for election. I would simply offer myself to the membership, and if God told them to vote for me I would gracefully accept the burden of responsibility and greatness that the Lord had thrust upon me. As long as Clive Ross didn't spread rumours that Lesley and I were up to anything more than kissing, and provided Tara Grace couldn't convince people that you had to be able to speak in tongues to be elected to the committee, I had a chance of winning a leadership role. I had played my part in the activities of the CU for the previous two years. I had put my acting skills to very good use, and at least here they were valued. I performed in sketches about devils and angels and I was given a leading part in a drama that compared giving away bananas to telling people about Jesus. It wasn't method acting, but my performances were warmly received and had raised my profile considerably. I was something of a Roger Moore in the CU. I had organised the bookstall in LT17 every Thursday night and book sales were up due to my clever marketing strategies, which included a legendary performance of *The Twelve Days of Christmas* to advertise the twelve different books on sale on the table at the back. *Growing Into Love* by Joyce Huggett sold out.

Some of my fellow undergraduates were less impressed by my possible elevation to the Christian Union committee. I dared not tell Conor O'Neill or Marty Mullen for fear of total rejection. After two-and-a-half years, Marty had only just started to say 'nay bother' to me in an almost-friendly fashion when I asked him to swap bookings in the television-editing suite so I could make yet another music video. Conor was so incensed by the continued dictatorship of Margaret Thatcher that I didn't want to risk upsetting him further with my possible leadership of another fascist regime. When I explained my aspirations to Byron Drake he predictably shook his head, flicked his fringe and his *Guardian* and turned up The Smiths on his Walkman.

'Don't talk to me, Tone,' he moped. 'You just don't get it, do you?'

'Don't get what?' I enquired.

'Sssh!' he said. 'Morrissey is just pure fucking genius.'

'Hey, what's the craic there, Tony?' Billy Barton asked in the canteen a few days before polling day. I was aware that Billy was also standing for election to the CU Committee, and as he was always very friendly to everyone I knew he was a possible threat. Hamilton Johnston and Johnston Hamilton were certain to vote for him. I hoped the voters had noticed that Billy was more interested in cars and cows than Christianity. I had never had a serious conversation with Billy in my life, and I was reassured by the fact that very few people got anywhere near a debate with him on justice and poverty in Christian mission.

'I'm standing for the CU committee,' I replied, in an attempt to gauge the mood of the electorate. 'God willing.'

'Good man yourself,' said Billy. 'Me too – God willing.'

'Really? I'd no idea,' I lied.

'It's some craic, hey,' Billy added, slapping me on the back.

That's one vote, at least, I thought. Two votes counting Lesley. Three votes if Aaron doesn't have a rugby match that night. Maybe ten votes if all the Heathers from Portadown want me.

'I'm standing for the committee, God willing,' several hopefuls said at the best-attended prayer meeting of the year, the day before the election.

'Dear Lord, we ask you to guide us to vote for the right leaders for the year ahead,' prayed Clive Ross.

'Yes, Lord,' said Tara Grace.

'And we pray that you will choose people worthy of the calling who are not caught up with the worldliness of materialism and the media,' Clive canvassed.

'Yes, Lord,' prayed Tara. 'And we pray that you will give us leaders who are baptized in the Spirit and are really just kinda on fire in a really beautiful kinda way.'

'Amen,' prayed Clive Ross.

After a few weeks of clandestine spiritual hustings, it came to pass that, lo, I was elected to the Christian Union committee. Clive Ross was not elected, an outcome he ungraciously compared to the crowd in the Bible choosing to free Barabbas the criminal and crucify Jesus the Saviour. I out-polled Billy Barton substantially, even though he was a right fella. My housemate Peter who liked guitars and prayer was also elected, which meant that our draughty house in Portstewart would become a nerve centre for student ministry. This only confirmed to Marina with the Daisy Duke shorts that I lived with 'a bunch of Holy Joes', which apparently was much worse than living with a mature student with a drug habit and a hygiene problem as she did.

Once elected to the executive committee of the CU this conclave of student spiritual leaders had to elect a president. This was the big job; the Pope of the Christian Union, except definitely not Roman Catholic. The president had to chair lots of committee meetings and lead prayers and welcome visiting speakers and never, ever get drunk in the uni bar. The president was supposed be a good leader and a 'thinking Christian' who read thick books by John Stott and understood really, really dark and really, really deep passages of the Old Testament. This election was carried out by secret ballot after a prayer meeting where God told us who to vote for. As the votes were being counted I noticed my heart was beating very fast, which suggested that I really wanted to win even though I was not supposed to covet such high rank and status. I promised God that I would stay humble if he let me win. When the result was announced, to my great surprise the committee had elected me president of the Christian Union. I was The President, so I was! I may have been just some wee lad from up the Shankill but now I was The President. I was like Ronald Reagan and Lesley was my Nancy. I phoned home from the red telephone box beside the sea in Portstewart and proudly informed my mother of my election. She said that it was lovely, so it was, but I should make sure to concentrate on passing my exams and not get distracted by too much coortin' or 'wee good livin' meetin's'.

Later, Tara Grace confided in me that God had told her I would be president. She promised me that she would pray every day that I would be baptized by the Holy Spirit so I could speak in tongues and heal people. Tara assured me that to be blessed with all the gifts of the Holy Spirit like her would be 'really just kinda beautiful', but I would have to give up all the hidden sins in my heart first. I was tempted to tell Tara that I hadn't lusted after Bo Derek in the sand dunes for weeks now.

Once I accepted my calling as a religious leader on campus I discovered that I would have plenty of opportunities to practice being a blessed peacemaker. This would prepare me for making peace between Catholics and Protestants, Jews and Muslims, Man United and Liverpool supporters. My greatest challenge was to persuade all the different types of Christian not to fall out with each other, which was very difficult, as there were more categories of Christian in the CU than flavours of Tayto crisps! I enjoyed all the different flavours coming together, but some members found it very difficult to accept the other members who were clearly in the wrong about so many matters of faith and practice. The Presbyterians and Church of Ireland members got on reasonably well once they discovered that the other side was not quite as theologically unsound as they had always been led to believe. The Methodists liked Wesleyan hymns and disliked too much money, while the Brethren members generally liked money and disliked women speaking. The Baptist members knew the Bible off by heart and disliked babies getting christened. The independent house church members liked praising Jesus with guitars and disliked organs. The Free Presbyterian members were few in number because they didn't mix with lesser Christians, but these members liked Paisley and disliked Catholics. The Catholic members were even fewer in number, and they mostly kept their heads down and hoped their priest didn't find out that they were mixing with heretics.

But, like how everyone in Northern Ireland was either unionist or nationalist, there were two main wings within the CU – the fundamentalists and the charismatics. These two rival blocs tussled politely for dominance in all spiritual decisions in the Christian Union. The fundamentalists liked Calvin but weren't too keen on women because God didn't want females to be in charge; the charismatics loved the Holy Spirit but hated Halloween because it promoted the occult. The fundamentalists tried to have all the Cliff Richard gospel music cassettes removed from the book table because Cliff sang the devil's music, while the charismatics demanded a better supply of gospel praise cassettes of Cliff singing about Jesus being really just kinda beautiful. I managed to reach a compromise on this major issue by agreeing that the book table should also include a book entitled *Pop Goes the Gospel* which explained how evil pop music was, especially if you played it backwards and were turned into a Satanist by subliminal messages. That way people could read the book and listen to Cliff and decide for themselves which of the two was more objectionable. Fundamentalists were very worried that we were on a 'slippery slope' to becoming secular atheists and this generally meant we should not change anything; on the opposite side of the theological peace wall, the charismatics were always demanding more contemporary worship songs, playing them on repeat and dancing and speaking in tongues at the CU meetings.

I believed that my role as president was to be a sort of mediator between the two sides, like the Alliance Party in Northern Ireland politics. This ran the risk that both sides would reject me, but I was determined to put my peacemaking into practice. To keep both sides holy and happy, I brokered a deal: for every modern song about really just loving Jesus for the charismatics, there would be a traditional hymn about reformed doctrine for the fundamentalists. I promoted mutual respect for the decision to clap along or not to clap along during 'Seek Ye First', and discouraged members from judging their fellow believers on whether they raised their hands in praise or kept them steadfastly in their Presbyterian pockets during 'Rejoice, Rejoice'. The charismatics loved the Holy Spirit as much as Jesus, and He gave them the ability to prophesy and heal each other. For some reason a high percentage of charismatics were born with one leg shorter than the other, so they often had to heal each other to make the shorter leg grow. Charismatics praised Jesus profusely for weeks after he lengthened their legs. The only miracle I was praying for was that I would be able to keep both the fundamentalists and the charismatics happy enough so they wouldn't break apart and start alternative Christian Unions with just their own sort. If there was a split in the Christian Union during my tenure as president it would be a sign of my failure as a peacemaker. If I couldn't keep evangelical Protestants from fighting amongst themselves, how on earth could I ever persuade Catholics and Protestants to stop killing each other? I had signed up as a volunteer to work on a summer scheme in North Belfast which would bring Protestant and Catholic children together so they could make friends and learn not to hate each other, no matter what their parents said. This summer scheme would be like the Westy Disco, but with Catholics and without the disco. It was going to be an enormous challenge for student volunteers to help children in Belfast do what politicians and paramilitaries and even their parents didn't want them to do, so helping rival groups of believers to get along in the Christian Union would be very good practice.

I was determined that my presidential year would be characterised by harmony and reconciliation, so when I wasn't trying to keep the fundamentalists and charismatics from engaging in all-out war, I decided to hold out the hand of friendship to the corpulent university chaplain who everyone said hated the Christian Union with a vengeance. Clive Ross said this man was an unrepentant anti-Christian chaplain who smoked, but Tara Grace insisted that he was simply being controlled by a demon of cynicism and if we prayed hard enough he would be delivered from this evil spirit. I thought the chaplain was just a little jealous because hardly anyone bothered with the chaplaincies. The CU was overflowing with members and it was controlled by student leaders instead of clergymen, so I wondered if the chaplain just didn't like people under the age of fifty being in charge. However, in spite of advice from my fellow committee members that I was wasting my time, I decided to request an audience with the chaplain. To my great surprise, he agreed to meet with me between busy rounds of cocktail parties and Holy Communions. I sensed a spirit of reconciliation was in the air. This would be the beginning of warmer relations between the jean-wearing Jesus followers and the dog-collared disciples on campus.

When the day came, I knocked on the chaplain's office door tentatively.

'Come in,' he called, with all the swanky authority that had intimidated previous presidents.

We shook hands and I introduced myself. Apparently, he required no introduction.

'What does your father do?' he asked immediately in an almost-English accent.

I was taken aback. No one had ever asked me such a question before actually trying to get to know me first.

Nothing you would think is of any importance, I thought.

I could tell that your father's profession was very important to this man, especially if your father happened to be a proper professional like a doctor or a lawyer. The obvious snobbery of the corpulent chaplain fanned the socialist flame within me, so I took a deep breath and stated proudly, 'My father is a foreman in a foundry in West Belfast.'

I could tell he was unimpressed as he moved swiftly on, relighting his grubby pipe as if I had said nothing of any consequence whatsoever. But I held his eye. I wanted to be sure that he knew how proud I was of my factory-working father; no son of my da would allow him to be put down by some stuck-up vicar who had never done a proper days' work in his life!

'Would you like to come and speak to some of the members of the Christian Union?' I asked, holding out a palm leaf.

The chaplain set down his pipe and stifled a patronising chuckle. I couldn't help but notice how pink his cheeks were, and his bulbous nose reminded me of a character in a *Noddy* book.

'Well now, I don't think that would achieve a great deal, would it, young man? Are you going to try to convert me? Get me "saved" and "born again"?' He spoke in a mock Belfast accent when using this evangelical terminology and his voice dripped with sarcasm.

Dickhead! I thought.

'Really?' I said meekly.

My attempt to extend the hand of friendship was not going well, but I knew I should turn the other cheek and persist.

'You see, you evangelicals are all the same,' he pronounced.

Arrogant shite! I thought.

'I'm not quite sure what you mean,' I replied respectfully.

'Well, you all think you're so high and mighty, but I have no doubt that the president of the Christian Union masturbates behind the bicycle shed as much as the next young man.'

Given the recent traumatic experience of losing a prized possession from the bicycle shed, I could not think of anywhere worse to risk exposing my most prized possession. Why was a man I'd only just met bringing up masturbation anyway?

Pervert! I thought.

'I'm really not a high and mighty sort of person, so I'm not,' I replied.

At this stage I decided that my attempt at reconciliation was doomed. I knew I should be gracious and forgiving and absorb the jibes and accusations for the sake of Christian unity, but after just a few minutes in the chaplain's office I was already having impure thoughts about telling him to stick his pipe up his fat arse. In my head I knew I should be asking 'What would Jesus do?', but in my heart I was thinking 'What would Granny do?' The Holy Spirit was prompting me to persist and pursue reconciliation with the corpulent chaplain, but the ghost of my granny was urging me to give the ignorant slabber a good dig in the bake.

'Well the offer is always there if you ever want to engage in a dialogue with fellow Christians,' I forced myself to say with as much sincerity as I could muster.

'Thank you, Mister President. How gracious of you to deign to meet me,' the chaplain smarmed, lifting his well-padded backside from his over-stuffed chair to indicate that the audience was over.

Bastard! I thought.

'Well, thank you for your time. God bless,' I said.

I smiled, shook his sweaty hand and left, humiliated and crestfallen. My attempts to negotiate a truce between faith rivals had failed miserably. How could I ever help children from opposite sides of the peace wall to become friends if I couldn't make friends with one sarcastic Protestant clergyman?

That night I found it very hard to get to sleep in my freezing bedroom. I pulled the many layers of blankets, eiderdowns and sleeping bag over my cold head, and when I finally drifted off I had a terrible nightmare. I dreamt it was end of the world and Jesus had returned in the clouds like a 'Thief in the Night'. The scene was every bit as apocalyptic as my Cliff Richard video, except it was worse because there were Daleks and Klingons on Portstewart Strand as well as panicking students. Jesus was the spitting image of Clive Ross and the corpulent chaplain was a big fat angel, and these two deities were separating the sheep from the goats. Lesley, Tara, Peter, Agnetha from ABBA and every single Heather from Portadown were all being brought up into heaven on the back of the big cuddly creature from *The NeverEnding Story* while Limahl sang the theme tune. Meanwhile, I was stuck in the bicycle shed at the university, and when I tried to escape, I realised to my horror that both of my legs and my jimmy joe had been chopped off. Darth Vader was standing in the doorway laughing a deep, rasping laugh and wielding a light sabre, and Buffy the hamster was running around on a squeaky wheel in the corner and singing like Morrissey. The ground was opening beneath my feet and me, Bo Derek, Marty Mullen, Byron Drake and John DeLorean were being sucked down into a flaming abyss, screaming for mercy.

I woke up in a cold sweat. My heart was thumping in my chest faster than machine-gun fire in West Belfast. Slowly, the terror subsided, and I prayed and repeated Psalm 23 until I drifted off into a less traumatic slumber. The next day I could remember every detail, so I tried to work out what the nightmare was all about. Though it was difficult to admit it to myself I knew what this dream meant – in spite of all my aspirations, I suspected I was a pitiful peacemaker, so I did.

19

CAREER MOVES

Time was running out, so it was. As my final year exams approached I realised that I urgently needed to climb to the next step on the ladder of my career. In the past I had graduated from paperboy to breadboy and then from breadboy to student with relative ease, but I knew the next step in my grown-up career was going to be much more testing. Many graduates in Belfast ended up on the dole and I was determined that this was not going to happen to me. I had worked hard to develop skills in journalism and filmmaking, so I researched further training and employment opportunities that could lead me to Hollywood in California or the BBC in London or at least to Downtown Radio in the Kiltonga Industrial Estate in Newtownards. My search proved fruitful, and in addition to my speculative letter to the BBC in Belfast asking if I could read the news like Rose Neill, I sent off applications for journalism courses in Belfast and Dublin.

My first glimpse of a possible future arrived in a brown envelope from the College of Business Studies in Belfast. This letter invited me to attend the college for a written test and an interview. The College of Business Studies had nine floors and was one of the tallest buildings in the city so was, by Belfast standards, considered to be a skyscraper – the weather in Belfast was usually overcast with low clouds so the sky itself seemed lower than it did in big cities like New York, meaning a relatively small building could in fact appear to be scraping the sky. The College of Business Studies even had a lift!

I was already familiar with this modern high-rise building because the School of Music orchestra used to rehearse there every Saturday morning. Every week, eager young musicians got to travel in a proper lift with sliding doors to the eighth floor where, on weekdays, students learned how to bake cakes. I myself had often contributed to the crucifixion of Beethoven from the back row of the second violins, performing with the ever-present aroma of self-raising flour in the air. So at least the venue for my interview was familiar territory, and I knew how to handle all the buttons and the sliding doors in the lift. Marty Mullen had warned me that the journalism teachers in the College of Business Studies didn't get on very well with the Media Studies lecturers at The University of Ulster and he said I was wasting my time, but I was certain that once they spotted my obvious talent they would put aside any minor institutional rivalries and let me on to the journalism course.

My mother warned me that as I had already been to university and received a student grant for three years, I would be given no further money to do another course at a college that you didn't even need A levels to get into. This led to some tension at home, and my father was appalled at the idea that securing a degree didn't actually train you for a job. Unlike the university, the College of

Business Studies taught the practical skills of journalism like how to take notes in shorthand when you were interviewing sneaky politicians and then type up your report for the *Belfast Telegraph* or the *Guardian* or the *Washington Post*. I had previously attempted to gain the typewriting skills required to be a reporter by signing up for a summer course at Cairnmartin Secondary School, but I arrived late for the first class and all the women laughed at a man wanting to know how to type so I never went back.

The written test at the College of Business Studies seemed to go well as I knew what to do and I had just enough time to write a report like a proper journalist. I was nervous about the interview, though, so I practiced taking deep breaths and said a wee prayer as I waited outside the office. When I was invited inside there was an older woman with glasses who welcomed me with lots of pleasant '-ings' and a man who seemed a bit fed up and didn't even look up when I entered the room and sat in front of him. It all started off very well. The woman asked me why I wanted to do the course, and when I explained that I wanted to be an investigative reporter like Bernard and Woodstein the man looked up at me for the first time.

'What's his background?' he asked the woman, as if I wasn't in the room.

She looked at my application form, frowned and said, 'I'm afraid he's another one from the degree course in Coleraine.'

The man shook his head. 'So what have you learned about journalism on your three-year Media Studies degree course?' he asked, in a tone of voice which suggested the correct answer might be 'not a lot!'

He doesn't like me, I thought, but this was my chance to impress. Having a degree from the New University of Ulster clearly put me at a disadvantage, but this was my chance to prove that, in spite of that, I could still make a brilliant journalist. I told him everything I had learnt about how the media was being used as a propaganda tool by the state and how journalists could never be totally unbiased because they had their own views like everyone else and whoever was paying their wages usually had an agenda anyway and how women and disabled people and all the other minorities were underrepresented in journalism and misrepresented by the media, even in soap operas. The more I spoke the wearier he looked, and every time I used the term 'feminist critique' he rolled his eyes.

'But can you give me any practical examples?' he asked.

'Well, the media in Northern Ireland think they are unbiased and just reporting the facts, but they are of course part of the system that sustains the conflict and they are only interested in bad news because they have negative news values, and journalists have their own sectarian biases the same as everybody else and the newspapers have either a unionist or a nationalist bias and when you read them it's obvious and you would think they are reporting on two parallel universes!'

Silence.

The woman took a sharp intake of breath.

No one had nodded since I opened my mouth.

The man coughed and put his pen down beside my application form. I had never before seen a ballpoint set down with such a sense of exasperation.

'They ruin good young people up there,' he said to the woman, once again as if I was not in the room.

I was pleased that he had acknowledged that I was once a good young person, but offended by the fact that I was now apparently ruined.

'His written test is surprisingly good,' the woman said, offering a morsel of support for my application, but shaking her head at the same time.

She doesn't like me either now! I thought.

I had obviously got it wrong and it was clear they didn't want me. The interview was mercifully brought to a conclusion within a few minutes. Within a week I had received my letter of rejection, which wasn't as rude as the interview. I was dejected. How would I ever become a journalist if everything I had learnt at university meant that no one wanted me? Maybe they had looked at my postcode and noticed that I was just some wee lad from up the Shankill? Maybe they'd spotted that I had been president of the Christian Union and didn't want a good livin' journalist? Or maybe I was just crap!

'Well, as one door closes another door opens, love,' my mother said after she noticed me biting my nails and not laughing even once the whole way through an episode of *It Ain't Half Hot Mum* on BBC1.

I needed a door in Dublin or in the BBC in Belfast to open very soon, or I would be consigned to Snugville Street forever.

'I've got a interview in Dublin!' I yelled down the phone when the good news arrived in an envelope with an Éire stamp.

There were a few moments of silence before Lesley replied. 'That's brilliant! Sure it's supposed to be a better course than Belfast anyway,' she finally whooped.

I could tell from her initial hesitation that she was concerned about what might happen to our relationship next year if we were to be separated by the border and the Newry hills. This was a good indication that she may not be able to live without me.

'Do you think I'll get in?' I asked, seeking reassurance.

'Of course you will, sure your wee fillums are wonderful.'

'I know, but they say it's very competitive.'

'Well if it's meant to be, it's meant to be,' she said wisely. 'Now I'd better go – Mummy's taking me to the big sale in Logan's in Cloughmills. You've no idea!'

Three weeks later I drove myself to Dublin in the green Simca for the first time. I bought cheap petrol with punts and followed the map in the college prospectus. After negotiating the traffic on the outskirts of Dublin, to my great surprise and relief I arrived on time without once getting lost. I couldn't help but think that this was a good sign. During the journey I wondered about the logistics of moving to Dublin for a year. How could I ever afford to live there? Would I manage to make new friends all over again? Would Lesley forget me and transfer her affections to a farmer from Broughshane with an XR3? Of course, some of my friends' concerns would be of a more religious or political nature. Titch McCracken would be appalled at the traitorous act of an Ulsterman moving to the Free State, but I hadn't seen Titch around for years. Boyd Harrison from the CU would give me a hard time for choosing to live in 'a priest-ridden country' whose government was controlled from the Vatican. Still, I saw the chance to live in a different country of a different religion as an adventure rather than a threat. At least as a Protestant in Dublin I would finally be a real minority, and I could discuss the rights of minorities without everyone accusing me of being an oppressor.

I arrived early for my interview and sat outside the office practising my answers and reading a book on how to do good interviews, which I had borrowed from the library following my disaster at the College of Business Studies. The book said that a good way to calm your nerves at an interview was to imagine the interview panel naked because they would seem less intimidating with their wobbly bits hanging out. This time round I was much better prepared and ready to stand up for myself if I had to. At last I was invited into a room full of books, recording equipment and smoke, where two men with stubble welcomed me in the same accent as Terry Wogan (though they were much less charming than the great broadcaster himself). It all started very well, and when they asked me what aspect of journalism I was interested in I said I wanted to be an investigative journalist and report from conflict zones.

'I'm also interested in becoming a consumer champion and exposing corruption like Esther Rantzen on *That's Life* on BBC1,' I explained earnestly.

I answered questions about my university course in as little detail as possible, just in case all journalism courses in Ireland hated Media Studies degree graduates. It was all going swimmingly until one of the interviewers began to examine my application form more closely. It was clear that something had caught his eye.

I wondered if it was my experience of producing a documentary on glue sniffing in Belfast or my voluntary work across the peace line during the summer holidays. After a few seconds of intense silence he looked up from my application form and said, 'So, why exactly do you people support Paisley?'

I was completely taken aback, as I had no recollection of mentioning Rev. Ian Paisley anywhere on my application form. I didn't support Paisley anyway, because he seemed to hate Catholics far too much and some people took that as an excuse to kill them. The interviewer was staring at me, waiting for a reply.

He doesn't like me, I thought.

'Well,' I replied slowly. 'I suppose people who support Paisley …' and I tried to remember what my granny would have said because she had supported Paisley until her dying day. 'Well, it's very important to them to be British and … they take the Bible very literally and only believe in a certain kind of Christianity and that you shouldn't play on the swings on Sunday and all …'

'I just don't get you people,' he interrupted. 'Paisleyites are the biggest fuckin' obstacle to peace in the North today.'

He thinks I'm a Paisleyite! I thought.

'Well, actually, personally speaking, *I'm* not …'

'What exactly do Paisleyites want?' he interrupted again.

This was not what I had expected in this interview. There was nothing in my library book about how to defend yourself for being something you weren't, and I was so flustered by this turn of events that I didn't even remember to picture the interviewers naked. The other interviewer returned to the scripted questions, but it was clear that his colleague had no further interest in me.

He set down his pen as firmly as the interviewer in Belfast had. As I stumbled my way through various questions about what I would do as a reporter on this story or in that circumstance, I noticed that the other interviewer was rolling his eyes. What was it that made interviewers for journalism courses want to roll their eyes at me? I rarely rolled me eyes at anybody – apart from Clive Ross and Irene Maxwell. The interview came to a quick and stilted end and I barely got a handshake as I left the room.

The rejection letter arrived a few weeks later and this time I was angry. I was certain it wasn't my fault this time – the interviewers hadn't even given me a fair chance. I had driven the whole way down the Dublin Road – in spite of being warned never to do so by Ian Paisley – and then when I got there they didn't want me *because* of Paisley! When I had got my first job as a paperboy with Oul Mac and when Leslie McGregor asked me to be his breadboy on the Ormo Mini Shop I was chosen based on my experience and skills alone. How would I ever get a job as a journalist if people kept assuming I was something I wasn't? What if no one ever gave me a chance? This was what John Hume called injustice.

It seemed that the BBC in Belfast was my last chance. I was sure the BBC would treat me fairly – after all, they produced *Blue Peter* and *Songs of Praise*, so I knew their moral standards were very high. I had almost given up when one day, to my great surprise, a white envelope with the BBC logo arrived. At first I thought my wee brother had applied for a *Blue Peter* badge, but when I noticed the Belfast postmark my heart leapt. Sure enough, inside there was a very pleasant letter inviting me to do a screen test.

'The BBC are goin' to try me out!' I shouted down the phone to Lesley.

'Oh. My. Nerves!' she shouted back.

The screen test took place in Broadcasting House in Belfast city centre round the corner from the Ulster Hall. When I entered the imposing building I had to go to the security desk and show my letter before they would allow me inside, presumably because they didn't want anyone hijacking the news. I waited for ten minutes until a nice lady in good clothes and make-up came over and welcomed me with lots of lovely '-ings'. I tried to respond with as many carefully pronounced '-ings' as possible – after all, if I were to become a newsreader I would have to soften my Belfast accent and try to sound more like I came from Cultra. However in all the excitement of walking past the real live Rose Neill in the foyer I forgot myself when the nice lady asked me if I had taken lunch.

'No, I'm starvin', so I am,' I replied.

She took me up in a lift to a proper recording studio like the one in the Band Aid video, only there was no sign of Simon Le Bon, Boy George or Bono. It was just me, a camera and a microphone in a little room with padded walls. It was so silent I could hear my heart beating. I was nervous. This was my last chance. Everyone else had rejected me. I took deep breaths, said a wee prayer and decided that I would do my very best. I would draw on my acting skills to enunciate my words and project my voice and look dead serious like the newsreaders between the bongs on *News at Ten*. The nice lady appeared behind a window to an adjoining room and sat next to a man wearing a sweater and headphones. Her voice crackled through a small speaker beside me.

'Okay, Tony. Are you ready, dawl*ing*?'

'Yes, please, thank you,' I replied.

'In front of you is a list of place names in Naawthan Ahland. I want you to read down the list as clearly as possible. Okay, dawl*ing*?'

This seemed very easy. I read down the list: Annalong, Ahoghill, Annahilt, Bangor, Ballycastle, Boho … I said the place names as if I was on the Eurovision Song Contest calling on all the different capital cities to cast their votes. When I got to the Ms there were one or two unfamiliar place names such as 'Maghaberry', but I tried to appear confident as I finished reading the list. When I looked up at the end, I noticed the nice lady and the man with the headphones were laughing. I couldn't hear what they were laughing at through the glass, but I thought the BBC must be a nice place to work if people were telling jokes and laughing all the time.

Once the nice lady had composed herself, she pressed a button on the other side of the glass and said, 'Now, Tony, dawl*ing*. Next you are go*ing* to be read*ing* from the autocue in front of you.'

'Okay, thanks!' I replied politely, feeling the need to give her a thumbs up through the window even though she could hear every word I said through the microphone.

'Just follow the words and look at the camera.'

'Okay, thanks.'

'Are you ready, dawl*ing*?'

'Yes, please, thank you.'

I read the autocue, which scrolled down with a news report

about a traffic accident, trying my best to sound authoritative but relaxed like John Craven on *Newsround*.

When I finished reading the report I noticed there was some smiling and nodding on the other side of the glass and I hoped this was an indication that they would at least want me to read the news when Rose Neill went on her holidays for the Twelfth fortnight. The nice lady told me I had done very well and said that someone would be in touch in due course. I was relieved that there hadn't been an interview this time.

For weeks I monitored the post for any sign of a white envelope with the BBC logo on the front. I understood now how Peter Davison must have felt when he had applied to be the new Doctor Who. Finally, one Saturday morning, the letter arrived at my house in Belfast shortly after the Ormo Mini Shop had passed. When it landed on the fraying hall carpet I knew this small paper packet would determine my future. I opened the envelope and read the letter.

'While we have no openings for you at present, we think you have some on-screen potential.'

I had failed yet again, but at least this time I had been given a fair chance, *and* the BBC thought I had some potential. I drove to Bellaghy that evening and showed Lesley the letter, and she agreed that I did have potential in many ways.

'Look, Mummy, the BBC says Tony has some potential,' she said, showing her mother the impressive letter on BBC headed paper.

Mummy was very impressed, and while preparing a mammoth spread of fancy pastries and triangular sandwiches she asked me about the screen test. As I attempted to decline offers of yet another chocolate coconut bun and more ice cream, I told her all about reading from the autocue and saying the names of all the places in Northern Ireland.

'Och, Mummy knows everywhere in Northern Ireland. You've no idea!' said Lesley. 'She makes up wee quizzes and all for the GB.'

'Well there were a few places I wasn't sure about,' I confessed.

'Like what?' said Mummy offering me a plate of perfectly symmetrical traybakes.

I wrote down 'Maghaberry'.

'How do you say that then?' I asked.

'Ma-gab-ree' she said.

My heart sank. 'I said Maka-Berry!'

'Oh, Lessley!' Mummy said, and put her hand over her mouth to suppress a giggle.

'Well, at least I got Bangor, Ballycastle and Boho right!' I protested.

'You mean Bow?' said Mummy.

My heart sank even further. 'I said Boo-hoo!'

Mummy set down her teapot and put both hands over her mouth.

'Oh, Lessley!' she shrieked.

'You've no idea!' Lesley replied.

Lesley and Mummy collapsed into fits of laughter. Now I understood the reason for all the laughter behind the glass at the BBC. I was a failure with no future in the media, and I was seriously scundered, so I was.

20

IT MUST BE LOVE

Where is she? I wondered.

I was standing at the model in my 'Feed the World' T-shirt and faded jeans, biting my nails and waiting for Lesley to accompany me to the canteen for a feed of sausage and chips and beans. Lesley had recently introduced me to new, exotic foods in Bellaghy, such as lasagne and another pasta dish with chicken and real garlic. This was completely new to my palate as my only experience of garlic prior to this was in Dracula movies on BBC2 on a Friday night. Italian cuisine was delicious, but I preferred to have the more traditional something-and-chips at lunchtime. I was listening to Agnetha's solo album on my Sony Walkman, but the batteries were low so she was starting to sound more like Björn. To complement my 'Feed the World' T-shirt I had two days worth of stubble on my chin. I was going for the Bob Geldof look because he was interested in saving the world too. My 'Feed the World' T-shirt had recently been at the centre of an unfortunate incident with my housemates, however, as, in a protest against the persistent allegation that I never washed the dishes, Aaron, Colm and Peter decided to teach me a lesson. I arrived home late one night after a particularly demanding CU committee meeting on whether or not healing should be allowed during the main weekly meeting. As I walked up the weed-strewn pathway to our student house, I saw that my 'Feed the World' T-shirt had been stuck to my bedroom window for the entire world to see. I knew immediately that my housemates had been up to some high japes, and when I entered the house and opened the door to my room I found several weeks of dirty dishes piled on my bed and a note on the back of my T-shirt which read 'But do the dishes first!' I was outraged at the suggestion that I was not pulling my weight in the kitchen. I had washed the dishes at least three times that semester, and I made a point of mopping the kitchen floor every few months. In spite of this unjust sullying of my T-shirt I continued to wear it with pride to tell the world that, not only did I want to feed it, I also supported Bob Geldof's endeavour to feed everyone in Africa from the proceeds of 'Do They Know It's Christmas?', even though Bob himself was a bit of a slabber and the Boomtown Rats had lost it.

It was not like Lesley to be late. I was the one who arrived late for our dates, usually as a result of something important, like an incident in the Middle East, or an argument over Nietzsche in the Students' Union, or an emergency prayer meeting in the Christian Union, or a brilliant cliffhanger at the end of *Doctor Who*. Even when Lesley had been in the library all day trying to complete her dissertation on stress in the RUC she was always on time, so this was very unusual.

'Stood up, Tone?' Byron Drake approached me with a broad smile and a folded *Guardian*.

'Just waiting for my girlfriend. This happens sometimes when you actually *have* a real live girlfriend. Has yours got a puncture?' I asked.

After three years at university I had mastered the art of the clever sarcastic put-down and I knew exactly how to stand up for myself. I was just as confident as Byron now and he knew it!

'Very droll, virgin, very droll,' Byron replied.

'I've just been reading that wee book you like.' I said.

Byron looked atypically impressed. '*The Catcher in the Rye?* Wow! You're getting there, Tone, you're getting there.'

'It's almost Nietzschean,' I replied nonchalantly as if I now understood what this phrase meant.

Byron patted me on the back, returned his attention to the Morrissey playing on his headphones and walked on with a flick of his latest Flock of Seagulls fringe.

'Here, Tony, can ye lend me your lecture notes from this mornin'?' asked a very hung-over Marty Mullen whose breath had just crept up behind me.

'Aye, dead on,' I replied.

'Dead on,' said Marty.

At this point in the conversation I noticed that Marty was wearing a brand new leather jacket, and I could tell by the smell that it wasn't a cheap plastic imitation like the one I had purchased from the bargain bucket in John Frazer's. The first time I sported my impressive but slightly-too-shiny faux leather jacket my big brother accused me of looking like 'that big fruit Freddie' from Queen. I never wore the jacket again and donated it to Shankill Methodist in a black bin bag, although I wasn't sure how many Freddie Mercury fans attended the annual church jumble sale.

'Can I have them back tomorrow?' I asked Marty.

'Aye, nay bother. Are ye goin' for a samich?'

'No, I'm meetin' Lesley.'

'Aye, nay bother,' Marty said, about to walk on.

'Like your jacket,' I admitted, even though I was feeling highly envious. How could he afford a leather jacket when he was always boasting about how many pints of Jack Daniels he had consumed the night before? I knew I should control my jealousy but I couldn't help myself. When would I ever be able to afford a proper leather jacket made of dead cows' skin and not PVC?

'I didn't think you were allowed them west of the Bann,' I added with pure student sarcasm.

'Sure you're only allowed te wear sashes and bowler hats where you come from,' he replied smartly.

I was determined not to allow this to descend into a sectarian spat because this would mean Marty would never accept an invitation to come to the CU and get saved, so I resisted my sinful urge to reply with a comment about balaclavas in Londonderry.

'Aye right,' I said.

'Aye right,' said Marty, deliberately pulling up the collar of his leather jacket as if he was a white Michael Jackson from Derry.

'See ya,' I said.

'See ya,' said Marty.

It was remarkable how Marty and I had become such dear friends in just a few short years.

By this stage Lesley was fifteen minutes late, and this was

fifteen minutes later than she had ever been – even during the January sales. I spotted Aaron Ward and two of Lesley's favourite Heathers from Portadown crossing the entrance hall and I dashed over to see if they had any information on my girlfriend's whereabouts. Lesley shared a big detached house in Portstewart (owned by a wealthy man who Mummy and Daddy knew) with these two Heathers and they were bound to know why she was so late.

'What are you like, wee lad?' said Aaron, looking me up and down. He disapproved of my heavily-gelled New Romantic hair, designer stubble and campaigning T-shirt just as much as I was bored by his rugby shirts and Pringle sweaters. He gave me a dead arm to indicate that he meant no harm.

'Have you seen Lesley?' I enquired.

'Ach, she's not well, so she's not,' chorused the two Heathers.

'Where is she?' I asked urgently, concerned that she had been rushed to hospital with another asthma attack.

'She's in bed at the house,' said the two Heathers.

Within seconds I was on my way to the bus stop for Portstewart. I was missing my lunch and a lecture on the terminal decline of cinema but I didn't care. My girlfriend needed me and she needed me now! The minute I arrived at the bus stop I began sticking my thumb out at passing motorists. Fortunately, I soon got a lift with a kind woman driving a Mini Metro with a picture of Charles and Diana on the dashboard and a strawberry-smelling cardboard tree hanging from the rearview mirror. Within ten minutes I had thanked her kindly, jumped out of the car and ran around the corner to Lesley's student digs, a large house with central heating and a sea view which was three times the size of my family home (although strangely lacking an avocado bidet).

I rang the doorbell.

No answer.

Then I rapped the brass knocker.

No answer.

What if Lesley was unconscious? I would have to knock the door down like Tubbs in *Miami Vice* breaking into a drug den. Then I remembered that in movies in such circumstances, the man always threw pebbles at his lover's window. I grabbed a couple of pebbles from the soil around the hydrangea bushes in the front garden and chucked them at Lesley's bedroom window. Unfortunately, I missed by several miles and had to search for more pebbles so I could have another go. A grumpy looking woman passed by and stared at me disapprovingly.

'Humph. Typical Belfast,' she said and walked on.

After three or four further stone-throwing attempts I noticed the curtains moving. A very pale-looking Lesley popped her head out, then motioned to indicate that I should go around to the back of the house. This was awful! What if I had forced my girlfriend to get out of bed at a critical point in her disease, causing her to relapse? What if I had to call an ambulance and she ended up in the Royal and the doctors had no time to see her because of a bomb or a shooting or something? What if she died?

How could I live without her? I wondered.

I ran around to the back of the house, past the hexagonal stones taken from the Giant's Causeway and placed attractively in the garden, and sure enough the back door was open. I entered the house and leapt up the stairs faster than Sebastian Coe at the Olympics. I burst into Lesley's bedroom.

'I'm not wearing any make-up!' were her first words.

I was very relieved as these did not sound like the words of a dying woman. Lesley was tucked up in bed in her Marks & Spencer's dressing gown with a million hankies, a hot water bottle and the pink cuddly dog I had bought her for Valentine's Day that year. Although just a few years ago I had received fourteen Valentine's Day cards, this year I had received only one.

'Don't look at me!' Lesley sniffled miserably.

'How could I ever not look at you?' I said, smiling. 'Is it your asthma? Do you need your puffer?'

'No, it's the friggin' flu,' replied Lesley, 'and my hair's awful!'

I was relieved that the illness was not life-threatening and climbed up onto the bed beside a mountain of used pink tissues.

'So I don't need to examine your big breaths?'

Lesley laughed weakly. 'I don't like you seein' me like this,' she said.

'Sure you saw me when I boked into your Mummy's beige bidet.'

'It's Sahara Gold.'

'Well I think you're just as beautiful without your make-up, anyway.'

Lesley let out six consecutive sneezes. 'Och, you're just saying that. You've no idea!'

'I'm not! I mean it, so I do.'

'Will you make me a Lemsip and a hot Ribena?'

I ran downstairs to the huge kitchen, boiled the kettle, prepared the remedies and carried them upstairs on a floral tray.

'There you are now,' I said, administering the healing potions. 'I'll look after you.'

'Will you, Tony?' Lesley asked, looking up at me with her lovely eyes as she sipped Ribena from her favourite mug with the ponies on it.

'I'll always look after you,' I added.

'What do you mean?' Lesley asked before six more sneezes.

What *do* I mean? I wondered.

Then suddenly, impulsively, I knew exactly what I meant. I cuddled up very close to my girl in bed; Joyce Huggett would have approved as I was fully-clothed and Lesley was wearing more layers of clothing than if she had not been in bed at all. I held her close in my arms, and realised that I was going to ask her a very important question. The most important question a man could ask a woman. The moment was spoiled slightly when Lesley sneezed again and the hot water bottle sandwiched between our bodies almost scalded me in the region of my jimmy joe.

'Will you marry me?' I asked lovely Lesley from up the country.

'Of course I will!'

'Really?'

'Yes!'

'No kiddin'?'

'Aye!'

'Even though I get on your nerves sometimes?'

'Yes!'

'Even though I'm just some wee lad from up the Shankill?'

'Yes, but you've got some potential!'

'Are you sure?'

'Yes!'

'So we're getting married then?'

'Yes! I love you, Tony.'

'I love you too, so I do.'

'What will Mummy say?'

'She'll say "What am I going to wear?"'

We laughed.

'I thought you were never going to ask. You've no idea!' Lesley said, beaming through a handful of tissues before launching into yet another sneezing fit. I was going to marry a beautiful serial sneezer.

We lay together on the bed and hugged and talked until we realised it was dark and we hadn't even put the light on. We agreed that it was better not to announce to the Christian Union that I had proposed while we were in bed together. We talked for hours about our hopes and dreams for the future. We would get engaged as soon as possible – if I could borrow enough money to buy a diamond and sapphire ring like the one Charles bought Diana – and on the one strict condition that the engagement ring would not be purchased in Argos. Then we would graduate and get jobs so we could afford to buy a house and get married. This would mean official sex – approved by Joyce Huggett – and I could leave Bo Derek behind in the sand dunes on Portstewart Strand forever. I'd get a job as a television presenter on *Blue Peter* and Lesley would become a trainee manager for Marks & Spencer and we'd earn so much money that I could afford my first real leather jacket and Lesley could continue to guarantee employment for the staff in Logan's boutique near Ballymena. Or maybe we would go to Africa to save the hungry children and sacrifice all our material possessions instead. Or perhaps we would move back to Belfast and live on the peace line and work to bring peace to Northern Ireland or Lesley could get a job as a prison governor and I could become a famous war reporter. Or we might buy a pebble-dashed chalet bungalow in Magherafelt with a Leylandii hedge and a bidet, or maybe move to a cottage in Glarryford and rescue a wee dog and Lesley would look after it in case I accidentally killed it. We could buy a brand new Renault 5 or a Porsche if we wanted to and buy nasturtium borders and variegated shrubs in garden centres and go on camping holidays to the Scottish Highlands or go to Egypt to see the pyramids.

Then after a few years, if Lesley could get over her fear of childbirth, we would have two perfect children and take them on day trips to Belfast Zoo on Bank Holiday Mondays and send them to an integrated school so they wouldn't grow up to hate Catholics. Then maybe I would become a famous film director and produce a science-fiction blockbuster that Stephen Spielberg would be proud of and the BBC would beg me to write an episode of *Doctor Who* and Benny and Björn would ask me to direct the ABBA reunion concert in the year 2000. I would win an Oscar and be so rich that we could start our own charity to save whole villages in Africa. Lesley would open a designer boutique on the Lisburn Road and it would be such a success that she would buy Anderson & McAuley's in Royal Avenue and change the name to Evans & Macaulay's. Our children would grow up to become even more successful than us but would never forget where they came from, and Lesley and I would become grandparents but still be trendy. Eventually when we were very old, we would retire and move back to Porstewart where it had all begun and live in a house with a lovely view of the Atlantic Ocean and the beautiful sunsets over Portstewart Strand and go for walks up and down the prom and buy pokes in Morelli's on a good day, if our arthritis wasn't too bad. Then finally one day when we were both old and tired, we'd die in each other's arms and go up to heaven and be together forever with God and Big Isobel and all the other wee good livin' folk that had ever lived.

Lying there together in the darkness, it was just the two of us. For now this was our secret, and our hopes and dreams were ours alone. We were proper adults now, about to take on proper grown-up responsibilities like sex (definitely), a mortgage (possibly), a job (hopefully) and a dog (riskily).

As I walked home that night I decided to take a detour and walk along the empty beach in the moonlight. I was completely alone under a sky full of twinkling stars with a carpet of soft sand beneath my ankle boots. The waves rolled in and out quietly and the sea spray shone silver in the moonlight. I said a quiet prayer, thanking God for creating this moon and the sea and Lesley and me. I whistled a happy tune like Anna in *The King and I* but more manly, obviously, like Yul Brynner. I walked to the end of the strand, climbed the Second World War sentry post and stood on top of it as if I was Marcellus in *Hamlet* and nothing was rotten in the state of anywhere. This was where I had got the green Simca stuck in the sand only a few short years ago! So much had changed since then. Big Isobel would definitely be proud of how 'all growed up' I was. I took deep breaths of moist, salty air and stood very still, appreciating the beauty of the moonlight reflecting on the River Bann. The west of the Bann and the east of the Bann seemed at peace with each other. I could almost imagine I was living in a place of absolute harmony, like the Westy Disco on a Saturday night.

I silently marvelled at how far I had come in my life since I was a wee paperboy delivering the *Belfast Telegraph* for Oul Mac up the Shankill. To think that just a few years ago I was a naive breadboy for the Ormo bakery burdened by nothing but handfuls of plain and pan loaves; now I was betrothed and about to become the first person in my family ever to graduate from university! In the post office on the West Circular Road my mother would tell Mrs Grant and all the women in our street how she would have to buy a hat for my graduation, and in the searing heat of the foundry on the Springfield Road my father would boast to his workmates that a son of his had got an Honours degree and would never have to work there.

I still had no job, no money and nowhere of my own to live, but I felt I had come of age – like *The Karate Kid* but without the violence. My head was bursting with excitement as to what was going to happen next, and though the future was a mystery, I believed it would be kind. I was about to go forth on a great adventure, just like Indiana Jones, but with fewer whips and Nazis.

I stood alone on the beautiful beach in the darkness, feeling happy and thankful. I searched for a slim stone to skim across the waves in celebration and found one that was perfect. As my stone skipped three times over the surface of the water and disappeared beneath the waves, I knew it was true. There was absolutely no doubt about it. I was all growed up now, so I was!

ACKNOWLEDGEMENTS

I want to acknowledge all the support I have received from bookstores, libraries, festivals, voluntary groups, universities and schools at home and abroad.

I am grateful to Kim Plyler and to all the team at Sahl Communications for managing my book tours in the USA.

Special thanks to Jane McCarter in the New York Irish Center; George Heslin of the 1st Irish Theatre Festival; Neville Gardner of Donegal Square in Bethlehem, PA; Pat and Mike O'Connor Thomas in Ballston Spa, NY; and the Moser Family in Goshen, IN for their generous support and hospitality.

I want to acknowledge the continued encouragement, support and advice of my literary agents, Paul and Susan Feldstein.

Last but not least, I would like to thank Patsy Horton, Helen Wright, Kerri Ward, Jim Meredith and all the team at Blackstaff Press for their enthusiasm, hard work and warm support in publishing *All Growed Up*.

ALSO BY TONY MACAULAY

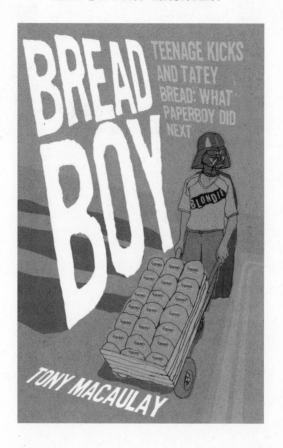

eBook
EPUB ISBN 978-0-85640-167-1
KINDLE ISBN 978-0-85640-170-1

Paperback
ISBN 978-0-85640-910-3

www.blackstaffpress.com
Follow Tony on Twitter @tonymacaulay